Seriously Useless Learning

The collected TES writings of Alan Tuckett
with introduction and narrative by Ian Nash

Published by NIACE

This collection © 2014 National Institute of Adult
Continuing Education (England and Wales)
21 De Montfort Street, Leicester, LE1 7GE
Company registration no. 2603322
Charity registration no. 1002775

Articles reproduced with kind permission of the TES.

NIACE is the National Institute of Adult Continuing
Education, the national voice for lifelong learning.
We are an internationally respected development
organisation and think-tank, working on issues central
to the economic renewal of the UK, particularly in the
political economy, education and learning, public policy
and regeneration fields.

For details of all our publications,
visit http://shop.niace.org.uk

Cataloguing in Publications Data
A CIP record for this title is available from the British
Library

978-1-86201-877-8 (print)
978-1-86201-878-5 (PDF)
978-1-86201-879-2 (ePub)
978-1-86201-880-8 (Kindle)

Printed in the UK by Marston Book Services, Abingdon
Cover design and typeset by Peter Batt – peterbatt.co.uk

Contents

Acknowledgements

A CONSIDERABLE number of people helped me compile this book and I offer them my sincere thanks. In particular I would like to thank Toni Fazaeli (who approached me to write the book), Sue Jones (for her painstaking advice and close scrutiny of the content) and George Low (who, as a journalist, has reported on the activities of Alan Tuckett for 40 years and contributed the final section of the introduction). Also, for the considerable time spent either in interview or contributing thoughts and ideas, I would like to thank David Hughes, Paul Mackney, Tim (now Lord) Boswell, David Blunkett, John Denham, Jay Derrick, Estelle Morris, Ursula Howard, Charles Clarke, Bill Rammell, Ruth Silver, John Field, Alastair Thomson, Peter Lavender, Julian Gravatt, Tom Schuller, Rob Wye, Nick Stuart, Carol Taylor, Gorge Low, Stephen McNair, Ed Melia, Dan Taubman and Peter Batt, who designed the book.

Foreword

David Hughes *Chief executive, NIACE*

AS WELL as the warm congratulations I received when I was appointed to head NIACE in 2011, almost everyone added: "...and you certainly have big shoes to fill." They were right, of course, as the glowing tributes to Alan in the introduction confirm. My experience of Alan before I took the job fits well with what others have said of his intelligent, passionate and charming persistence, even in the face of some of the most egregious policy announcements and mistakes.

As Alan's successor at NIACE, I have a unique perspective to add. I never doubted that Alan would be gracious about leaving NIACE and that he would be supportive. I am not sure, though, that I had expected him to be as generous as he has been, and that says a lot about the man. Imagine the scenario: having built up an organisation so powerfully over a quarter of a century and having become 'the voice of adult learning', you have to let go and trust that a new broom will not sweep too clean. I think that is tough and yet Alan has been hugely personally supportive, an enthusiastic sounding board yet distant enough to allow me and NIACE the space and leeway to grow and evolve.

The columns make fascinating reading. They track an extraordinary time in learning and skills in England. They record enormous hope and so many missed opportunities. Whilst Alan was writing these columns, I was working in the further education funding bodies and got to see first-hand a lot of the struggles and debates covered. Like many inside the Government machine, I shared the enormous hope when the Learning & Skills Council was established, as well as the frustrations when the powerful rhetoric of the Learning Age Green Paper failed to materialise on the ground.

Alan's columns provide an important commentary on the difficulties all governments face in implementing good policy. My experience over this time has taught me many things, not least that good policy is not enough. There has to also be good implementation. Too many times in the 2000s I found myself in heated exchanges with senior civil servants, and sometimes

Seriously useless learning

ministers, about how their beautifully-crafted policy would not result in the changes they were seeking.

History shows that the New Labour/Whitehall response to policy not delivering results was to tighten the national and central grip. We saw far too much well-intentioned but ultimately futile effort to control and command, and not enough understanding of how to change behaviours at the delivery end. As it became clear that centralised control was not working, institutional change was seen as the answer and the Learning & Skills Council and the Government department were split and re-organised. The lessons from all of this still need to be learned.

The NIACE response to all of this and the effects of funding cuts in the last five years has remained passionate, evidenced and optimistic, despite the profound misgivings we have with the impacts on adult learners. Our work continues to focus on developing new practice and policy proposals, gathering the evidence of what is happening and what works, and being the critical friend to Government and influencers. I think that is the legacy of which Alan should be most proud; that we have continued to operate in the spirit of what can be seen in his columns; that we retain the pessimism of the intellect and the optimism of the spirit which others have remarked on.

Please enjoy reading these columns and let's make sure that we do two things. Firstly, that we learn from the columns the lessons for policy and implementation. Secondly, that we remain passionate and dogged in our fight for opportunities for all adults throughout their lives to be able to participate and benefit from learning.

Ann Mroz Editor, Times Educational Supplement

IN HIS impressive body of work on adult learning for the *Times Educational Supplement* (*TES*), Alan Tuckett drew a unique perspective on an area of education too readily sidelined or neglected by politicians of every hue, who continue to downplay its importance and undermine its potential as an agent of positive and lasting change. The blessing and the curse of adult learning is that it is not easily categorised or defined; it cuts across settings, formal and informal, from the college lecture theatre and workshop to the village hall and community centre. It is found scattered across the post-school terrain of further and higher education and comes under ill-defined departments, areas and labels such as "extra-mural studies" and "other" learning.

Alan, more than almost any other commentator, helped us at the *TES* keep a watchful and constructively critical eye on adult education in its broadest sense for over 15 years, charting its ups and downs, calling politicians and policymakers to account and reporting in detail on the strengths and weaknesses of policies and strategies that seemed to change with the wind. As his columns show, he does so not through dry observation, but by giving tantalising perspectives and telling the stories of how people who have underachieved at school have been helped to return to learning. His writing has an abundance of evidence on how adult learning restores dignity; how it helps build (or rebuild) careers and how it sustains health and active participation in society among people of all ages.

I am pleased to be able to offer a comprehensive selection of his writings for this book because it reminds us of the need for, and value of, constant vigilance when reporting on the way education and training are shaped by those in power. Alan was able to do this and to communicate successfully with a wide variety of audiences because, as commentators in this book note, he had a unique ability to hold a conversation with his readers – an essential attribute of good journalism and of good commentary.

I hope that the readers of this collection of his works will feel rewarded by their reading. I also hope that they will see this not as a definitive statement on adult learning or the end of the conversation, but as the beginning of a new chapter in the constant struggle to create and sustain a rich entitlement of learning for all.

Introduction
by Ian Nash

ALAN TUCKETT wrote for the *Times Educational Supplement (TES)* throughout one of the most turbulent periods in recent decades for adult education. When he started as a columnist in the mid-1990s, there was the promise from a New Labour government of legislation for post-school education to match reforms achieved for young people through the 1944 Education Act – a well-mapped, broad road for progress with clear entitlements for all.

By 2008, neoliberal economics and the financial crash had narrowed any such provision to training designed for a skills-driven utilitarian agenda, with the notion of entitlement limited to those seen as having the greatest need of the most basic skills.

Tuckett, more than anyone else, charted in detail in his writing the vicissitudes of adult (or lifelong) learning as the pendulum swung between vocational training priorities and what he called 'other' learning. However angry he may have felt about what was often blatant denigration of other learning, he always wrote – and still writes on occasions – with a sense of wonderment and fun. "It is not a question of either/or, but a need for both," he said repeatedly, never once elevating one educational pathway over the other.

Nevertheless, he sees the purpose of education as fundamentally political, a position well described by him in a 2009 interview with Ekkhard Nuissl, director of the German Institute for Adult Education:

> *"Adult learning is about helping people themselves identify the nature of power relationships or the nature of the direction of change they want to undertake, and making sure the system doesn't stop them getting there."*

While Tuckett is clearly a man of the Left, his writing is never partisan because he is careful to distinguish between the pragmatic and the political. Whichever party is in power, he views its policies as the new starting point for whatever strategy will achieve his purpose. In other words, he is always prepared "to start from where we are, wherever we find ourselves". And that purpose is always the goal of winning the broadest possible entitlement to adult learning for all.

As a result, he is widely respected – and people like him. They listen, too, and read him because he is interesting and interested in everything. Like a polymath who seems to have taken full advantage of every adult learning course under the sun, he ranges widely, in order to reinforce his argument in print and speech, from the lyrics of Bob Dylan and offerings of the tourist markets around the Taj Mahal, to the Unesco initiative, Learning Without Frontiers, and the empty anti-adult-education polemics of former Ofsted chief inspector Chris Woodhead.

For Paul Mackney, founding general secretary of the UCU, this combined *idée fixe* and ability to see reason is what has always driven Tuckett and helped him achieve much. "Measured against Engels' first law of dialectics – the interpenetration of opposites – Alan Tuckett is dialectical man," says Mackney. "He once told me how he loved the Newport Folk Festival duets of Joan Baez and Bob Dylan because they united the sweet perfection of the former with the rasping tones of the latter. His practice as a 'critical friend' of government is similar. Just when you think Alan's prose is leaning to the saccharine, he lets loose a phrase penetrating enough to sink a battleship."

A typical example of this from a *TES* column in 1999 is the way Tuckett conveyed so much anger over what he saw as the destructive utilitarianism and elitism of a decade, without ever getting personal. "The obsessions of the 1990s have bleached out delight and creativity from too many organisers' thinking," he wrote. "People still struggle to make sense of poems, capture light on paper, make music etc. But this is not seen as a curriculum fit for the excluded."

Mackney sees this as more than some literary flourish or gainsay; it is part of Tuckett's method. "In conversation, Alan's [Cornish] burr lulls you into a sense of comfort, just before a sharper tone disconcerts you into questioning some easy pre-conceptions. But these are not the vapid games of a controversialist. There is purpose – the defence and extension of education for adults. If you are committed to that, other differences can be parked. He once said to me, after a disagreement: 'OK, you're right from your side and I'm right from mine', recycling, perhaps unconsciously, a line from Dylan's third album, *The Times They Are A-changin'*. Alan was central to the defence of adult education against the idiot winds of neo-liberal economies in the early 1990s, bringing together the most militant union branches with the Women's Institute in a campaign which was so successful that, a decade later, eight out of ten FE college students were adults."

Living in a political world

What then of the politicians of the time? Under the Tories, Gillian Shephard, the Education Secretary, woke up to the idea of wider adult learning and, taking a shine to Tuckett, kept hounding him to help create a Learning City in her Norwich constituency. He liked them because, he said, post-school education and training was not a coherent system, and cities brought together disparate initiatives to secure a culture of collaboration.

"Gillian Shephard asked me and others at an adult learners' week celebration to help her make Thetford a learning city in three weeks. We said it might take a bit more than three weeks for Thetford to become a city, but we would help."

The notion of learning cities goes in and out of political favour and was very much 'in' at the time, says Nick Stuart, then director-general for employment and lifelong learning at the Department of Education & Employment. "I went with Christopher Ball to Washington DC hoping to persuade the Kellogg Foundation to give us big money to set up a learning city in London." It never came off and the intervening election changed the political map.

From 1992 to 2006, Tim (now Lord) Boswell was Parliamentary Under Secretary at the Department for Education and then shadow spokesman with responsibility for adult education. While Tuckett may have railed against the utilitarianism of the decade, he quickly developed a rapport with Boswell, who would continue his commitment to adult learning when in Opposition and beyond into the House of Lords. In 2010, he chaired the NIACE-supported Independent Inquiry into Adult & Youth Literacy. Over two decades, he admits, the basis of his commitment to creating a lifelong learning society shifted "from economic necessity to moral duty". Tuckett played no small part in his change of thinking, he says.

"To me, Alan will always be most closely (and almost uniquely) identified with the cause of adult education. Of course, others have championed the cause, but he has in a sense made it his own," Lord Boswell says. "In part, this in my view derives from his high 'seriousness' and integrity in seeing education as an essential vehicle for liberating talent and securing personal fulfilment. Part of this reflects a view of a healthy economic model in which those beginning from disadvantage – or simply missing out along the conventional school path as a result of circumstances – may reclaim their right to participate in society and to share in its good things, including empowerment through work, with the income they can derive from it, and also the full use of their talents to work and share with others."

This point is eloquently reflected by Tuckett, writing in the *TES* in 2000, when he urged the Learning & Skills Council to maintain spending on learning support to back neighbourhood renewal strategies. "...It is only when people in the poorest communities feel empowered and supported in shaping the regeneration of their communities that significant change can happen. And effective outreach work, backed by enough patience and flexibility, can support the gains in confidence and agency for that transformation to happen."

Yet that is not all, says Boswell. "Alan always sees the intrinsic moral purpose of his passions. He is eloquent on the benefits to society of participation in adult education, in terms of better health, lower rates of offending, greater social tolerance and a more positive tone to our common life. He believes in democratic participation, for which literacy (and confidence) are essential. He sees people as 'goods' in themselves, rather than as instruments of production."

This perhaps explains the way he has approached the subject at the many conferences and meetings, as well as in his writing, says Boswell. "I have held with him over almost a quarter of a century. He has that underlying seriousness and faith as a 'given' – and can persuade others of it. Yet, at the same time, he enjoys playing the iconoclast and cheerfully subverts those who like to impose templates of learning and models of its finance. The situation in adult education is always 'desperate', because it is always hard even for ministers who have some empathy with him to persuade colleagues and the Treasury to provide the essential resources, even on a shoestring.

"Yet the position is never 'serious', because consistently he has won the case by the force of his argument. Even 'Schedule 2' [part of the 1992 FHE Act that excluded non-vocational courses from government funding] has had its day – and we respect and love him for it. The struggle continues…, but so does the lightness of touch."

The political influence of NIACE under Tuckett's leadership was also recognised when New Labour came to power. When Alan started his *TES* column in *FE Focus*, he was already at the centre of things and, while under no illusions, became vice chair of the Education & Employment Secretary David Blunkett's National Advisory Group for Continuing Education & Lifelong Learning (Nagcell – an appropriate name for lovers of puns). "The contribution that Alan Tuckett has made to continuing and adult education (lifelong learning) is immeasurable," says Blunkett:

"Not only his tenacity and stay-ability in terms of devoting a very large part of his life to the promotion of adult learning, but also his ability to persuade others of the importance of maintaining a national commitment at times when all the pressures were in the other direction. I was extremely proud to work with him in the four years I was Education & Employment Secretary in mobilising those committed in this area to restoring what had been severely damaged, and to giving both resources and backing to the developments of the future."

A huge amount of Tuckett's work was and continues to be on the international scene. For example, he was responsible for turning the ingenious idea of Adult Learners' Week from a national celebration of adult learning success into an international phenomenon. "The report that he produced for the international meeting in South America a few years ago was an example of how well he was able to pull together positively what had been done, whilst pointing a way forward at a time when attention on adult learning and the resources available to invest in it were extremely scarce," says Blunkett.

"I believe that the foundation he laid, reflecting as it did the heritage that we have in communities across Britain of adult and family learning, of evening classes (and in the past, day release) will stand us in good stead for protecting as best we can what we have, and looking to a more positive future."

When necessary, however, Tuckett was quick to put ministers in their place, as in 2006 when Alan Johnson, Education & Skills Secretary, denigrated 'other' learning in order to justify Labour's volte face and unravelling of a key part of the vision conveyed in The Learning Age. But, as ever, the tone of his writing was more than fair-minded. "Governments are elected to make their priorities clear, and Mr Johnson's were straightforward: 'We must rebalance taxpayer's money towards the subjects where there is greatest need.' My problem lay with his illustrations. 'More plumbing, less Pilates' makes for a good headline – it is alliterative and rolls off the tongue. 'Subsidised precision engineering, not over-subsidised flower arranging' – government apparently wants hard vocationalism, not soft leisure courses. Then, remembering that there is more to the British economy than manufacturing, he backpedals: 'Except of course where flower arranging is necessary for a vocational purpose'.

"Just in case we have missed the point, he concludes: 'Tai Chi may be hugely valuable to people studying it, but it's of little value to the economy.' And here is the rub. Anyone looking at the statistics on days lost to the British economy through bad backs will conclude that more Pilates might lead to more productivity. And if Tai Chi has little to offer the economy, why is the Government campaigning so hard to limit obesity? But the real point is that you don't need to denigrate learning for personal and community development to make the case for a skilled economy."

Time and again Tuckett finds himself challenging ministerial pronouncements denigrating 'other' learning. He drew on powerful evidence from research, cited extensively in this volume of his writings, and he fought – and continues to fight in semi-retirement – a war of attrition; a man with the patience of Job. In pursuing his quest, Tuckett proved to be the master of irony, as with his judgment about the value of active creativity, when he coined that phrase "seriously useless learning", without which, as Jay Derrick, co-editor of the book *Remaking Adult Learning*, put it:

Seriously useless learning

> *"...he [Tuckett] believes that a society without it is damaged goods lacking in democratic resilience, justice and fun."*

The book was written in 2010 in tribute to Tuckett and his lifelong commitment to adult learning. Irony and gentle evidence-based persuasion were essential weapons in his armoury since Tuckett knew what he was up against.

Tuckett's notion of 'seriously useless learning' has deep historic roots in English culture and education. Eddie Playfair, principal of Newham Sixth Form College in east London, spelled out, in *Culture, tradition and values in education*, his blog of March 23 2014, what really lies behind the phrase. "In the first half of the 19th century, the chartists called for 'really useful knowledge' which would help working class people understand their situation and do something about it. Perhaps we need to describe a 21st century version of 'really useful' knowledge and skills which help people fully realise themselves as individuals, nurturing family and community members, citizens and workers." In this, he sees nothing wrong with a utilitarian view of education "as long as our view of usefulness is broad, social and humanistic and not narrow, purely economic or individualistic." Playfair sees it a mistake to talk of education for *its* own sake and argues instead that we engage in learning for *our* own sake."

Estelle Morris, who served as minister, then education secretary, from 1997 to 2002, points candidly to the cause of Tuckett's dissatisfaction:

> *"It [adult learning] had never been the top of the political education agenda, particularly following the financial cutbacks of the last Conservative government. However, the flame was kept alive through people like Alan and, when the political focus did turn in that direction, his experience and wisdom became indispensible. He has a wonderful combination of optimism about the power of lifelong learning with an understandable frustration about a stop-and-start approach to its development. For policy makers, it was powerful – he didn't let you off the hook but enthused you about what was possible."*

A retreat from big promises

From the start of his time writing for the *TES*, Tuckett's narrative exuded a firm belief and confidence in the idea of 'entitlement', one that New Labour had appeared to buy into. On Labour's partial retreat from this in the 1999 bill following Learning for Success, he delivered a firm rebuke to ministers. "Until we have an explicit charter of rights and entitlements for adult learners, there must be a clear public commitment to securing a minimum curriculum range and access to learning facilities, guidance and learner support, within reasonable reach of home. Without a commitment of this kind, we will not get the learning society we are all after. Defining adequacy is a tortoise that could do with help in overtaking the hares in the Government who are preparing the Bill." He concluded: "The best time to change bad law is before it appears in a Bill."

It is easy to forget how Alan led the vanguard of a new movement for such change in the 1980s. Ursula Howard, a compatriot in that movement and director of the National Research & Development Centre for Adult Literacy & Numeracy from 2003 to 2008, explains just how fundamental a change he wrought: "Inventing 'adult learning' was probably Alan Tuckett's greatest contribution to education. It was a game changer. When Alan took over at NIACE in 1988, the image, if not the practice, of adult education was stuck in the past, invoking school-room classes, chalk-and-talk and wearying once-a-week two-hour classes. Policy-makers habitually refused to make adults a funding priority, with the glorious exception of the Inner London Education Authority (ILEA) and a few other city authorities. Although working-class and ethnic minority adults, as well as 'women returners', were growing in number, the state grew meaner and meaner about funding the acquisition of knowledge for its own sake, seeing basic language, literacy and workplace skills as their priority."

Not that the priority was misguided; just misplaced, too often to the undue exclusion of wider learning, Howard says:

"Adult learning cut through educational discourses with dynamic effect, creating the idea of the learner, whoever they are, whatever and whenever they learn. It freed up thinking and broke divisions between formal and informal, teacher and taught, active and passive, skills and knowledge. Learning was what adults did, throughout their lives, supported and stretched – or not – by society and the state.

"The timing was good. Learning through technology was taking off, with huge potential for autonomous learning, which is still developing. Adult learning was quickly understood in countries across the world, creating an international movement encapsulated in Adult Learners' Weeks. Adult learning has not opened short-sighted policy makers' purses as much as practitioners and intellectuals would like. But it has made everyone think more respectfully and hopefully about how everyone chooses to develop our lives. That is what Alan has brought about."

Seriously useless learning

Not everyone accepts this vision of Tuckett as the radical reformer. Charles Clarke, who was Education Secretary from 2002 to 2004, saw something of a conservative in him. Like many ministers, Clarke holds him in high esteem. "He was the most articulate and clear-minded person on the worth of adult education in all its senses and in seeing the need for individuals to fulfill themselves. Because he was so persistent in that view, he was a constant reminder that this had to be recognised." Clarke then talks with more caution. "Is it something economic or social, of value in itself? He was very strongly on the latter side and, therefore, found himself in very difficult political waters when arguments of utility were going up the agenda with issues around the money spent." Then Clarke points to what he sees as the real Achilles' heel:

> "If anything, he was slightly pre-occupied with traditional forms of education. By that, I mean institutional. I would say there was a tendency to assume that what had been done for the past 30 years was right for the future. Alan was protecting what had been rather than providing for needs in the modern arena. Argument sometimes got fixed in pro-change and anti-change."

Is Tuckett deep down a traditionalist or is Clarke's view any more than a snapshot at a particular time? If his writing reflects anything, it is of a more radical tendency. Defensiveness usually emerges when he lobbies against the dismantling of what he sees as 'essential support structures'. For the informal learning desired by Clarke, someone in central or local government (preferably in both) must champion (and pay for) training and retention of skilled outreach workers. As he wrote in November 2001: "Another lesson is that many people have forgotten the skills of outreach and negotiation necessary to such work. As the Social Exclusion Unit report on skills recognised, many of the poorest communities have little contact with any institutions." And again, in November 2004, reflecting on wide-scale LSC cuts and erosion of local services: "How will outreach and guidance services be paid for? Will good quality provision survive for people with learning difficulties and those recovering from mental health problems? How can we support learners to strengthen literacy, language and numeracy skills while they pursue other studies? How do we support teachers to deal with change? The questions are legion."

Part of Clarke's argument for the informal over the institutional rests on the value and power of new technology and the internet to support informal learning. But as Tuckett pointed out in February 2005: "Annual NIACE surveys show that the gap between the two halves has been deepened by a digital divide. Those who don't succeed in formal education are rarely skilled in information technology, and so fall further behind."

And when the Labour government finally showed its commitment to a genuine expansion of informal learning under the stewardship of John Denham, secretary of state for innovation, universities and skills from 2007 to 2009, he had the resolute backing of Tuckett. The instrument of change was to be the white paper on informal adult learning. Almost a decade earlier, in January 1999, Tuckett had praised Denham's strong commitment to adult learning when he wrote:

> *"John Denham moved jobs from social security to health in the ministerial reshuffle provoked by Peter Mandelson's borrowing arrangements [Mandelson had failed to disclose a secret loan of £373,000 from colleague Geoffrey Robinson to buy his London home]. Fortunately, to judge from his impressive speech at the launch of the United Nations' Year of the Older Person in London this week, he (Denham) has held on to his role as chair of the inter-ministerial committee which is overseeing the Better Government for Older People initiative. He highlighted the importance of supporting older people's choice to have as active a life as possible, and made lifelong learning one of four priorities for the year."*

In May 2008, Tuckett was pressing home the case for informal leaning "beyond the institutional" when he wrote: "In the wake of the recent local election results, ministers have promised to pay more attention to what people think. It is to John Denham's credit that he has already created the perfect opportunity for this through the consultation on informal learning. As Secretary of State for Innovation, Universities & Skills, he understands that there is a good deal to be listened to and acted on."

Not that they always saw eye-to-eye; Denham, like preceding secretaries of state, admired the "simple persistence with which he (Tuckett) kept arguing doggedly the case for informal learning. It was enormously important and he would not let it go". However, on occasions, he also found him exasperating. "There were times when he had a way of seeing the cup being half empty rather than half full; you had struggled to achieve something only to be told it was not good enough – it could be most dispiriting."

However, the mutual respect and integrity they shared overshadowed everything else. Yes there were differences, says Denham. "But the most productive part of my work with him was on the white paper, *The Learning Revolution*, in which I presented quite a challenge to traditional models of adult learning characterised by the ten-week evening course starting at 7pm on a Monday." There was also a need to make a virtue of necessity since the days of expansionist budgets were over. Regardless of the finances,

Seriously useless learning

however, Denham insisted technology had changed things and that adult learning needed to reflect this. "*The Learning Revolution* aimed to transform things for people using technology. Ten years ago we never had the iPad; now we do and it is changing relationships between teacher and learner. Technology is not about teaching; it opens the door to a process of inquiry where one area of interest can lead to another." He cites the genealogy programme as a good example. Someone makes an inquiry using computers at the local library about their family tree, they find a history group of like-minded people and find themselves getting more deeply involved, doing something you never expected. Multimedia interest stimulates new desires to know and it sets people on a totally new learning journey." There were other players too besides the colleges. "We had the National Trust, Channel 4, the Eden Project and others making massive investment in adult education but never really thinking of themselves as being part of the bigger adult learning picture," he said.

Denham secured £20m for a 'Transformation Fund' to built on the potential of technology, connect organisations and develop partnerships between institutions and groups such as the Eden Project in the hope of removing some of the barriers to learning. The initiative reached across generations and cultures, such as work in Denham's own constituency where a Sikh Elder group linked with a largely white Sure Start group. "Alan became enthused in all this. Once he understood what it was we were trying to do he really got involved; he said yes we are opening new routes."

But was this a newfound enthusiasm on Tuckett's part or was he simply giving credit where due? His insistence on the power of technology, the role of community groups and others and his belief in the power of learner as teacher, as espoused by the radical Latin American educationist Paulo Freire can be found in his writings a decade or more earlier than this. In the end there was a synergy, a meeting of minds between Tuckett and Denham.

Paying to speak English

An issue over which Tuckett had serious run-ins with Labour ministers was that of English for speakers of other languages (Esol). At times, he considered spending cuts to be an act of betrayal and, by 2010, cuts had sparked the national Action for Esol campaign. One such minister was Bill Rammell, minister for education and then skills from 2005 to 2008. He was the man charged with making radical cuts that, Tuckett argued and wrote about, revealed a serious flaw in the government's entire skills strategy.

As Rammell was arriving on the education scene, Tuckett was spelling out his position. In May 2005, he wrote:

"English for speakers of other languages was excluded from the Moser

Report in 1999, and when information and communications technology was added to the suite of basic skills, the official press release called it 'the third basic skill' – so invisible was language. Esol needs sustained investment to build a tutor cohort large enough to meet the thousands ready now to learn, and to reach out to all the UK's linguistic minorities."

Rammell was immediately impressed with the man and says: "He was an immensely powerful and persuasive leader. What was really attractive about him was the way he accepted your premise, in terms of the need to drive up skills, and then used the argument to make a case for the link between learning for leisure and personal development – crucially, to get on those first steps of the skills ladder. He came at it from the point of view of: 'I understand your agenda and we (at NIACE) can help you drive this agenda forwards'."

When it came to Esol, however, Treasury strong-arm tactics and a demand by the Department for Innovation, Universities & Skills to reduce funding won the day. NIACE had commissioned a national inquiry into Esol in 2006 and Rammell had accepted two-thirds of the recommendations, but not those on funding. "I used the NIACE report on the subject to make the changes I felt were necessary. Alan was pissed off but he did not stop communicating with us. They [NIACE] had readily identified that expenditure had gone through the roof but that the hardest-to-reach learners had been pushed to the back of the queue. Alan was frustrated when we insisted on containing spending. He believed our analysis but did not accept our solution. That said, you never fall out with Alan. You could always continue the dialogue. He would say the government had reached conclusions he would not have reached but he never stopped engaging."

Indeed, that persistence paid off, at least in part. That November, Tuckett said that Bill Rammell made a significant and welcome impact on Esol – but only after a compromise, cutting all courses for asylum seekers. "We argued that where the Home Office failed to process a decision within eight weeks, it should pay for the Esol until a decision is made." Also, NIACE had said those who could pay should pay but that everyone should have free provision to level 1.

But the government decided to charge for all not on income support or benefits, regardless of their skills. The impact on the low paid with weak language skills proved to be significant, as Tuckett had warned. "While making a welcome commitment to prioritising those in need, the government decision risks further punishing the poor."

By March 2007, however, the government had relented somewhat on Esol. After considerable lobbying and an impact assessment on race, Rammell

Seriously useless learning

modified fees proposals. Tuckett wrote: "The changes to Esol funding are welcome, of course, but as Paul Mackney, former Natfhe [predecessor to the UCU] general secretary, says, it is not a matter of shuffling the limited budget for adult learning, to give privileges to some learners at the expense of others. The time has come to squeeze serious money from the spending review." And with a note just short of sarcastic, he completed the column saying: "Maybe this prospect explains the gallows humour abroad in the land."

So, was Alan too institutionally-minded and conservative? Blunkett was strongly influenced by him and saw him as the voice of adult education, using his ideas in shaping the Learning Age and subsequent legislation on adult learning; whereas Charles Clarke, around in leaner times, says he could be rooted in the past rather than open to change, and Bill Rammell points to problems over Esol. For John Denham, the bringer of the newer ideas in informal learning (or at least new to Parliament), Tuckett Alan was in fact, very receptive to these. Again, the writings testify to the strength of support he gave.

A safeguard on some funding

His persistence also ensured that funding for informal learning would be further safeguarded throughout and beyond the 2008 financial crisis, to survive draconian cuts under the Coalition government. There is a question of whether or not Labour left it too late because, by Denham's time, the party looked set to lose the election, which of course it did. (Ivan Lewis, minister for young people and learning, secured the safeguard in 2003. Set at 3% (£300m) of the LSC budget, it would shrink year on year to £210m. The fund was, however, consolidated under Denham's watch in the light of the informal adult learning green paper.

With a new government to persuade, Tuckett continued to press home the message. In October 2010, he wrote: "The safeguard was initially set at 3% of the Learning & Skills Council budget, then about £300m, and shrunk each year to its current cash-limited £210m. Without it, and a fund for innovation like the Transformation Fund, it is hard to see how ministers' vision can be realised, or local aspirations met."

John Hayes, the new minister for FE, skills and lifelong learning, was not difficult to persuade. He had spent five years as shadow minister before the Coalition and Tuckett had worked hard to convince him. In July 2011, Hayes wrote to all MPs to say: "We have protected the £210m year budget for Informal Adult & Community Learning." The new Zealot on the block for informal learning went on to ask whether providers could link together and get a 'multiplier' effect from the £210m. It spurred the Workers Educational Association on to ask: "Is John Hayes the nicest man in Parliament?"

One of the best descriptions of the power of Tuckett's prose comes from Jay Derrick, a perceptive writer himself. Many have commented on what they see as an almost schizophrenic mix of remarkable optimism and stoicism in Tuckett's writing.

But Derrick argues that, in the man and his writing, these qualities are in balance:

> *"I don't see these traits as being opposites. Alan's politics are both utopian and realist: he is utopian in that he believes a better future is possible, but a stoic realist in believing that it is up to us, imperfect as we are, and starting wherever we are, to try to make it better – without much of a blueprint and with no certainty of success."*

Because of this, struggles that followed the early heydays for adult learning under New Labour never defeated Tuckett, Derrick suggests. "For obvious reasons, a great deal of his work over the period since the New Labour election victory in 1997 has been damage limitation. My judgement is that the damage would have been much greater without Alan's leadership, optimism, patience and persistence." A line from Tuckett's favourite artist Bob Dylan in the song *Idiot Wind* would not go amiss: "In the final shot he won the war/ After losing every battle".

However, the war goes on; with the replacement in 2012 of John Hayes by Matthew Hancock as minister for FE and skills, the clear signal was of a Coalition Government in retreat from anything but the narrowest work-based notion of utilitarianism. In March 2014, announcing cuts to public spending on 'low value' vocational qualifications, Hancock told the House of Commons: "Small qualifications in coaching angling, aerial balloon displays and self-tanning are not a good use of taxpayers' money or learners' time." In an earlier comment, he had included 'instructing pole fitness' in his list.

Unfortunately, this only served to make him look foolish since some of the examples he chose had never qualified for state funding. Hancock had joined the long line of politicians from all parties who, faced with a lack of firm evidence to support their argument, play to the gallery by rubbishing 'other' learning. Critics had already been muttering about him as a minister not fully on top of his brief and now leaders of FE told him to so his face. Association of Colleges chief executive Martin Doel said:

> *"It's unfortunate that there's little understanding or recognition that some of the courses derided in this announcement are those which are important in encouraging vulnerable adults, for example those who are recovering from mental or physical health issues or redundancy, back into work-related training and into employment."*

Seriously useless learning

And David Hughes, chief executive of NIACE, said:

> *"Often, people find so-called 'low-value' courses a great way to step back into learning, to help them rebuild their confidence and they then go on to take further courses and qualifications."*

Intimate conversation with a gentleman

Throughout his years for the *TES*, Tuckett drew a more significant postbag than most columnists. For Ruth Silver, former Lewisham college principal and a senior adviser to successive governments, the reason is obvious: "He conducted a very intimate personal conversation on the page with his readers, believing always that you could convert people through reason and sound argument, unlike today's commentators whose writings are too often less about hard evidence and more what sociologist Richard Sennett describes as 'the fetish of assertion'." His commentaries were well-informed philosophical and political reflections on the state of post-school education and governing policies, she says. "As a result, politicians, senior civil servants and policy makers use him as a sounding board."

Tuckett used this style of writing to shift the focus away from politicians, from the Great and the Good, and to reminding ordinary citizens that they have the power to change things "if only they would wake up and use it". Writing in October 2005, he asked whether we have become over-reliant on think tanks for our critical judgment, and intellectually lazy as a result. To illustrate the point, he evokes the notion of the 'awkward citizen'. Awkward citizens ask questions and are disruptive.

"Such people learn as they go, as John Field [professor of lifelong learning at the University of Stirling] points out in his study *Social Capital & Lifelong Learning*. It's true of people in the environmental movement or 'Make Poverty History'. The college space where such people gain this 'other' learning is slowly disappearing in the target-driven culture," says Tuckett.

"Yet we need awkward citizens every bit as much as we need a skilled workforce to test existing policies and come up with better ways of doing things. This is not a task to be delegated to think tanks. And all the blame for the marginalisation of such work cannot sit with government or its funding agencies. Some must lie with local providers, who move at the speed of light to adapt to changing priorities."

For some reason, Tuckett's 'dual' personality evokes thoughts of Gramsci in several people who were interviewed for this book. For example, Bill Rammell commented:

> *"His manner and tone of voice were in no sense an artifice; he was very engaging and got people to listen to him. He reminds me of*

Gramsci's observation: 'Pessimism of the intellect; optimism of the spirit'. He recognised the barriers and difficulties and recognised you could have impact."

Similarly, John Field, who has worked closely with Tuckett over many years, also spoke of "pessimism of the intellect, optimism of the will". This well-known paraphrase from the Italian Marxist Antonio Gramsci applies more to Alan Tuckett than to anyone else I know. As director of NIACE, he encountered every policy maker, however unreconstructed, and discovered common ground with them, before engaging them in a constructive discussion about why they supported (not why they should support) adult learners. And he met some pretty unreconstructed characters during his long tenure of the hot seat in Leicester [NIACE HQ]. During the time he was writing for *TES*, Alan dealt with governments of both political colours, as well as civil servants who shared few of his views, tastes or instincts. Some tried to cut adult learning to shreds, others wanted it narrowed down to skills development, some loved and defended it. In all cases, Alan spotted opportunities for persuasion along with cause for exasperation.

"I remember a discussion with a friend who had joined the staff of NIACE a year or two earlier. I asked her how she was enjoying her new role. She reflected, smiled and said: 'I am still adjusting to a culture of generosity.' A two-edged sword, then, which helped protect adult learning in harsh times."

What makes a good columnist?

Tuckett possesses the two essential qualities of a good columnist: an insatiable appetite for the written word and a passion for communicating what he has learned – interpreting, not parroting. Virtually everyone who has worked with him will testify to this. Alastair Thomson, principal policy officer at NIACE, said: "Looking back on Alan Tuckett's commentary pieces, I'm struck by the consistency of the values and principles behind the words, and the fluency with which he makes the case to politicians of all persuasions, that the education of adults will not only improve the lives of individuals and their immediate families but also enrich the economy and wider society.

"Working alongside Alan from when he joined NIACE in 1988 until he retired in 2010 was a pleasure, a privilege and, most of all, an education. Alan has an enormous appetite for ideas and is able to assimilate a large volume of oral and written material quickly and make connections. He also has a compulsion to share what he knows. Whether in conversation or on the page, he has the ability to construct a persuasive narrative which helps others to make better sense of the world. A

Seriously useless learning

recurring feature of his writing is his way of humanising points of policy with references to individual students, teachers or examples of practice, anchoring theory to practice and lived experience. Other themes to which Alan's writings return repeatedly are solidarity with the poor (globally as well as nationally) and with the marginalised.

"One of the reasons people look forward to reading Alan's words or listening to him is that, invariably he inspires hope. In difficult times for the public funding of adult learning, he reminds us that education is something more than a public service to be closed down, sold off, rationed or shaped to ever-more instrumental ends. Education is not wholly owned by the state – it belongs also to people themselves. In this way the act of both teaching and learning can empower and liberate. That positive message encourages people to believe that another, better, world is possible."

To achieve such ends in his *TES* columns (and subsequent writing), Alan is never afraid to take a side-swipe at ignorance and lazy rhetoric from the Great and the Good. Such was the case in his *TES* column of March 2000, after witnessing a jaw-dropping, inane lecture by the then Ofsted chief inspector Chris Woodhead at the Royal Society of Arts. Tuckett wrote: "Chris Woodhead had chosen to ask: 'Is lifelong learning a utopian ideal?' It was both characteristic and astonishing as a presentation: characteristic in that he gave a raucously polemical defence of the status quo; astonishing in the skimpiness of its frame of reference and the research undertaken in preparation.

"Chris Woodhead berated moves to improve educational opportunity for older adults, suggesting they had earned the right to be left in peace. Behind his remarks was a bleak view of what learning can do to enrich life, let alone your health. Yet research by Fiona Aldridge and Peter Lavender [*Learning and Health*, National Institute of Adult Continuing Education] shows nine in ten learners see positive effects on physical and mental well-being."

Globe-trotting

Tuckett accepts no boundaries or limitations in his worldview of adult learning, and this had a big influence on his writing for the *TES*. As David Blunkett observed earlier in this piece, Tuckett produced a report on an international meeting in South America that pointed the way forward for any country looking to further adult learning. He spread the word of adult open access in a truly international way – éducation sans frontiere.

Julian Gravatt, assistant chief executive of the Association of Colleges, tells an amusing tale of Tuckett gliding with ease between national and international arenas in pursuit of his goals. He met him regularly in Coventry, which housed the HQs of successive government funding agencies.

"Coventry was one of England's finest medieval cities; it was a symbol of post-War renaissance and, for the last 20 years, has been where people assemble from across England to discuss technical details of further and adult education. Hundreds of thousands of hours have been spent – in a developer's attempt at a post-modern office built on an old Coventry engineering site – discussing ALF, GLH, QCF and ATJz [acronyms of deathless, will-sapping jargon from the pens of bureaucrats talking about average funding and guided learning hours etc].

"Occasionally, at one of these meetings, you'll see Alan. Possibly in a white suit. Just back from somewhere more interesting. He may or may not have studied the spreadsheets or the carefully written consultation papers, but you can rely on him to take the meeting beyond the processes and the targets to the fact that we're talking about real people of all ages and background organising and taking courses to improve themselves, their families and their communities.

"Sometimes it can be irritating. Not everyone gets a gig in Germany or a trip to Brazil. But Alan's use of his experience and his focus on the moral purpose of education provides a heat source in the current ice age. It helped successive ministers protect the £210m community learning fund in successive budgets, inspired researchers to look at the wider benefits of learning and gave NIACE an inner energy at a time when other national organisations have stumbled and fallen.

"None of this should distract us from the current crisis in English adult education. Twenty-five years ago, the UK led the world in evening class enrolments, programmes to open access and innovative thinking about adult learning. Much of that work survives but much has been lost and we lack a sustainable model of paying for group learning for everyone. For some people, digital TV, smartphones and computer games fill the gaps, but for many others they don't. Alan continues to help people work through these issues as a college governor and international NGO leader. It's not easy but it's always worth a try."

While Tuckett has battled against the erosion of open access in England – so acutely observed by Gravatt – his ideas were adopted internationally with remarkable alacrity and not a little success. Adult Learners' Week is

Seriously useless learning

a good example. Writing in June 2000, he describes a visit to NIACE HQ: "Just before Adult Learners' Week this year, a group of adult educators from across the globe met in Leicester. They were there to help the United Nations Educational, Scientific & Cultural Organisation prepare advice for countries considering starting a festival of adult learning. The results will be published on September 8 at the launch of the first International Adult Learners' Week." This has to be one of the biggest understatements in Alan's writing: they were in Leicester because Tuckett was seen as the world leader, almost a guru; he was the architect of Adult Learners' Week, which is marked across the world.

That said, he travels widely in order to bring ideas home as much as to export (he would say "share") good practice. And the questions he raises always ask more than is immediately apparent. For example, writing in June 2000, he says: "'What's the use of a centre of excellence among a sea of poverty?' Sam Isaacs, head of the South African Qualifications Authority asked my breakfast companion last Sunday. The question invites you to think about how much is appropriate to spend on higher education in a country where 12 million or more lack basic literacy skills." When you consider recent international reports on the state of adult literacy, the question becomes pertinent much closer to home, as does the question: "So what are we doing about it?"

Take the issue of adult literacy and numeracy and Claus Moser's report, with its headline finding that seven million adults in the UK lack basic skills. Writing in August 2001, Tuckett said the work that followed persuaded the Treasury to release unprecedented sums of money, and Labour promised to achieve targets for strengthening basic skills for 700,000 adults. But, he asks, how generous was this? To find out, he looked overseas and the International Adult Literacy Survey – undertaken since the mid-1990s. With his always-critical eye, he questioned just how valid the research was. "From the beginning, the survey's methodology was questioned, but its impact cannot be denied. In countries such as the UK, which did poorly with 23% of adults having difficulties, this was, perhaps, unsurprising. But in Sweden, which came top by a long way, with just 7% of adults having difficulties, a new measure was introduced, offering an entitlement to everyone without school-leaving qualifications to a year's full-time study on full pay, with the state picking up the bill. At a UK-Sweden conference I attended, the Swedish education minister explained that the issue was a civil rights concern. 'If the survey had shown there were only a thousand, a hundred or just 10 adults needing help, it would be just as much a priority,' he explained."

Learning is a civil right
Adult learning as a 'civil right' pervades the thinking, evidence and recom-

mendations in the biggest-ever two-year inquiry into the future of lifelong learning, Learning Through Life, from 2007-09 and directed by Tom Schuller, former head of CERI (Centre for Educational Research and Innovation) at the OECD. While it was independent of NIACE, it was very much Tuckett's brainchild. The blueprint it offered of changing entitlements to adult learning through four stages of life was visionary and stands alongside *The Learning Age* for its far-sightedness. Schuller says of him:

> *"I think of Alan as someone who was able to keep repeating the same messages with extreme persistence, but also to absorb new thinking and produce his own original thoughts. His commitment to lifelong learning as an inclusive and transformative activity has always been total. He is an internationalist, egalitarian enthuser.*
>
> *"I benefitted personally from his courage and vision in committing NIACE resources to the inquiry. Although it was his baby, he managed to allow us a very fair degree of space in taking it forward. Perhaps the impact has not quite been what we would have hoped, which I feel is a poor reward for his risk-taking, but he's a pilgrim who is never discouraged. If there is one word that captures Alan, it is 'relentless'."*

A place where adult learning as a 'civil' right became most embedded – under the guidance of NIACE in the way Tuckett wished for – was, ironically, in the British Armed Forces. A major programme was embarked on in the early part of the new Millennium to help its personnel improve their literacy, and numeracy research and a long-term study conducted by NIACE and NRDC showed also how such sustained programmes improve professional development and operational effectiveness. It also showed how broad a canvas NIACE worked on.

A voice to be reckoned with

"In many of Shakespeare's plays, you see the stage direction 'A Tuckett Sounds' – presaging the entrance of some grandee. Well, A Tuckett has been sounding across the world of adult education for my entire working career – and that is now a very long time."

This observation from Rob Wye, former chief executive of the Learning & Skills Improvement Service, is interesting in several ways. First, it underlines the theatrical nature of Tuckett the performer; second, it reminds us of the man's love of words; and, third, it says that he had a voice with a resonance that can be 'heard' in the minds of people when reading his columns. It is the 'conversation' he has with his readers that Ruth Silver spoke of. Wye points out that the 'sound' is one of strong commitment.

Seriously useless learning

"Alan has a fundamental and unshakable belief in the power of learning to change lives, and its importance throughout lives. It is through that belief and enthusiasm and his strong political nous that the adult education agenda and the adult education budget has remained – albeit under pressure, but still there."

Equally, Tuckett reinforces that commitment with strong presentation. "I also relish Alan's turn of phrase – seeing the value, yes, in instrumental learning and work skills, but also for the 'seriously useless learning' that instils a joy in new things and a sense of wonder at the world. Long may our favourite Tuckett continue to sound!" This sense of Alan's 'voice' also comes through strongly in comments by Peter Lavender, an education consultant and senior research fellow at NIACE, who has worked more closely Tuckett than most:

"When Alan wrote his first column for the TES, his voice was already known in the post-compulsory education sector. It was a mellifluous Cornish voice, arguing for 'adults too', celebrating their learning in all its variety, persuading you that learning could transform lives, change policy and build a civilised society. And we knew this to be true. It was a challenging voice: challenging the narrowness of skills strategies, the foolishness of endless policy change ('like pulling up the roots to see if the plant has grown yet') and the damaging impact of inequality. Without Alan's voice from NIACE, we might never have had key images to make sense of widening participation for adults; might never have experienced the celebration ('posh frock days') inherent in Adult Learners' Week or the creative power of the concept of (again that phrase) 'seriously useless learning' (the emphasis being on 'serious').

"When adult learning opportunities were threatened by the Bill leading up to the 1992 Further & Higher Education Act, Alan took delight in organising opposition and discussion, particularly enjoying the impact of the National Federation of Women's Institutes. Much of the argument Alan made has won the hearts and minds of successive governments, winning support right across the political spectrum, with enormous success. That is, until this minister and this government, where policies for learning exclude adults returning to learn in later years, ignore the power of learning for frail and elderly people, and restrict community learning to the voluntary sector. We need Alan's voice back again – more than ever before. It is hugely missed."

Qualities that shape the writing

This work is essentially Tuckett's collected writing, though that is clearly inseparable from the man. On the personality side, there is much that could be said. For all his gentle demeanour, many of the people interviewed for this work recall that he could get angry – 'sometimes very angry', as several recalled. He very much admires Nick Stuart, the former civil servant and chair of NIACE who helped shape NIACE, too (see below). And while many say that, as a man of the Left, he never really recognised 'New' Labour, he strongly admired and liked the Labour Government's approach to lifelong learning under David Blunkett.

For those who want more on the personal perspectives, there is the book mentioned earlier, *Remaking Adult Learning*, the tribute – or festschrift – written when Tuckett left NIACE. There is a whole chapter there on his management style, with very many comments on the person. They reinforce Paul Mackey's idea of Tuckett as dialectical man. This comes through in comments from those who worked and often still work closely with him. He liked nothing more than a good argument, says Carol Taylor, NIACE director of development and research, who was CEO of the Basic Skills Agency when, in 2007, it moved to merge with NIACE – where its origins lay.

> *"Alan could not have been more welcoming. I, like so many others, found him intellectually challenging, passionate about adult learning, candid, funny, warm-hearted, and far-sighted. We had a few robust exchanges, which he enjoyed – he liked nothing better than to be challenged! He was splendidly eclectic and thrived on controversial debate. His public persona of dignified advocacy was underpinned by a healthy realism born equal measures of hope and despair. Whilst he was forced to kow-tow to the monetarist utilitarianism that reduced the intrinsic value of everything to figures on a spreadsheet, he nonetheless remained resolutely upbeat about the justice of his cause."*

Dan Taubman, former national officer at the UCU, has worked with him ever since Tuckett was appointed to be principal of Clapham & Battersea Adult Education Institute. "Alan's charm and charisma worked wonderfully well with what we called 'mainstream' provision. He was able to be simultaneously radical and reassuring. This sprang from his love and commitment to adult education as empowering and liberating process. When Alan became director of NIACE, he demonstrated a remarkable ability to make penetrating analyses and critiques of government adult learning policy whilst hoovering up lots of government money."

Whether it's the dialectical process, robust argument or general debate, for Stephen McNair, President of the National Association for Adult Guidance and NIACE senior research fellow, the key strength of Tuckett – written or spoken – is the power of persuasion.

> *"He has an extraordinary ability to charm even the most entrenched opponents, appealing to their better natures and making them feel that they are part of a worthy cause. He can usually persuade you that the outcome of a conversation is not only necessary, but right – what you had always really wanted, but only now understood."*

Despite an apparently anarchic approach to management, says McNair,

> *"He was also a very good judge of risk, and where to draw boundaries. His approach to fundamental disagreements on policy was always that, when a decision is simply unacceptable, he has a duty to say so clearly, but an equal duty to warn his opponent in advance and they respected the fact that, in his own phrase, there are 'no surprises'. Principled views must be expressed, but never with rancour, and relationships were rapidly rebuilt afterwards. He also never shied away from tough managerial decisions: he allowed individuals remark-able freedom, but was quite capable of explaining very clearly when performance was unacceptable. Over 40 years of major change, he has always continued to believe in the cause of adult learning and the possibility, whatever the political, social and economic climate, of making it better."*

. . . .

THE JOURNALIST who reported most on work of Alan Tuckett is George Low, former editor of *Education*, which for most of the post-war years was known in the trade as the '*Private Eye* of education'. What follows is his account of Tuckett's progress in the years prior to the arrival of the Coalition government.

Alan Tuckett, by George Low

I first got to know, like and admire Alan Tuckett in 1974. This was a time of economic and social recovery after several bitter years of inflation and industrial disputes; when the lights went out (literally) at the end of the Heath government. Harold Wilson had come back as Labour prime minis-ter and was trying to embark on a period of economic recovery and social reconstruction.

In this climate, the Right to Read movement had started in the adult educa-tion centres, based mainly in the cities. It was also taking off in the BBC with a startlingly successful series on adult literacy. The Open University and various university institutes had spawned a slightly mad new movement known as the Association for Recurrent Education, which had picked up the virus from the United States and Scandinavia and wanted to spread the message nationwide.

This was the background scene when a meeting of various campaigners was held in London to decide how to take the Right to Read campaign. Among the most eloquent was a young settlement head from Brighton, who called for a national campaign in the media to spread the word and muster public support for adult literacy. "What's that guy's name?" asked Arthur Stock, the director of NIACE. "Alan Tuckett", came the reply and various people in high places – and the press – made a note of it. It was not long before he joined the committee of the Adult Literacy Resource Agency (ALRA). That voice came to be well known on the circuit. His words reverberated round the education press; they were original and often surprising. His writing also had style, vigour and a certain poetic quality. He sometimes got carried away in both spoken and written language, but he always had an adult educator's ability to engage and stimulate his audience.

Alan's campaigning zeal made him some enemies in high places, especially when he moved to ILEA as an adult education principal. But he also made some good friends and supporters. Among them was Roy Harding, chief education officer of Buckinghamshire and later general secretary of the Society of Education Officers. Roy was one of the founders of the Open University who also had a profound and intimate knowledge of the FE sector at local government level. He was greatly respected at the Department for Education & Science (or DES, as it was then called). He had a long involvement with NIACE through the Association of County Councils. When Alan became director of NIACE, Roy Harding was his president and generously offered him all his contacts and experience of central and local government. He was able to steer Alan round some of the threats and pitfalls of Whitehall and Westminster.

Another key adviser was Nick Stuart, a very able senior civil servant at the DES who had a great respect for adult learning – his father had resorted to self-study as a prisoner of war in Germany during the war. He became chairman of the NIACE board when he finally retired from his top job as director general at the DES. Alan was lucky to have him, especially because not all the DES civil servants were either friendly or well-informed. Indeed, some were even malevolent towards 'quangos' such as NIACE.

With the benefit of these wise and benevolent advisers Alan was able to survive some of the darker days of the Thatcher regime, when adult education had to sell itself for funding in the marketplace and find new sources of income. Opportunities for growth and expansion came only rarely when there were friendly ministers in post at the DES, and then they had to be seized. With the help of such advisers, Alan was able to make attractive and affordable policies temptingly available on a plate which ministers could boast of as their very own recipe. Alan founded the Adult Learners' Week as a public campaign for adult education locally and nationally, which proved such a startling success that it became an annual event for NIACE, and for tutors and students throughout the country.

With the arrival of David Blunkett as the first secretary of state for education in the Labour government under Tony Blair, Alan enjoyed a rare and magical window of opportunity for new projects. From his own background as a disabled student and his time as chairman of Sheffield education committee, Blunkett was a true believer in adult recurrent education and open to all sorts of ideas for projects, especially for the disabled, literacy and numeracy, as well as citizenship and English as a second language. Alan basked for three or four years in the warm favour of Blunkett's generosity and NIACE had the badge of ministerial approval.

Alas, the benign era did not last into the second New Labour term, when Blunkett moved to the Home Office and certain civil servants took over at the Department for Education & Skills (the DFES, as it became known). The Basic Skills Agency was abolished as a tiresome quango and its director Alan Wells was forced to resign. Tuckett took the leftover remains back into NIACE, but the BSA was a shadow of its former self as an engine for tackling adult illiteracy. The ambitious programme devised by Alan Wells and Lord Moser for abolishing illiteracy by the year 2020 was consigned by the DFES to the dustbin.

Nevertheless, Alan has proved amazingly resilient, even under the current Coalition regime, and his reputation has grown steadily as an international figurehead. The publication of Tom Schuller's blueprint for lifelong learning will prove a worthy monument to Alan's long tenure at the head of NIACE, even if the dream never comes to pass. He can take comfort from the old Biblical saying: "A prophet is not without honour, save in his own country" (St. Matthew xiii, 57).

But in adult centres up and down the country, Alan the great campaigner will always be freshly remembered. And in retirement, we continue to hear Alan's voice in fervent support of adult learning and social justice each time Alan picks up the pen to reflect and write from the long view and from many global vantage points.

From optimism to audit

REFLECTING THE air of optimism and expectation around the New Labour government – not least in pledges to adults made by the education secretary David Blunkett – Alan Tuckett wrote of expansive days, of Blunkett securing cash in the comprehensive spending review with arguments drawn from *The Learning Age* and the Helena Kennedy report, *Learning Works*. He was encouraged, knowing these measures should ensure 'widening participation' in further and higher education and in community learning, built around partnerships and joined-up local government – exactly what so many people yearned for.

From the start, however, he sounded a note of caution about a tendency towards bean-counting by a party still needing to restore public confidence in its ability to manage the economy. He wrote:

> *"And partnerships work best when all the participants recognise the politics of generosity – that the more you give away, the more gets given back to you. Of course, that sits uneasily with audit culture."*

Later, he would write:

> *"The first Adult Learners' Week was held in 1992. It began at a time of struggle, when adults had to assert that they could be the best judges of what was worth studying, and that they had a right to claim modest investment from government to back them in their choices."*

He further warned how readily a less generous administration would reverse any such gains.

He was right on both counts. First, obsessive audit soon put paid to many of Labour's promises to support a broad adult learning entitlement as provision accelerated, slowly at first and then with remarkable speed and alacrity, towards narrow utilitarian goals. Second, a political generation later, lack of generosity would increasingly be the hallmark of a Coalition government whose ideological fix on neoliberalism allowed little room for even modest investment, especially where public spending was concerned.

Seriously useless learning

Throughout the first period of his writing for the *TES*, Tuckett set out his stall of entitlements for the marginalised: a creative and inspiring curriculum to bring the socially- and economically-excluded back into learning; loans for the over-50s to study at university, since "they have decades to make use of new intellectual stimulus"; and, most of all, a breadth of learning on offer to all adults. His notion of 'the excluded' applied at every level from basic skills to HE, wherever unjustifiable barriers hampered progress. His vision was one of "raising all boats". If this all appears a bit scatter-gun and difficult to pin down, that is the nature of post-compulsory learning, he writes.

> "Adult learning is not a tidy business and I am nervous that, in pursuit of coherence, we may squeeze out diversity. Nowhere is that risk clearer than in Gordon Brown's throwaway remark in the [April 1999] Budget, that vocational tax relief is to be phased out and, with it, public support 'for non-vocational courses like diving and flying lessons'."

Tuckett calls for "a dialogue to overcome its [the Treasury's] desire to demonise learning which leads to no obvious short-term economic benefit, to protect the widening participation agenda, and to persuade economists that learning is the key industrial skill, and it can be picked up in unlikely contexts."

However, then as now, he never argued in favour of one form of learning over another. On the one hand, he was clearly irritated by "a panjandrum in the [civil service] system who said: 'Surely we might agree that the primary purpose of education is preparation for the labour market'?" On the other, he lobbied hard for learning in the workplace:

> "All the evidence shows that most adults still get access to learning at work, and we need a closer link between work-based learning and learning in colleges and community contexts."

A battle he pursued but lost by September that year was for a clear definition of 'adequacy' and 'sufficiency' when it comes to adult education entitlement. The Tories had veered away from any such commitment in the 1992 FHE Act and now Labour, all too early in its first term of office for 18 years, was doing much the same.

Halfway through Labour's first term, Tuckett expressed concern that not all was going well. Looking at promises in *The Learning Age*, he questioned whether the white paper, *Learning to Succeed*, would deliver on them. Problems were looming. For example, voluntary-sector agencies felt excluded and he predicted how localism and personal empowerment would suffer as a result. Big money was now going to the colleges, which was creating its own demand. But is it getting us where it ought to? he asks.

By the end of 1999, the scale of demand on colleges was dwarfing even the big money finally going into further education. There was evidence of a growing gap between the haves and have-nots – the work-rich/time-poor, as against time-rich/work-poor. An hour-glass economy was emerging, characterised by a preponderance of high-skilled and management posts at the top, and cleaners, carers and caterers at the bottom, while skilled manufacturing jobs were being ripped out of the middle – an accelerating trend that started under Thatcherism. Moreover, it was clear that as with the health service, educational benefits went disproportionately to the best-off. "The inescapable conclusion is that getting people into jobs is not in itself enough," Tuckett argued.

The scale of the challenge was apparent in the work of the government's Social Exclusion Unit, about which he writes extensively during this time. It found three reasons why neighbourhood renewal strategies failed: the systems were focused insufficiently on needs of the disadvantaged; local capacity to sustain initiatives was weak; and the socially-excluded felt they had nothing to gain from joining in.

Tuckett's conclusion? We need "patient, sustained work on a number of fronts over an extended period. It is not cheap work, and it does not quickly and predictably lead to easily-auditable outcomes." Numerous warnings about over-reliance of audit were coming thick and fast from government agencies, NGOs and voluntary organisations.

By the new Millennium, there was the Learning & Skills Bill. However, he wrote, it gave inadequate status to lifelong learning partnerships in shaping policy and strategy, put no duty on local authorities to provide for adults, created a divided inspection model with too few quality checks on adult learning, and offered little of substance about the role of the youth service and adult guidance. Tuckett was disappointed and, moreover, unconvinced that any developments would be free of Downing Street interference:

> *"To return to lifelong learning partnerships: they are given a critically important role in consulting learners and liaising with the voluntary sector. How will that survive a policy change in Sanctuary Buildings or Number 10? There is altogether not enough about accountabilities to stakeholders, users, local communities – and there needs to be if we really are committed to revitalising and sustaining active civil society."*

We see also a rowing back from Kennedy's call for an adult learning entitlement at level 3. The second report of the government's Skills Task Force had come to the same conclusion as Kennedy in respect of 19- to 24-year-olds, but the third report settled for Level 2 for other adults, albeit with Level

Seriously useless learning

3 as an aspiration. "Neither argument has yet won the day with the Department for Education."

Tuckett drew on a considerable bank of evidence when he wrote that the nub of the issue is, as all the social policy reports and government work shows, that "for neighbourhood renewal to succeed and social exclusion to be beaten, all age groups must be involved in local communities". He accepts that, whether it's on funding or on inspection, it's clear that 16-to-19 entitlement is paramount.

> *"But it is, I think, essential that the same symbolic commitment is given to the creation of a society in which old and young have a right to learn. An adult entitlement might need a different balance of expectations about who pays. It might not be achievable all at once. But it is as necessary to making the policy work as is the welcome supply-side measures in the Bill."*

By mid-year, his frustrations spill over.

> *"The audit culture has given priority to the needs of funders and institutions. In public, inspection has focused on accountability and judgment, leaving advice and encouragement to private conversations."*

BY THE summer before the general election, the Learning & Skills Bill is all but wrapped up. Primacy is given to the young as expected, with few of the promises to adults remaining beyond free basic skills training. "After that, they will get what's left once the promises to the young are met," Tuckett writes in July 2000. Hoped-for entitlement up to and including Level 3 have vanished.

> *"The commitment to give what's left over to adults is all well and good while cash flows into education. Yet, as Baroness David remarked in the Lords, it would be better if ministers stated a clear aspiration to introduce a proper adult entitlement. Tessa [Baroness] Blackstone's reply to Baroness David was interesting. 'At this stage,' she said, 'I am not able to make any commitment about there being an entitlement to adult learning. However, I shall certainly take away her suggestion, which may in the longer term be desirable.'"*

Tuckett notes that the Baroness would go no further than saying it 'may' be desirable, fearing that the "old-fashioned Treasury view – that adult learning is an optional extra – lingers near the heart of government".

Nevertheless, he still retains some optimism and insists there's still much to go for – for an adult and community learning curriculum to be built in from the beginning and better briefing for voluntary agencies to play their part:

> "I think, though, that the largest challenge lies with those committed to widening participation. To serve the needs of the learning poor, who have their best chance of learning at work, new alliances will be needed. The new learning and skills structure will bring education and training closer together. But the trick will be to think how we can better serve the needs of part-time and temporary workers, who often have too little free time to study outside work."

When Blunkett came into office, he said patience was needed to change policy affecting adults and compared the task with turning round an oil tanker. Tuckett reminded his readers: "Much has been achieved, but little is written into the Act. As a result, another administration, or different ministerial priorities in this administration, could easily reverse many of the gains." He then reiterates:

> "And that is the source of my gloom. So much to feel pleased about that it feels churlish to point out that there is not enough in the Act to secure the future adult learning deserves."

Commentaries
8 January 1999 to 28 July 2000

8 January 1999

All we wanted for Christmas

by Alan Tuckett
Section: FE Focus. Issue 4306, p34

JUST OCCASIONALLY, Christmas brings you just what you wanted, and more besides. It was a bit like that this year for Lewis, my son, when his godfather sent him an Action Man who repeats the last thing said into his communications unit, and another friend gave him a dig-your-own-dinosaur kit, so he could do archaeology like his sister.

For me, the weeks leading up to Christmas had much the same effect. Governments seldom do more for adult learners than they promise to do – but David Blunkett's team have taken the framework of issues addressed in *The Learning Age*, imbued them with the spirit of Helena Kennedy, and won real extra money in the comprehensive spending review. And there is a good deal more money.

However, it is firmly linked to widening participation in higher, further and community education, and to partnerships. At a National Institute of Adult Continuing Education conference in December Jane Cowell, a key adviser to the Kennedy committee, talked of being 'partnershipped out'.

It is a feeling that will become common, as the government seeks to secure joined-up government at a local level, and to overcome the mad inter-institutional competitiveness of the 1990s. Taking part in partnerships, and building the trust to make them work, takes a lot of time. And partnerships work best when all the participants recognise the politics of generosity – that the more you give away, the more gets given back to you. Of course, that sits uneasily with audit culture.

If the widening participation agenda is to work then investment in community-based work is essential, and three initiatives will help.

First, the small but significant Standards Fund budget for the development of local education authority lifelong learning plans should halt the decline of LEA-adult education spending.

The second positive development is the clarification in the 1998 Education Act of the Further Education Funding Council's powers to fund leisure courses. Given the patchwork of courses currently available, that was an essential precondition to opening the system to 700,000 more and different learners.

Finally, the £130m available to create a Community Grid for Learning should give everyone access to local learning centres linked to the web, and offering a combination of face-to-face and distance-based learning facilities, in libraries, church halls, and adult education centres. This development is an important precondition for the University for Industry to be able to contribute to the widening participation agenda. A second precondition is an effective network of local guidance services. For that we await an early announcement!

Along with the Moser report, developments on individual learning accounts, the review of the training and enterprise councils, and the University for Industry corporate plan, it should make for a busy New Year.

But there remains a great deal to do, if current policies are to work for adult learners. Sixty per cent of the new places for adults are for 'Kennedy' students. That is admirable, but not everyone is skilled in the outreach work needed to persuade many adults that learning really can help.

You can see this in a number of the bids to the Adult & Community Learning Fund which show little appreciation of the time that needs to be taken to create a climate of confidence, or of the negotiation of the curriculum adult educators used to talk convincingly about. Not all of them recognise the challenge in retaining new returners. But, as Helena Kennedy said at a NIACE conference, you cannot retain students you have not effectively recruited.

Veronica McGivney's powerful new study, *Excluded Men*, published this week, points to the scale of the challenge. The publication launches Sign Up Again, a campaign to help institutions recruit, particularly among men and older people.

Veronica's study shows that many men believe that learning is something for women to do. She points to the feminisation of the curriculum, and the need to develop strategies that address men's scepticism, and start from their current aspirations.

Institutions have something of a mountain to climb to make learning work for everyone, but the new co-operation and partnership culture also poses stiff challenges to the inspectoral tribes of post-school learning.

In Wales, the same HMI undertake inspections for LEAs, the Welsh Further Education Funding Council, and for the Training Inspectorate. Why can't we have the same rational system in England, where boundary problems get in the way of supporting adult learners, with coherent quality assurance services? It would be good to see improvements in the new year.

Seriously useless learning

22 January 1999
Allow for the old invisibles
by Alan Tuckett
Section: FE Focus. Issue 4308, p36

John Denham moved jobs from social security to health in the ministerial reshuffle provoked by Peter Mandelson's borrowing arrangements. Fortunately, to judge from his impressive speech at the launch of the United Nations' Year of the Older Person in London this week, he has held on to his role as chair of the inter-ministerial committee which is overseeing the Better Government for Older People initiative. He highlighted the importance of supporting older people's choice to have as active a life as possible, and made lifelong learning one of four priorities for the year.

If John Denham was good, the Age Exchange theatre company was stunning. A troupe of some 15 older people led the policy works and voluntary agency staff through a funny, sharp and engaging review – in ten minutes flat. Their work – on this occasion a wry look at Christmases before the war – was the product of active participation in the creation of drama, growing out of reminiscence work and oral history with other older people.

They use it to stimulate other older people to make sense of the changes they have experienced in their lives, and to lead inter-generational dialogues with children. Watching the performance reinforced one of the clearest messages of the launch – that many of our attitudes to older people are shaped by their under-representation on television in active and interpretative roles.

Age Exchange retains its base in Greenwich, south east London, although it now works all over the country and in Europe. Pam Schweitzer, its animateur, has a single-minded passion for the work and its capacity to demonstrate the energy, brio and wisdom of older people as learners. She shows here what Augusto Boal's work demonstrated so well in Peru – that theatre provides the most creative tools for stimulating dialogue to give voice to marginalised groups.

It is striking, as Sue Cara observes in this month's *Adults Learning*, how few of the bids for funding from the Adult & Community Learning Fund involve theatre, the arts or music. The obsessions of the 1990s have bleached out delight and creativity from too many organisers' thinking. People still struggle to make sense of poems, capture light on paper, make music etc. But, she argues, this is not seen as a curriculum fit for the excluded.

Formal systems can lead to funny priorities. When I worked in south London, I was involved with a weekly crafts class in a hospice. There was inevitably a large turnover of students during the year. The tutor was, I felt, brilliant – sensitive and inspiring; giving her students what might be one of life's last achievable challenges.

I thought you needed a special kind of capacity to do the work well, and asked for the post to be regraded. After a visit the fashion inspector told me the class could not be regraded because the work lacked sufficient difficulty. I think there are lessons here for the Qualifications & Curriculum Authority, and for that matter the Moser Committee. We need flexibility and fitness for purpose in thinking about what constitutes quality and how you can measure it. Too often policy is developed for the people who are visible. It is a key demand of Jim Soulsby and Sheila Carlton's timely *Learning to Grow Older & Bolder* that we stop ignoring older people when we think about lifelong learning. Why can't people over 54 get loans to study at university when they have decades to make use of new intellectual stimulus? Too often the arguments seem narrowly economic – the assumption is they will not be able to repay. Interestingly, their study shows that most people over 75 who are studying are doing so for work-related reasons.

Education on television fares rather better. The BBC leads the way in making a range of programmes that stretch beyond the narrowly domestic, aimed at older people, put out at lunchtimes, and backed by study material and access to Open College accreditation. Of course, far more people send off for the material than seek formal accreditation. But the offer is there, linked to courses at short-term residential colleges – creative new partnerships, driven by curriculum. Just what the doctor ordered to offset sclerosis in the education system, and to foster the kind of lively older age we ought to have the right to look forward to.

26 February 1999

Money talks, but we need a good speech

by Alan Tuckett
Section: FE Focus; Comment; Opinion. Issue 4313, p32

At last. Tessa Blackstone has announced that part-time higher education students living on low incomes will be eligible for loans of at least £500. For too long there has been an easy assumption that since many part-time students in higher education get support from an employer, there was no need to fund them.

The acceptance of that view was the biggest disappointment in Sir Ron Dearing's report on higher education last year. Mike Fitzgerald, former vice-chancellor of Thames Valley University, told a finance meeting of the National Advisory Group for Continuing Education & Lifelong Learning that most 'full-time' students had jobs in term-time to make ends meet.

Seriously useless learning

This year's figures for student applications have been revealing. Despite the hype, more young people applied for higher education than last year, even after the funding changes. However, full-time mature applicants were down by about 10%. A degree may be the best investment you can make in yourself, but mature students already take on substantial debt, for themselves and their families, in order to study.

Two in three mature students study part-time, fitting study alongside other demands on their lives. They have always had to pay fees, and always had to find their own living expenses. What is welcome about this decision is that it makes the part-time option more affordable for more learners, and is a major step towards an adult-friendly system.

Of course, it is never enough. There are still adult students whose only realistic option is to study full-time, and for whom the risk threshold will be too forbidding. A study of Access course enrolments by John Field, professor of lifelong learning at Warwick University, shows a marked shift towards utilitarian subjects and out of the humanities – just when the case for liberal education is back on the policy agenda. But then, if the risk increases it is no surprise if people choose what look like the safer options.

For poorer people there will be a need for scholarships to be available, widely advertised and publicly supported – though there is nothing to inhibit others from offering parallel support. This needs to be on top of institutional Access funds – which can be great, but are only available when you have taken the plunge and joined a course. In addition, there still needs to be a major push to make learning a right for unemployed adults in their first 18 months on the dole.

I was able to make some of these arguments to David Blunkett and Tessa Blackstone, along with the case for parity of treatment for part-time students, when the National Institute for Adult Continuing Education met ministers a week before Tessa's announcement.

There was, of course, not a word to indicate that we might soon have some of our concerns addressed. I was impressed by the discipline you need to be a minister in this government with good news to tell. But I also reflected that there is a broader message ministers need to deliver. Given how much the government has set in motion since the publication of *The Learning Age*, there is a need for a major speech joining up the thinking – not only to make clear the range of measures the government has taken to widen participation, but to underline their importance to others.

Despite clear signals that local education authority adult education is a statutory duty to which government attaches importance, Surrey, for example, is gaily planning to decimate public support for its service. I don't think that would happen if the secretary of state gave a strong policy steer in a major speech.

This is an odd demand to be making. We need more talk to go with the action. With so much going on, why can't we encourage the politicians to claim credit for the larger picture?

2 April 1999

Spring may be a difficult step
by Alan Tuckett
Section: FE Focus. Issue 4318, p24

The clocks went forward, and I lay in bed puzzling how my son's time clock had adapted to this change instantly, while mine resisted with great force. I stumbled grumbling to breakfast to find a glorious fresh spring day, forsythia smiling cheerfully in the garden, magnolia buds burgeoning on the neighbour's tree. Marvellous, but I could not quite adapt my mood.

I felt much the same at the end of NIACE's annual Study Conference this weekend. I came back exhausted, of course, from staying up too late imagining how the world might be better for adult learners. Still, much of the argument had been enlivening. There were dozens of examples of creative practice, much of it developed in spite of the external environment. There was also a clear sense that things were getting better, and that we might look forward to the day when creative new work happened because of enlightened policy.

But Bob Fryer, chair of the government's continuing education and life-long learning group, reminded us that while a great deal has happened to improve matters for adult learners in the past two years, we must not expect it all to happen overnight. Cultural change, he argued, results from a long haul.

Sue Waddington, the European Parliament's spokeswoman on the Leonardo education project, dropped in to report on the slaying of the commission, and how best we can preserve a European dynamic for lifelong learning.

Accounts of the current work and future challenges facing the University for Industry were also impressive. This was the first time I had heard the shapers of the initiative talking to key partners in a convivial and exploratory way. The UFI is the government's flagship initiative, and it is essential if it is to work for the benefit of adult learners that it gets its relationships with other providers right. On this evidence there is much to be cheered about.

Even Individual Learning Accounts – where individuals, employers and government invest – were made attractive in minister George Mudie's vision of trade unions bargaining on behalf of cohorts of members to pool accounts to secure learner-friendly provision.

George was funny, warm and steeped in commitment to giving those who

Seriously useless learning

have benefited least from the chance of education of a quality worth having. He instinctively trusts practitioners and challenges policy-makers to be less territorial in their thinking, and their practice. He invited us to help the government to address the overlapping but discrete needs of adults learning in the formal system, in the workplace and the community by having equally robust and demanding strategies for each. Far from receiving a hostile reaction, he sent practitioners back to work with their values confirmed, and ready for the challenges ahead.

It was, in short, the sort of conference you dream about: coherent, stimulating, flexible.

Why then am I so out of sorts? Easter exhaustion plays a part, linked to a big new task, and a sense that some critically important voices are not engaged with our agenda. The extension of the training and enterprise council review to include all of post-16 education gives a vital chance to shape future policy. I accept George Mudie's view that there is a need for coherent overlapping strategies for community learning and for workplace learning to go with further and higher education. It was, said differently, a key conclusion of the National Advisory Group for Continuing Education & Lifelong Learning. But adult learning is not a tidy business, and I am nervous that in pursuit of coherence we may squeeze out diversity.

Nowhere is that risk clearer than in Gordon Brown's throwaway remark in the Budget, that vocational tax relief is to be phased out, and with it public support 'for non-vocational courses like diving and flying lessons'. Translated, that will mean a return to the old divisions in employee development schemes with only approved subjects attracting tax relief. Old Treasury beliefs die hard.

Somehow we need to develop a dialogue with the Treasury to overcome its desire to demonise learning which leads to no obvious short-term economic benefit, to protect the widening participation agenda, and to persuade economists that learning is the key industrial skill, and it can be picked up in unlikely contexts.

But the Treasury is not alone in having misconceptions about lifelong learning. The Audit Commission's local authority performance indicators document suggests wrongly and crassly that adult education is not a statutory duty for LEAs, and finds it unsurprising when services are cut. Hardly surprising then when Surrey excises financial support for what was always one of the best of services.

Away from conference debate, the sunshine is still intermittent for lifelong learners. It will be a long haul.

7 May 1999

Other parts of the forest lead out of the woods

by Alan Tuckett
Section: FE Focus; Opinion. Issue 4323, p36

Consultation, consultation, consultation. It is now more than a year since the publication of *The Learning Age*. Apparently it generated thousands of replies, but we are still waiting for the publication of the government's summary of the issues raised. We also await a government statement on what will happen next, and for that matter we are still expecting the second report of the National Advisory Group for Continuing Education & Lifelong Learning. Things are happening, of course, but too many people are left with the sense that we are engaged in a dialogue of the hard of hearing.

Much of what is good for adult learners has been achieved almost by stealth. Slowly, the needs of part-time students are being addressed. Modest, practical steps make a difference. The latest good news is the decision of the Higher Education Funding Council for England to maintain an annual development fund for widening participation projects, at double the current size, alongside the additional cash for the same purpose to be built into higher education institutions' mainstream funding. The project funding amounts to about 15% of the allocated total.

While more money is needed to make a real difference to the system, the strategy is surely right: an adult-friendly HE system needs institutional managers to recognise the need for change, and to devise strategies to that end. But at the same time, project funding gives permission to highlight the needs of groups under-represented in the system, to work with them in new ways, and of course to fail on a scale small enough for lessons to be learned without putting institutions at risk overall.

The same principles will need to inform the Kennedy agenda in colleges. In the light of the highly-publicised problems of Halton, Bilston and the Wirral, the temptation may be to avoid risk at all costs. Yet without risk many adults whose needs are not currently met well by colleges will continue to be excluded.

As our institutional relationships move from the sharp-edged world of competition to the cuddlier world of partnership, confidence to get some things wrong will be as important as ever. Reflection on what went well, what could have been done differently, what produced unexpected outcomes is the stuff of learning. Still, reflection on its own is not enough. You have to tell stories for others to have the chance to understand what you have learned.

I was struck by this at two different consultation meetings in the past fortnight. The first was convened by the Department for Education & Employment to offer national organisations a chance to consider issues that will (or do I mean might, or could?) be addressed in what seems now to be called the post-16 review. I was struck by the remark of a panjandrum in the system who said: "Surely we might agree that the primary purpose of education is preparation for the labour market?" In Pinochet's Chile perhaps, but in a democracy?

Competitiveness remains a major commitment of government. But the context has changed. There is an impressive range of strategies to address social exclusion and community building. Yet if your work is focused on labour market concerns, it is possible that much of the change may have passed you by. You need people in other parts of the forest to tell you the wonders they behold. One of the benefits of consultation at its best is that it gives the space for people to tell each other useful stories. This was illustrated at the consultation meeting, hosted by the Local Government Association.

People are more open to listening to one another, and learning in an atmosphere of trust. And surely government at its best should, like the LGA, host a good conversation, in which different interests explore the maximum possible area of agreement. Still, trust grows slowly and you need plenty of time for everyone to feel they have had a chance to join in. Some will wait until there are clear options to consider. Some will change their minds. But if you take time you can secure wide ownership of change.

The temptation when you are busy is to put your head down and get on with it. But given the aspiration to create a learning society, I don't think that is an option open to any of us in partnerships, institutions or, for that matter, in government.

16 July 1999

Learning to live with 'Learning to Succeed'

by Alan Tuckett
Section: FE Focus; Opinion. Issue 4333, p42

LEARNING to Succeed is the best white paper for adult learners since the magnificent Report of the Ministry of Reconstruction's Adult Education Committee in 1919. While the writing of the 1999 white paper lacks the elegance and lyricism of the earlier paper, much of which was written by RH Tawney, it shares with it a determination to put learners at the heart of the system. Yet, curiously, Learning to Succeed has little to say about the curriculum, beyond the welcome end of the nonsensical schedule 2/non-schedule 2 divide.

The complex muddle of overlapping responsibilities in post-school education and training was bewildering to learners and, in places, indefensible. Sorting out the muddle has led to a paper that focuses on structures.

I like the way it recognises that the system needs to combine coherence and diversity. It allows for national strategic planning, for national priorities, and for industry specific needs. At the same time there is provision for planning on a travel-to-study and travel-to-learn basis, which makes sense for much of the work of colleges.

The proposed remit of the 50 sub-regional learning and skills councils should enable European funding, regional development agency initiatives and the skills needs of local communities to be synthesised.

The new duty given to local government will be critical to the success of the structure. Effective strategies for work with many older people, tenants groups, people with disabilities and minority linguistic communities rely on the creative co-operation of different arms of local government. All in all, the paper proposes a structure in which power and decision-making can flow up and down the system, and where learners can hope for equitable support wherever they learn. Of course, a huge amount of detail needs to be got right for the system to work in practice. And people who work with learners need confidence that their concerns will be heard.

It is important that the sub-regional councils impact effectively on learning in the workplace. All the evidence shows that most adults still get access to learning at work, and we need a much closer link between work-based learning and learning in colleges, and community contexts. The issues of motivation, the recognition of prior experience, fitting learning into busy lives, issues of assessment, and of the transferability of skills learned in one context to another, are all shared across the different contexts adults learn in.

The only merit I can see in the new inspection arrangements is that they will make those connections easier to make, as will the new adult sub-committee of the national council. Still, colleges will face the happy prospect of at least two sets of inspectors crawling over the same provision, because learners will be untidy, and learn in mixed-age settings. We have to be careful that we do not replace the inanities of a curriculum divide with too rigid a distinction between 16-to-19 and adult learners.

Given the energy driving the 16-to-19 agenda, an adult qualifications framework, which recognises the importance of small steps of learning, and the need to give them credit, is a necessary protection. Now we need to sort out appropriate ways of measuring such learning. It would be good to move beyond the excesses of audit culture, where the needs of the external observer seem paramount, to involve learners in understanding their own learning gains, in the way the pioneering work of the Workers' Educational Association has done.

Seriously useless learning

It may be understandable that the government left higher education out of the planning, given the complexity of the task. But the boundaries are increasingly blurred. With so much higher education now taking place in further education, it would be a good idea if a follow-up paper could join up the thinking. Both higher and further education support learning at work. Widening participation is central to the concerns of both. And both have roles to play in fostering a rich, creative civil society.

Another omission is teacher training. The omission of learning support for the people who will need to make the system work is serious. Our current arrangements, where large numbers of part-time workers get little or no staff development or training, are not adequate to the task.

For adults, the relationship between funding for uncertificated work, provision supporting progression and work leading to qualifications will need teasing out, so that each is properly supported. Thank goodness there will not be a single super tariff to cover everything, but until the details are on the table, real anxieties will continue. Sorting them out will make for a busy summer.

24 September 1999
Speak out now to change bad law quickly

by Alan Tuckett
SECTION: FE Focus. Issue 4343, p5

GOVERNMENT sometimes works with impressive speed and purpose. Sometimes, progress is slow and negotiations feel like treading through treacle. To start with the treacle: for as long as I can remember, adult educators have been wanting the government to define 'adequacy and sufficiency'.

The 1992 Act, taking a lead from the 1944 Butler Act, requires the Further Education Funding Council to secure sufficient 16-to-19 provision, and adequate facilities for adults to undertake courses covered by schedule 2 of the Act. A parallel duty requires local education authorities to secure further education for adults in areas not covered by the schedule.

Try as we might, we could persuade neither minister nor bureaucrat to lift a pen. The result has been, at least in the case of local authority adult education, that councillors talk of it as a 'non-statutory' service. Faced with government pressure, many authorities put money allocated (at least notionally) for work with adult learners into schools' budgets. Of course, many honourably resisted the pressure.

More than a decade ago, the Unit for the Development of Adult & Continuing Education did groundwork on what adequacy might mean. In the early

1990s, Bryan Merton, then a senior HMI, carried on the work.

This last winter, there was money in the Standards Fund for LEAs to audit their services, to provide baseline data which might be useful in defining adequacy. Now I hear appalling rumours that the people preparing the Bill arising from Learning to Succeed are considering dropping the words from the legislation.

This will not do. Until we have an explicit charter of rights and entitlements for adult learners, there must be a clear public commitment to securing a minimum curriculum range, and access to learning facilities, guidance and learner support, within reasonable reach of home.

Without a commitment of this kind, we will not get the learning society we are all after. Defining adequacy is a tortoise that could do with help in overtaking the hares in the government who are preparing the Bill. There is still time to respond to the white paper, and it is worth readers' while to do so.

As my organisation says in its response, on the subject of the proposed arrangements for inspection, the best time to change bad law is before it appears in a Bill. Thinking about inspection, and the rampant growth of audit culture during the 1990s, I have been prompted to think how much I relied on my institute inspector, Bill Carter, in the Inner London Education Authority when I was a principal.

It seemed that Mr Carter was sent to me from heaven, to ask good questions, to help me hear things when I was not listening, to challenge our academic board to be more adventurous, in designing learning opportunities – in short, to set our sights higher. It felt as if responsibility for serving adult learners in Clapham and Battersea was shared by both of us, and of course my colleagues. There are echoes of that role in the current work of college inspectors. I think the test of the new legislation will be how quickly it helps us all move back to thinking about learners and learning, and how to support them better.

But to return to speedy and purposeful government. Sir Claus Moser's report on literacy and numeracy, *A Fresh Start*, was published in the spring. Since, the government has put in place a technical implementation group, affectionately called TIG, to oversee work leading to practical implementation of the report's proposals. It is backed by smaller work groups looking at English as an additional language, research, standards, learning difficulties, and so on.

I am impressed at just how much has been achieved – and how open, and consultative, the work being undertaken and how serious some of the discussion is. Nevertheless, there remains a tension at the heart of government thinking between its commitment to standards, and its determination to widen participation. Of course, opening the doors to poor education is unacceptable. But so, too, are needless hurdles to participation.

Seriously useless learning

Happily, pluralism is winning out – so far at least. But with legislation imminent, I would like to see the publication of the Social Exclusion Unit's paper on skills, and a fresh prospectus from the University for Industry. We need all the fuel we can get to protect the rights of hesitant learners to study at their own pace, working to their own agendas, gaining confidence and voice as they go.

22 October 1999

Tea-timely reminder of power of collaboration

by Alan Tuckett
Section: FE Focus; Opinion. Issue 4347, p6

THERE IS a small wicker basket, full of peppermint tea, on my desk. It is the kind of thing you might buy as a gift for an aunt. Indeed, it is a product for the tourist market, and is sold exclusively at the Taj Mahal and its associated hotels. The basket was given to me by Christine Nathan at a Unesco adult learning conference in Manila, as a reminder of the scale of the challenge facing adult learners in many places.

Christine is an impressive person. She is general secretary of the building workers and allied trades union in India, an organisation with 20m members. She is also general secretary of BanBandhu, a coalition of non-governmental organisations that supports tribal people living in India's forests.

The peppermint tea is one of the products that previously unwaged forest workers have developed and now market direct, cutting out middlemen. It represents the end of a long learning journey – supporting the workers by understanding their situation in working unwaged for landlords and middlemen; fighting local administrations for the right to receive a return on their labour; resisting violence and intimidation; resisting loan schemes that trap them in poverty; building confidence, and learning about the market. The role of support workers – adult education development workers by another name – was critical to the success of the initiative. This was recognised by angry landlords in Chandraphur, who saw the educators as a threat to their supply of free labour. They reacted by killing and cutting up one worker and leaving pieces of the corpse at the edges of the forest.

It is easy to forget what a dangerous business learning can be, when it challenges existing power relations. The story sets our own concerns in context, too. Still, in the green paper *The Learning Age*, David Blunkett recognised that many of our institutions resulted from people's courage, co-operation and their imagination in overcoming their problems. He saw the need for us to rebuild the confidence to trust our collective imagination, to address the new challenges for our society to be productive and inclusive. This is not a primary focus of the white paper *Learning to Succeed*, which attempts to reconcile the tension between widening participation and narrowing measures of gains in quality by focusing on structures and procedures. This week, workers in consumer and producer co-operatives asked me: "What will these structural changes do to help revitalise learning for citizenship, or to regenerate our communities?"

The white paper has strengths. It proposes a structure in which strategic planning can happen nationally, sub-regionally and locally. But power and decision making has to flow from the expressed demands of local communities, as well as from the top downwards. That will only be achieved if the local arrangements are sorted out creatively. The experience of the best local learning partnerships over the past year show that strategic planners, with cash in their pocket, can co-operate to improve the mesh of learning support at local levels. But many voluntary sector agencies and small providers feel excluded from those initiatives. The role of the partnerships proposed in the white paper is different, and provides the chance for providers of all sorts to collaborate. There will still be a need for the partnerships to offer the local Learning & Skills Councils strategic advice, and partnerships will need an effective planning mechanism to develop this. They will also need new forums to engage voluntary and community sector providers.

No single representative can speak for the voluntary sector's overlapping interests, without the support of a consultative forum. For learners, too, there will be a need for imaginative mechanisms to help them to shape the system, building on this September's Adult Learners' Forum. Planners addressing these questions could do worse than to look at the strategies developed earlier this century by the Women's Co-operative Guild, led by Margaret Llewellyn Davies, to engage a mass membership in meaningful debate, and to capture the complexity of their views on the great questions of the day. Mutuality has, perhaps, more to offer than the market in ensuring that the learning society we want to create has a place for everyone.

The renewal of organisational forums is a major theme in Charles Leadbeater's book *Living On Thin Air*. One chapter makes an interesting case for adult learning. He celebrates Delia Smith's recipes, showing how the consumer (learner) provides the last stage in the production process, turning the recipe into a chocolate cake – much less messy and less risky than making and marketing cakes. Of course, in a weightless economy, media exposure matters. That, surely, is the main case for the University for Industry. Still, I can't help thinking that the basket of tea is more eloquent than a recipe could be.

Seriously useless learning

19 November 1999

Claiming your stake in the knowledge society

by Alan Tuckett

Section: FE Focus; Further Education; News & Opinion. Issue 4351, p2

TO COVENTRY for a conference on participation, run by the National Institute for Adult Continuing Education and the government. The event was to present findings from the institute's 1999 participation survey, and to mark the publication of *Pathways in Adult Learning*, the follow-up to the 1997 national adult learning surveys.

Taken together, the surveys confirm that about a quarter of the population say they have done no learning since school, and that another third may have done some learning, but cannot remember it without extended prompting – hardly the best platform for the knowledge society.

The danger with snapshots, however, is that they fail to capture dynamic change. The most encouraging finding, for me, of the Pathways to Learning study is that 28% of the people who defined themselves as non-learners in 1997 said they had done some learning when re-interviewed 18 months later. Taking a four-and-a-half year period, 81% of those surveyed reported learning episodes. This suggests that the number completely excluded from access to learning is smaller than we thought.

On the other hand, the survey showed how quickly the learning habit can be lost. People were asked about their learning plans. Two in three who reported learning in the 1997 survey, and by the follow-up survey, had learning plans. Yet 70% of those who had done some learning in the 1997 survey, but nothing since, said they were unlikely to return.

Clearly, where the learning habit is so fragile, the participation target adopted by the government is a challenging one.

At the conference, Naomi Sargant complicated matters further by observing that, while 20 years ago more than 20% of learners said they were learning sports or keep fit, that number was now negligible. The same pattern was apparent in DIY. Yet the boom in the leisure industry, and in home-improvement retailing, suggests that people no longer think of keep fit and upholstery as 'learning'.

John Field and Tom Schuller's work for the Economic & Social Research Council on the patterns of participation in Scotland and Northern Ireland also suggest that different people take different views about what counts as learning. A major study in south Wales by Gareth Rees and his colleagues finds that there is less learning going on now than in the heyday of the coalfields.

What does all this suggest we should do to create a learning society in which everyone feels they have a stake? In a characteristically iconoclastic

contribution to the conference, John Field drew attention to one answer –
from the Dutch ministry of education, culture and science: "A chain is only
as strong as its weakest link." There are echoes of similar thinking in the
New Deal programmes. Yet as John Field suggested, taking a horse to water
does not automatically lead to drinking. Bad experiences of a first return to
learning can put you off for good. A study in the 1980s found that if the status
of student is less attractive than that of worker, it does at least give you a
context for engaging with a wider society.

One lesson was clear. The workplace is a key site for engaging previously-
excluded groups. The government makes that more possible, at least, in
linking learning for community and economic development in the work of the
new Learning & Skills Councils.

17 December 1999

It is not enough merely to get people into jobs

by Alan Tuckett

Section: FE Focus; Further Education; Opinion. Issue 4355, p28

IN THE last weeks before my granddaughter Rosie was born, my daughter
shifted from excitement and expectation to an impatience to get the birth
over with. I have been feeling that about the Bill on post-16 reforms.

Yet the Bill itself will not be the last word. A prospectus will tell us what
the policy means, and then there will be a funding principles document, for
widespread consultation, followed in late spring by the funding proposals
the government means to adopt. Meanwhile, the government may introduce
amendments to improve the Bill in Parliament. And then there is the comprehensive spending review – lots to argue about for a new millennium.

And it is worth arguing. It is possible to lose Parliamentary votes and still
win the argument, when administrators come to make the system work.
There is also plenty of evidence that once the government is convinced, it
backs its policy with serious resources, as the million pounds a day of new
money for college sector work announced at the Association of Colleges
conference makes clear.

Spending the money well to widen participation and achievement will
create demands of its own, but the scale of need dwarfs anything yet available. This was brought home to me at a work and lifestyles seminar at the
culmination of the Debate of the Age, organised by Age Concern. The afternoon began with the welcome announcement of Third Age Apprenticeships,
to tackle age discrimination in the workplace. They fit well with the range
of measures that see access to work as the key welfare strategy, and the
government has good news to tell about the growth of jobs.

Seriously useless learning

This was followed by Ray Pahl and Jonathan Scales, who reported on their work for the Debate of the Age study group on work and lifestyles.

Their analysis was devastating. It demonstrated the gap in Britain between the work-rich and time-poor and time-rich but work-poor, and pointed to four interconnected social trends that produced a sharpening divide in Britain.

First, they showed that there is a sharp rise in administrative and managerial jobs; a similar if less marked increase in low-skill service-sector jobs (cleaning, hairdressing and so on), and a dramatic fall in jobs in the middle, with the decline of skilled manufacturing jobs. They showed that in households with two adults, 70% of men in administrative and professional work had partners with similar jobs, while only 15% of men in the lowest-paid work had partners in the more skilled sectors of the economy.

Two-job households contrast with no-job households. More and more of the new jobs are taken by women – and many of them pay wages insufficient to maintain an unwaged partner. Health care and educational opportunity are more likely to benefit the relatively successful. And globalisation is strengthening these trends.

Taken together, Ray Pahl suggested, the trends show that where the absolute living standards of the poorest may rise, those of the mobile and affluent rise ever more sharply. The inescapable conclusion of the study was that getting people into jobs is not in itself enough.

The scale of the challenge is apparent, too, in the final report of the Policy Action Team on Skills, led by the Department for Education & Employment for the Social Exclusion Unit, in response to its neighbourhood renewal strategy. The report looks at the reasons for the failure of successive measures to open learning opportunities to socially excluded communities. It suggests that there are three main reasons why current arrangements fail the most excluded communities. First, the system is still not adequately focused on meeting the needs of socially disadvantaged adults. Second, local capacity to develop and sustain initiatives that can help people to improve their skills is usually weak. Finally, people who live in socially disadvantaged areas believe they have nothing to gain from joining in.

What is impressive about the report is its recognition that the complexity of the problems facing such communities will not respond to a single solution, but to patient sustained work on a number of fronts over an extended period. It is not cheap work, and it does not quickly and predictably lead to easily-auditable outcomes. Hard but necessary lessons for the Treasury during the Comprehensive Spending Review.

28 January 2000

Bill needs lifelong partners to be complete

by Alan Tuckett

Section: FE Focus; Further Education. Issue 4361, p5

THE LEARNING & Skills Bill, like Vladimir Nabokov's *Pale Fire*, comes with its ready-made explanatory text. It is just as well. Without the prospectus you look in vain for any mention of lifelong learning partnerships. They are absent on the face of the Bill – yet the new thinking requires partnerships to play a critical and much changed role in making sure that the FE system is responsive to pressures on the ground as well as to central initiatives.

Again, the white paper held out the prospect for local education authorities of a changed "duty to contribute to provision for adults". Yet, while the proposals in the Bill meet the substance of this policy goal, there is no mention of a duty. Apparently, Parliamentary Counsel won't have split duties on the face of legislation. I have never met a Parliamentary Counsel, but they are clearly powerful souls, telling government what is and isn't possible.

Powerful, but not always clear. From 1944 on, we have looked unsuccessfully for a government definition of 'adequate' further education for adults.

The new Bill redefines adequate as 'reasonable'. And what is reasonable? Easy. "Facilities are reasonable if ... the facilities are of such a quantity and quality that the (Learning & Skills) Council can reasonably be expected to secure their provision." This might work, but is hardly a comfort if cold winds blow, under a different administration, or a less benign secretary of state.

Still, I think this administration, and this secretary of state, have done adult learners proud. The ludicrous Schedule 2 that differentiates between leisure and vocational courses is to go – though no one should suppose that that will mean the end of differential investment in the curriculum.

The establishment of national statutory committees for adults and for young people will help the Learning & Skills Council in its work. There is a clear and key strategic role for local government. There is a recognition that quality assurance is important outside the qualifications framework, and local education authority services can look forward to the rigours and the support of regular external inspection.

And they can sleep at night during this budget round, safe in the knowledge that ministers guarantee that the Learning & Skills Council will maintain spending for the first two years of operation. All good stuff.

There are, inevitably, worries. First, the inspection arrangements must be changed – at least to make sure that colleges with a majority of adult learners are inspected by teams led by the new adult inspectorate. But a single post-school inspectorate would be better. Second, if young people's work is to be inspected on an area basis, so should provision for adults. Third, the local learning and skills councils will have just as much need of adult and young people's committees as the national council, and it is a weakness of the proposals that this is left to local discretion.

On the subject of committees, there is surely a case, too, for the establishment of a quality recognition and improvement committee to wrestle with the complexity of capturing learning gain across the full range of the LSC's activities.

Another concern affects one of the successes of the last decade. The introduction of Investors in People relied on the local teams that fuelled the expansion of the programme, yet the prospectus would split them between support for IiP in small firms and that offered to others. It would be better to keep the expertise together in my view.

Again, there is still work to be done to recognise that young adults use youthservices for learning, but we are promised another new paper on this. The papers could say more about adult guidance, too.

Each of these issues can be addressed, and would improve the Bill if they are.However, the major worries relate to securing the policy gains of the Bill in the long run.

To return to lifelong learning partnerships: they are given a critically important role in consulting learners and liaising with the voluntary sector. How will that survive a policy change in Sanctuary Buildings or Number 10? There is altogether not enough about accountabilities to stakeholders, users, local communities – and there needs to be if we really are committed to revitalising and sustaining active civil society.

In the same vein, the Bill and the prospectus have too little to say about the social and economic benefits of joined-up social policy – notably in the field of health, but also in the co-ordination of our many technology initiatives. Without such links, many adults will still find their learning needs missing in the gaps between complementary but unrelated social policy dynamics.

Put all that right, and win the resources to back it in the Comprehensive Spending Review and adults will start the millennium with a bang!

11 February 2000
All generations have the right to learn
by Alan Tuckett
Section: FE Focus; Further Education; Opinion. Issue 4363, p2

HOW FAR should the government go to support the creation of a lifelong learning culture in Britain? The Kennedy report was clear. *Learning Works* argued that there should be public support for everyone to level 3 (A-level).

At that level, demonstrable benefits to individuals from further investment in learning kick in. Below that level, we have workers inadequately skilled for the vast bulk of the new technology-rich jobs on which economic prosperity rests.

The second report of the Skills Task Force came to the same conclusion in respect of 19 to 24-year-olds, but the third report settled for level 2 for other adults, albeit with level 3 as an aspiration. Neither argument has yet won the day with the Department for Education & Employment or the Treasury.

The first technical report on funding, January's contribution to the stream of government consultations on the Learning & Skills Bill and related policy, recognises the need for an entitlement for 16 to 19-year-olds.

If the Skills Task Force has persuaded the government on 19 to 24-year-olds, it seems we shall have to wait until later in the year to find out, as the Chancellor's spending review works its way through the system. In this, as in much else in the detail of the policy, the aim seems to be to create a two-tier system, in which overwhelming priority is given to the needs of labour market entrants.

There can be no argument against a policy that seeks to make sure that all young people access the confidence, skill and choice learning offers.

It must be one of the cornerstones of an effective lifelong-learning culture. But a focus on labour market entrants will not be enough for the economy.

And as *Local Solutions*, the Skills Policy Action Report on learning for neighbourhood renewal, shows, social exclusion will only be overcome through the patient involvement of all ages in local communities.

The government recognises this in many of the supply-side measures in the Bill and accompanying policy paper. The bringing together of adult learning in the workplace, in the college sector and in community settings, will lead to less haphazard and fragmentary gains. That the Employment Service signed up to the funding document holds out the prospect that the New Deal will soon be joined up with the wider DFEE policy.

The increased resources committed to further education makes possible a reinforced priority for 16 to 19-year-olds without adults needing to lose out. And the decision to make bursaries available for mature students in higher education shows a willingness to shift policy that has negative consequences.

And yet the loose drafting of clause 3 of the Bill tells a wider story. This is the clause that says adults are entitled to 'reasonable' provision. It then explains that 'reasonable' means provision of a quantity and quality that the council can reasonably be expected to make in the light of its resources.

The clause ends up suggesting that, while standards for young people are inviolable, they don't much matter for adults.

A case of never mind the quality feel the width.

Seriously useless learning

The same approach informs the government's proposals over inspection, where the Adult Learning Inspectorate risks looking like a second-string operation. It would take just a small tweak to the Bill for Office of Standards in Education to lead joint inspections in sixth-form and tertiary colleges, and for the Adult Inspectorate to lead in general further education.

Though the change would be small, it would have the powerful effect of showing that it is possible to have a policy that emphasises young people's needs without sacrificing the aspirations of adults.

The importance of entitlement for 16 to 19-year-olds is the recognition it gives that there can be no going back on the resources needed to include every young person in the learning society.

The Skills Task Force does a useful job in making clear that the same pressures are there for the next age cohort, and that they will need a similar commitment. The case for older adults is more complex. We do need to sort out fees.

The government certainly needs to think through what to do next in those sectors of the economy where the latest incitement to employers to train voluntarily fails again to secure learning opportunities for workers.

But it is, I think, essential that the same symbolic commitment is given to the creation of a society in which old and young have a right to learn.

An adult entitlement might need a different balance of expectations about who pays. It might not be achievable all at once. But it is as necessary to making the policy work as the welcome supply-side measures in the Bill.

10 March 2000
Woodhead will help adults who help themselves

by Alan Tuckett

Section: FE Focus; Further Education; Comment; Opinion. Issue 4367, p4

LAST MAY, during Adult Learners' Week, the Campaign for Learning set up job swaps for Learning at Work day. At one award ceremony, I mentioned I had not taken part. Immediately, Carlisle College challenged me to swap with Hugh Waddell, who had just completed the college's doorkeeping course. We agreed to wait till 2000.

Hugh ran the National Institute for Adult Continuing Education (NIACE) for a day this week, and I will have done my duty as a bouncer at Buskers night club by the time this column appears. I know already that Hugh has the harder job, but there are similarities. In both jobs, there are times when a word early on can save trouble later.

Hugh brought a rich portfolio of skills with him. A distinguished career as a rugby-league international and coach gave him a wealth of teaching and learning strategies. He listened well, moved meetings at pace, and shaped me up gently over delays in my work that affected other people.

After an Adult Learners' Week meeting and chairing our directorate, he and I took the train to London for an all-party parliamentary group meeting for the adult and further education groups. Later, we dashed to the Royal Society of Arts just in time for the chief inspector's annual lecture.

Chris Woodhead had chosen to ask: "Is lifelong learning a utopian ideal?" It was both characteristic and astonishing as a presentation; characteristic in that he gave a raucously polemical defence of the status quo, astonishing in the skimpiness of its frame of reference and the research undertaken in preparation.

There was, of course, a lot of sense in the central contention that getting schools right is essential in creating a learning society. But that is hardly a revolutionary idea and, as Nyerere recognised, it is not enough.

Before we got there, we were told that the poor will always be with us, despite educators' best intentions. Taking Frank Coffield's discussion of a light-hearted proposal of mine in these columns two years ago, he came to the brave conclusion that compulsion was not a good idea for adult learners.

He was sceptical about the Campaign for Learning's celebration of neurological science breakthroughs and what they might tell us about teaching and learning. Above all, he wanted to set up clear oppositions between teaching and learning, product and process. He wanted subject disciplines to be protected and all students to have clear goals.

He told us early that there was little space in the talk to address adult and continuing education – extending a tradition of benign neglect of this part of his statutory duty and kept up throughout his term of office, it seems to me.

This might not have mattered if he had grappled with the real challenges of bringing school and community together in the creation of a learning culture. But there was nothing of the powerful role of inter-generational learning and its benefits to adults and children.

There was no recognition of the scale of the task of adapting a society, where one in four learns early that education is not for them, to a world where more and more work requires the confidence to learn and skill in learning.

There was a good deal of slapstick about the right of older people to be left in peace, spared the attentions of lifelong learning zealots bearing prospectuses and a gleam in the eye. No more promotion; motivation is not curriculum. Yet there is more and more evidence that engaging in learning has a positive effect on health in older age.

The view of the chief inspector, on the cusp of wider new duties for securing a learning society, is that the state is too ready to impose solutions and infantilise the people. He clearly felt that we should concentrate on those who make it through the doors unaided. The others have made their choice.

Seriously useless learning

What price Kennedy? It is a bleak and narrow view, and I prefer the generosity and vision of David Blunkett's.

I am a little nervous about my night as a doorman. With luck and Hugh's help, I will learn just what to say to pre-empt trouble. Perhaps then I could transfer the skill to encourage Chris to 'try a bit harder' with adult learners.

14 April 2000

How we forgot adult lessons
by Alan Tuckett
Section: FE Focus; Further Education; Opinion. Issue 4372, p5

MALCOLM MCLAREN dropped out of the race to be mayor of London when Ken Livingstone decided to stand as an independent. I was sorry to see him go. This was partly because of his distinctive contribution to our culture, but mainly because his manifesto was fresh and surprising. One key demand was for the restoration of adult education services in the capital.

It is ten years this month since the Inner London Education Authority was closed down. I have a photo of Neil Fletcher, the ILEA's last leader, leading the remnants of the final party from the building.

I was proud to be among them – because the ILEA had developed an adult learning service unparalleled in the UK, and much of Europe. Its policies were successfully tackling social exclusion.

The story of the authority's end is not just one more of the periodic spasms of institutional upheaval in local government. It marked the end of the most serious experiment we have yet seen in securing mass participation in life-long learning.

You can argue about whether primary and secondary schools have done better or worse with the loss of the city-wide authority – but no one can suggest that adult learners have benefited.

Adult education was 'the jewel in the crown' of the ILEA's work. Indeed, I wrote a pamphlet with that title to mark the passing of the service.

With 5% of the country's population, the authority's service recruited 15% of the country's students, and spent more than a quarter of the money committed to adult education. And that was just the dedicated adult education institutes. Colleges offered more opportunities, as did the polytechnics, which helped pioneer university access courses.

A lot of money was spent – but ILEA recruited hard-to-reach students and gave them successful learning experiences. In 1987, 47% of adult students nationally had post A-level qualifications; but only 22% of the ILEA's learners.

The ILEA recruited more black people, unemployed people, people with disabilities and, above all, more pensioners. Retired people could study any number of classes for a pound a week, and with the cheap fares policy they ranged the city – shoe-repairing in south Lewisham, studying carnival arts in Notting Hill, or learning one of 57 languages on offer.

The contrast today is stark. Of the 12 buildings that made up the core of Clapham-Battersea Institute when I was principal, none is now used for adult learning. Some were knocked down, others sold off. The pottery at Latch-mere is now apparently a posh flat for a minor royal.

So where are the 12,000 to 15,000 learners who used the places? Some, of course, will have migrated to the new palaces of certificated learning. But statistics suggest that the bulk of older students quietly went away. All in all, then, I thought Malcolm McLaren had a good point.

Cities worth living in have ways of weaving community and learning that catches your interest, that works and builds social capital.

Of course, the damage done to learning in London has been paralleled in many other places.

A decade on we need to recover the volume, range and richness, and above all the skills in outreach work to open doors to excluded groups. That is the key message of the Social Exclusion Unit report on skills.

Too few who work in institutions share the understanding many voluntary bodies have about how to relate to hard-to-reach communities. We need to help the voluntary sector develop those skills and support them in growing diversity. Otherwise we will end up serving mainly those we already know how to help.

The one key lesson I learned in the ILEA was that trusting learners to shape programmes reaps rich rewards. That trust, allied to policies promoting social justice, can make a mighty difference.

5 May 2000

Don't leave out the learning volunteers

by Alan Tuckett
Section: FE Focus; Further Education; Opinion. Issue 4375, p2

DAVID BLUNKETT recognised the importance of the voluntary sector in one of the more lyrical passages of his preface to *The Learning Age* when he reminded us of the way working class Victorians formed organisations to overcome their problems. He is not alone: both the Further Education Fund-ing Council and the Social Exclusion Unit would agree.

Why, then, is the voluntary sector so marginal to the arrangements for establishing the Learning & Skills Council? Two rumours illustrate the prob-lem: one with implications for local voluntary bodies, the other affecting national agencies.

Seriously useless learning

First, the local problem. I hear that the arrangements to create transitional task forces leading to the new local learning and skills councils explicitly ruled out the recruitment of voluntary-sector representation onto local planning bodies. If this is true, it is crass. Certainly, there is a complicated job to do to make sure that the system works on April 1, 2001 – also to ensure stability for existing providers.

But the reason for the changes is to make learning accessible to all, which will not be achieved without the voluntary sector. To mobilise the sector effectively will not be easy. Voluntary bodies come in all shapes and sizes, crossing public-policy boundaries. They are strong in some areas and weak in others. They have different capacities for engaging with planners and bureaucracies, but their experience seems invaluable in planning a more inclusive and consultative system than the one we have now.

Engaging them will be a vital role for lifelong-learning partnerships and some have made a good start. Others will need help to change from being strategic planning bodies, where everyone at the table has large budgets, to the kind of place where providers large and small can be involved. But do the partnerships have enough resources to involve everyone while responding to the massive volume of planning that is going on?

Despite the government's real efforts to consult widely on the Bill and the changes that flow from it, most voluntary agencies do not know where and when to make representations. The risk is that their experience will be under represented on the new councils and that rules written with large providers in mind may not work for smaller ones. Of course, not all voluntary bodies are small and the larger ones have enormous reach. The WEA is the largest single provider in FE, and thousands of parents re-engage with learning through the Pre-School Learning Alliance.

Single-issue environmental groups are the major source of adult-learning opportunities about sustainable development, while the Big Issue Foundation and the Foyer movement have been more successful in involving homeless people in overcoming their exclusion than many statutory providers. The sector is citizenship in action.

Last summer, the learning and skills prospectus promised that national voluntary bodies, much like national multi-site employers, could apply to the national council for funding for their national work.

But piecing together a national plan through 47 local negotiations would be a nightmare. Recent consultation meetings suggest that, unlike business, national voluntary agencies might have to apply to the local council serving the area in which their headquarters are located. This would be unacceptable.

The case for a national employers' unit is surely that the council would develop an expertise in the common issues affecting employers contracted to the LSC. By contrast, officials dealing with voluntary bodies would be dealing with them in the margins of time otherwise focused on the needs of a single area. Expertise would be scattered and consistency of treatment hard to guarantee.

I can see no villains in this story. The DFEE has less experience of focusing on voluntary agencies than the Home Office. As a result, perhaps too little attention has been paid to making the reforms work well for voluntary agencies. There is still time to put that right.

2 June 2000

If we can't dance, we don't want your revolution

by Alan Tuckett
Section: FE Focus; Further Education; Opinion. Issue 4379, p4

JUST BEFORE Adult Learners' Week this year, a group of adult educators from across the globe met in Leicester. They were there to help the United Nations Educational, Scientific & Cultural Organisation prepare advice for countries considering starting a festival of adult learning.

The results will be published on September 8 at the launch of the first International Adult Learners' Week.

We all agreed there was no template – except, as Joe Samuels from South Africa suggested, there should be celebration, eating, drinking and music. Certainly the week here includes many parties. But it also highlights a number of lessons worth transporting to quieter policy forums.

The first related to the contrast between the exuberance learners bring to the week and the rather utilitarian focus of much policy debate.

As a distinguished civil servant said to me recently, merging the departments of education and employment five years ago has improved links between education and the labour market. But, he went on, it has left people feeling uneasy about supporting learning that enriches quality of life, without obvious economic benefits

Policy-makers could do well to remember the dictum of anarchist and feminist Emma Goldman: "If I can't dance, I don't want to join your revolution."

This would be well understood by the minister for lifelong learning, Malcolm Wicks, who has led the government's recent recognition of the second lesson: the importance of learning later in life. Unfortunately, other senior figures are less understanding. Earlier this year, in a contentious and at times facile annual lecture, Chris Woodhead berated moves to improve educational opportunity for older adults, suggesting they had earned the right to be left in peace.

Behind his remarks was a bleak view of what learning can do to enrich

Seriously useless learning

life, let alone your health. Yet research by Fiona Aldridge and Peter Lavender (*Learning and Health*, National Institute of Adult Continuing Education) shows nine in ten learners see positive effects on physical and mental well-being.

I don't suppose the minister had Mr Woodhead in mind when he organised a reception for England's oldest learners. Fred Moore, the oldest learner, is now 107, born in the 19th century and still learning in the 21st. The enthusiasm he and his colleagues shared for learning was palpable.

Later, my taxi driver asked me what Fred was studying. "Art," I said. "Shouldn't someone tell him he probably won't make it as Picasso now?" said the taxi driver, before adding: "Still, he sounds as if he has more sense of purpose than many people half his age."

The third lesson I drew arose from the publication of several inspection reports on the work of education authorities with schools in their areas. It was a sharp reminder of the way the new Learning & Skills Bill focuses on the young, not just through entitlements but also through inspection arrangements.

Listening to the delicacy of the chief inspector's judgments on the BBC's *Today* programme, I was struck again by the need for 'area' inspections of services for adults, as well as 16 to 19-year-olds.

For a decade, we have seen league tables of the achievements of just 20% of students in further education. Colleges' great successes in serving adults have been less visible. If we cannot convert the government to the need to provide area inspections for adults in the Bill, we may have to organise our own convivially, from below.

Tessa Blackstone provided the fourth issue, in her speech to the National Adult Learners' Forum conference. She challenged us to create a 'Listening to Learners' quality standard like Investors in People, as a benchmark of institutions' commitment to giving learners a proper voice in shaping provision. This is a timely challenge. Hopefully, local learning partnerships will get the support they need to make effective consultation of learners a reality.

30 June 2000
Why excellence should not be our only goal
by Alan Tuckett
Section: FE Focus; Further Education; Opinion. Issue 4383, p2

"WHAT'S THE use of a centre of excellence among a sea of poverty?" Sam Isaacs, head of the South African Qualifications Authority, asked my breakfast companion last Sunday. The question invites you to think about how much is appropriate to spend on higher education in a country where

12m or more lack basic literacy skills. It invites thinking about quality that includes social value. Mr Isaac's organisation combines the functions of this country's Qualifications & Curriculum Authority and the Quality Assurance Agency here. His agency does include questions about the social impact of education in their national qualifications framework. These issues are as relevant, if on a different scale here. They are recognised by the CBI in its concerns about the long tail of under-achievement and the way this might affect the skills of the future workforce. But will they impact on current debates about quality here?

I was able to listen in to the conversation because I was recently on honeymoon in Cape Town, and we were catching up with friends. We had a wedding party at the Co-operative College at Stanford Hall, a people's palace dedicated to the value of the learning we do together beyond the individual learning most of our systems measure.

A good deal of the fun at the party was had retelling old stories – marking shared memories, illustrating how things have changed, how we make sense of life. Most of our stories made connections that highlighted common experiences. Many of them captured a warm sense of the ridiculous – affectionate reminders of the gap between how we are and how we seem. I was reminded of the time I interviewed someone for a part-time job in adult education in 1973, and spent nearly four hours grilling the candidate for a one-off two-hour-a-week short course in popular planning.

Events like this are convivial and the source of new stories, to be distorted, refashioned, remembered on other occasions. They draw on and strengthen trust and social capital. It's hard, of course, to measure the learning we do together, but it is nonetheless palpable that we learn as well as live it up.

I came back to work thinking how impoverished we have let debates about quality become. The audit culture has given priority to the needs of funders and institutions. In public, inspection has focused on accountability and judgment, leaving advice and encouragement to private conversations.

But learners' perceptions about quality – of courses, institutions, or the services in an area – have not been part of the discussion. The *Learning to Succeed* white paper began a process that can change this.

Local Learning Partnerships are required to consult learners – 16-to-19 'area' inspections should do likewise. We can ensure that learners have the chance for informed reflection on the quality and accessibility of guidance, progression routes, and learning support, and on mechanisms to ensure that institutions are responsive to community demand. They will have views on the balance to be struck between excellence and inclusiveness. And help, perhaps, to answer Sam Isaacs' question.

Seriously useless learning

28 July 2000

Bill leaves us feeling insecure

by Alan Tuckett

Section: FE Focus; Further Education; Opinion. Issue 4387, p2

THE LEARNING & Skills Bill has been put to bed, the budgets are bulging and, slowly, the shape of the new system is becoming clearer. There has been enough consultation for many of the remaining flaws to be our fault. Yet I'm sloping off to summer feeling a bit gloomy.

Despite the commitment of ministers to policies that provide learning opportunities from cradle to grave, the new Learning & Skills Act preserves the primacy of the young. Unlike 16- to 19-year-olds, adults have to make do with an entitlement to free basic skills. After that, they will get what is left over once the promises to the young are met.

We should remember that the Skills Task Force suggested there should be entitlements for young adults, up to level 3 (equivalent to A-level), and for adults over 25 to their first qualification at level 2 (GCSE-equivalent). Helena Kennedy was more ambitious in *Learning Works*, suggesting that adults needed free education up to university entrance.

The commitment to give what's left over to adults is all well and good while cash flows into education. Yet, as Baroness David remarked in the Lords, it would be better if ministers stated a clear aspiration to introduce a proper adult entitlement. That is what Tony Blair has done with his goal that 50% of young people should be in higher education. Such a statement concentrates the minds of policy-makers.

Education and employment minister Tessa Blackstone's reply to Baroness David was interesting. "At this stage," she said, "I am not able to make any commitment about there being an entitlement to adult learning. However, I shall certainly take away her suggestion, which may in the longer term be desirable."

I should, of course, feel pleased by the hint of a better future. But it is the word 'may' I have a problem with. Of course, it might merely be evidence of the fiscal caution. I hope it does not mean that the old-fashioned Treasury view – that adult learning is an optional extra – lingers near the heart of government. There is still plenty of work to do to turn the Act into a workable system.

Many of the details of the funding formula are still to be sorted out. I hope that as much as possible of the adult and community learning curriculum gets built into it from the beginning. That will involve modelling work, to make sure that there are no unintended financial consequences for providers.

Voluntary agencies need much better briefing to play their role in the new arrangements, and many local learning partnerships have some way to go to include the full range of providers.

I think, though, that the largest challenge lies with those committed to widening participation. To serve the needs of the learning poor, who have their best chance of learning at work, new alliances will be needed.

The new learning and skills structure will bring education and training closer together. But the trick will be to think how we can better serve the needs of part-time and temporary workers, who often have too little free time to study outside work.

Workplaces and community settings alike can be sites to tackle exclusion. But using a workplace might raise a question about who pays for what. Hence the case for defining what the state will provide in an adult entitlement.

When he came into office, David Blunkett talked about the patience needed to change policy affecting adults, and compared the task with turning round an oil tanker. Much has been achieved, but little is written into the Act. As a result, another administration, or different ministerial priorities in this administration, could easily reverse many of the gains.

And that is the source of my gloom. So much to feel pleased about that it feels churlish to point out that there is not enough in the Act to secure the future adult learning deserves.

The battle for entitlement

IN OCTOBER 2000, Tuckett reminded readers that the battle for entitlement and space to learn went on not only in class, workplace and community, but on the airwaves – broadcasting. Ten years on from Margaret Thatcher's Broadcasting Act, that ended the duty of independent television to educate and inform, the creeping influence of digitalisation – depriving two million people of the right to view the Open University casually – created further threats despite the advantages. Once prime-time quotas went from ITV (though not Channel 4), educational schedules were pushed back later and later on BBC.

> "The power of television to change behaviour is perhaps best illustrated by the BBC's family literacy shorts, made to back a Basic Skills Agency campaign. One weekend of exposure prompted 300,000 people to ring for help, and family literacy found a permanent place on the adult curriculum overnight."

While Tuckett was writing this, hopes were still high for a successful University for Industry (UFI) – the creation of Gordon Brown that, he promised, would do for adult learning what the Open University did for higher education, using the airwaves and digital access. Time would prove this to be a false hope – for political reasons rather than the question of access.

Meanwhile, Tuckett continued to stress the importance of the broadest possible access to adult leaning.

> "While dedicated channels are great for aficionados, the struggle to widen participation relies on reaching and surprising the viewer who is not yet looking for learning. Without programmes on the main channels, at a time of day most people watch the box, it is going to be a stiff challenge."

Concern was rising, too, for the effectiveness of the government's basic literacy strategy. All the evidence pointed to allowing either qualifications or a portfolio of evidence when assessing learners, he wrote. So there was dismay when the Qualifications & Curriculum Authority (QCA) restricted such flexibility to entry level, while those at levels 1 and 2 were expected to take external tests if they want the qualification.

To achieve this, in any case, there has to be considerable support from outreach staff, which had been lost over the previous 20 years, described by Tuckett as "a dark age for progressive adult education". Outreach work was lauded in the government's Social Exclusion Unit report on the role of what were called 'community champions'. As Tuckett reported, the report said:

> "There are real 'resource' people in the community who can relate to their neighbours and teach them a thing or two. They may not have strictly bona fide recognised educational qualifications, though they may have considerable industrial/commercial service experience over a number of years, and skills which they can share with other people."

Just as QCA restrictions were driven by audit and target-setting, so too the deployment of staff. The report, *Recovering Outreach*, by Veronica McGivney, principal research officer for NIACE, showed the need to empower people who had the persistence locally to do the job of neighbour-hood renewal. "You can talk to people and raise their awareness, but it may be six weeks or six months before they come back." And there was the rub, said Tuckett.

> "We have a system impatient for results, and a world where catastrophe can happen at speed, but you cannot force the pace at which people choose to reshape their own experience."

Come January 2001, and any hope that the long-awaited white papers on urban and rural renewal might give a spur to adult learning were fading. There was some indication in the urban paper of opportunities for creative providers to give community-based learning for adults a key role in regeneration, he said. "By contrast, the rural white paper has almost nothing to say about learning, despite emerging from the same department..."

A section of the first white paper relating to broadcasting touched on the issue and said:

> "With the growth of new technology, there is a real risk of a digital divide, which public service broadcasting can bridge by offering new and interactive services of information and education, and ensuring the development of the Internet is not purely commercial."

But, said Tuckett, "the paper does not, alas, recognise the key role broadcasting can play in shaping attitudes towards learning". He illustrated the value of carefully-targeted support and persistence in April 2001 when he wrote:

> "Another feature of Adult Learners' Week is the encouragement every unemployed person receives with their Giro cheque to ring learndirect (0800 100 900), the free telephone advice service run by UFL. It is highly effective. For the fortnight in May, there is a major surge in enquiries and a third of those people take up courses."

As with empowerment for neighbourhood renewal, give people a sense of entitlement linked to clear mutual benefits and they will be more readily convinced of the value of learning.

Without clear entitlement and support for UK residents in need, what chance was there of meeting the needs of refugees and asylum seekers? he asked, contrasting attitudes at home and in the US where strong support led to "concomitant benefits of migrants to the wider economy". In Leicester, where NIACE has its head office, he had seen Idi Amin's exiled Asians, who gained UK government support in the early 1970s, help to lift the city's entrepreneurial drive.

> "The lessons of its experience, though, have been slow to spread. Geoffrey Howe's panic to avert the arrival of large numbers of Hong Kong's population at the time the colony was handed back to China is replicated regularly. More recently, Jack Straw's Home Office has obliged asylum seekers to live below the poverty line, and to use vouchers instead of cash."

Work by NIACE at the time highlighted how wasteful were the employment constraints on migrants and it asks whether a more enlightened Home Office would not use the time more wisely to strengthen their language and vocational skills.

By August 2001, following the general election victory for Labour in June, target setting and audit ruled everything. Moser revelations of 7m functionally-illiterate adults helped persuade the government to release cash, with initial targets to strengthen basic skills for 700,000 adults. The International Adult Literacy Survey (IALS) supported Moser's evidence that led to the fears. But the response from different countries was striking. "IALS put the UK at 23% of adults with problems," Tuckett noted.

> "But in Sweden, which came top by a long way, with just 7% of adults having difficulties, a new measure was introduced, offering an enti-

*tlement to everyone without school-leaving qualifications to a year's
full-time study on full pay, with the state picking up the bill."*

When Tom Stitch, US literacy expert and author of *Literacy in War and
Peace*, questioned the IALS figures, suggesting numbers were half the
level estimated, the UK media immediately questioned the wisdom of such
expenditure, while the Swedish spoke of it as a civil rights issue. The Swedish minister explained at a conference attended by Tuckett:

*"If the survey had shown there was only a thousand, a hundred or just
ten adults needing help, it would be just as much a priority."*

Meanwhile, in the UK, NIACE was challenging UK government threats to
withhold benefits from the unemployed who did not take part in basic skills
training. The move was wholly unjust, Tuckett wrote. "Literacy and numeracy
are rights, not obligations." Also, compared with Sweden and the US, the
time is too limited anyway, he said; the offer was two to four hours a week, in
the belief that it was 'output' – getting the numbers through at low cost – that
mattered, not what they learned. "Also, there was an obsession with passing
the tests over and above what was learned in a lasting way."

Returning to the issue in September, he supported government demands
for a language proficiency test as a pre-condition for citizenship. "As long
as the state provides access to education for all asylum seekers, refugees
or domiciled speakers of other languages, it seems a reasonable demand.
It guarantees that all who share responsibility in a democracy for shaping it
have access to the learning necessary to do so in an informed way," he said.

*"But any such measure should be accompanied by greater oppor-
tunities. Countries that invest in new arrivals reap rich rewards in the
economy and civil society. No bad goal for us this year – to recognise
the rich treasures that migrants bring."*

Tuckett's arguments in print are never a one-way street. The leitmotiv in
so much of his writing in this period is that spending on adult learning is not
mere expenditure but an investment that always brings greater returns to the
state, returns that unintended consequences of ill-thought-out target-setting
and audit tend to undermine. By late autumn, things were looking up. It was
easy to forget how hard it had been to have access courses accepted as a
route to higher education, he said. The fund set up by Helena Kennedy was
providing HE bursaries to the previously excluded, Margaret Hodge, minister
for education and employment, had announced a major review of HE finance
and work for the Fryer committee suggested that a mechanism to introduce

codes of agreement between employers and workers for training in the workplace was close.

Unfortunately, within a month, the Treasury's heavy hand of audit was closing in again. Rather than rail against it, Tuckett chose yet again to look for international comparisons. This time, he wrote of how Singapore reacted to the downturn when the US shifted manufacturing to cheaper sites elsewhere in Asia. The Ministry of Manpower hosted events focusing on culture and creativity – "to give a different set of skills to those displaced by economic restructuring". One course was Dr Madan Kataria's practical session in 'Learning Through Laughter'. The idea was that laughter improves your immune system; it reduces stress and makes us more flexible in responding to change. Evidence suggests "the way we live now means we spend less time laughing", said Tuckett.

IN THE midst of the most depressing measures at the hands of the Treasury, "we should all learn to laugh out loud," he insists. "It's hard to feel quite so cross when you have wagged your finger in someone's face and roared with laughter at them, while tears stream down their face as they laugh back at you." The problem was that Brown was effectively re-imposing the old iniquitous Schedule 2 of the 1992 FHE Act by dictating what would or would not count as entitlement for state funding at Level 2 – "no laughing matter".

By 2002, there was general concern that the focus on basic literacy skills was becoming narrower than ever; only those who passed an approved qualification counted towards the 750,000 target. Years of experience warned Tuckett that this approach was not for "learners who had been failed by education where teaching had been narrowly focused on preparing them to pass tests". What he wrote then was prescient, though it was soon to become obvious:

> "We risk letting a tool to measure progress distort what is taught and learned. Targets galvanise systems into action, and that is a good thing. But when they are allied to too narrow a system of audit, they can get in the way. What we need is for every course in the workplace, in colleges and communities, to offer basic skills support and for people to take confidence from the skills they gain. That will need different measures.
>
> "In this case, everyone is trying their hardest to do their best for people failed by the system. But we should trust good tutors to tell us the balance needed to measure the progress that we are all committed to secure."

Commentaries
20 October 2000 to 8 February 2002

20 October 2000

Removed to the margins by prime-time pressure
by Alan Tuckett
Section: Further Education; Opinion. Issue 4399, p32

IT IS ten years since the Broadcasting Act changed the face of television for adult learners. Until then, all terrestrial broadcasters shared the obligation to educate, inform and entertain. (Incidentally, not a bad obligation for educators everywhere.)

The BBC's schools programmes were regulated, but its adult output was left to the corporation, advised by an advisory council. By contrast, independent television companies had to satisfy regulators on quality thresholds and quotas for children and adults alike. For adults, this meant so many hours of approved programmes a week in prime time, and so many hours during the day.

I was privileged to sit for some years on the adult advisory panels of the BBC and the Independent Television Authority. Good conversation, good lunches and, on one of the panels, better wine than I was used to.

You could see clearly the pressures educational broadcasting was under – to be moved to the margins of the schedule to make way for blockbuster movies or high-rating quiz shows.

Sometimes, the boundaries of the educational and the educative were difficult to sort out. So, at the BBC, none of David Attenborough's visually-rich and informative natural history programmes counted, since they were made by the natural history unit in Bristol rather than by the education department.

And we developed a family game trying to guess which eight-minute slot of the ITV morning magazine programme, *This Morning*, was the educational programme. Another heated debate related to back-up material: was any programme that was supported by off-air material or a phone line automatically educational?

Meanwhile, wonderful and inspiring things appeared regularly on the screen. And the fact that ITV was obliged to screen programming on the mass channel in prime time meant the slots were kept safe on the BBC, too.

Margaret Thatcher changed all that, with her determination to set independent companies free from regulation. The imminent threat posed by satellite and cable channels was, apparently, set to fragment the television audience in the early 1990s.

Seriously useless learning

It is easy to believe people caught in the excitement of a new technology, as this year's dotcom mania showed. As it turned out, satellite and cable ended up aping the structure of the mass-channel terrestrial broadcasters for their flagship channels. Viewers, it seems, like a mixed menu of programmes.

Education needs a place on that menu because television reaches people free at the point of use in their own homes and, for many, quickens a mild curiosity into a decision to take an interest further. As Bridget Plowden memorably said, broadcasting is democratic – there are no reserved seats.

The power of television to change behaviour is perhaps best illustrated by the BBC's family literacy shorts, made to back a Basic Skills Agency campaign. One weekend of exposure prompted 300,000 people to ring for help and family literacy found a permanent place on the adult curriculum overnight. Once the prime-time quotas went from ITV, though thankfully not from Channel 4, educational programming on BBC1 was pushed to later on the schedules, then into night-time – where, astonishingly, it attracted a substantial audience of first-time viewers alongside those 'time shifting' with the aid of a video recorder.

The 1990s have presented a conundrum. The distinctive role of educational programmes has been slowly eroded, while marvellous learning campaigns have been developed – from Second Chance and Brookie Basics to Webwise and Generation Sex, television has shown new ways of identifying and meeting the needs of new learners, often using the techniques of advertising.

It is encouraging, too, if unexpected, that regional independent companies have strengthened their education officer force over the past ten years.

But the technological magicians are back in force. The same qualities once ascribed to satellite are now bestowed on digital and online programming.

The BBC has an innocuous-sounding consultation out on transferring all its schools output on to digital. Apparently, the same thing is to happen to the Open University programming, depriving the 2m people who eavesdrop OU programmes each week of a learning opportunity.

And now there are rumours that the BBC will end its dedicated educational production capacity, and change the role of its education workforce.

If this is true, it is serious business. For all the high hopes for the University for Industry, it is still mass-channel television that can create the passion for learning best. And, while dedicated channels are great for aficionados, the struggle to widen participation relies on reaching and surprising the viewer who is not yet looking for learning. Without programmes on the main channels, at a time of day most people watch the box, it is going to be a stiff challenge.

17 November 2000

New assessments are not ideal for a fresh start

by Alan Tuckett
Section: Further Education; Opinion. Issue 4403, p32

WHEN I was a boy, I grew up on air force stations. More or less every day, a group of airmen marched by, not quite convincing in their military discipline, but having to follow the rules. I was led to think about this in a recent conversation about qualifications and basic skills. The great debate that engaged the committee that produced *A Fresh Start* was about the necessity for testing. Some argued that all publicly-funded provision should lead to qualifications, secured through externally-set and marked national tests. 'Objective' qualifications would motivate the mass participation of people having difficulties with writing, reading and with numeracy. Others disagreed, and the happy outcome of the Moser report was a plural approach.

Achievement could be demonstrated by tests leading to qualifications. Alternatively, achievement could be assessed through portfolio-based work. As a literacy teacher, a long time ago, I felt the key to success lay in drawing on student experience and being alert to their purposes, and the contexts in which they sought to strengthen their skills. Building on this, learner and tutor had to make sure that skills were systematically strengthened. This approach had the merit of focusing on learning relevant to learners. I was pleased the portfolio route remained an option in the post-Moser report era. Or so I thought.

I was dismayed to hear this week that while this remains true at entry level, learners wanting a level 1 or 2 qualification have to take an external test, because the defining characteristic of a qualification, accepted by ministers on the advice of the Qualifications & Curriculum Authority, is that it includes externally-set and moderated tests. Now, literacy students can still pursue studies and have their work assessed outside the qualifications framework. But if, as an adult, you want to have your work assessed by other means, you cannot have a qualification.

This would make sense if we had no means of securing rigour in other forms of assessment. But we do know how to do that. Of course, many people may welcome tests, but for others they symbolise a system of selection that has already failed them. Why don't things change? It is a bit like the airmen marching around the camps where I grew up. Their military competence lay in their technical skills, flair and capacity to interpret principles. Yet, because marching was a precondition of other forms of military activity, they were obliged to march.

With David Hargreaves leading the QCA, it may be time to revisit the defini-

Seriously useless learning

tions. His work in the Inner London Education Authority *Improving Secondary Schools* showed vividly that different aptitudes are strengthened in different ways. We learn more than one sort of thing, in more than one way. That is as true of literacies as of anything else. Perhaps ministers should ask QCA afresh if we can safely take a variety of routes, to different ends of equal quality, and measure them in different ways.

Thinking about childhood, I was reminded too of the fad for watching *The Woodentops* that obsessed my early teenage friends near Lincoln. I had just come back from Singapore and was bewitched by rediscovering television, and the new choice of stations. I found it hard to understand why my friends wanted to watch a children's programme I'd left behind years before, when there might be a sports programme on the other side. Still, to be agreeable, I watched too without understanding my friends' enthusiasm.

For some reason, Chris Woodhead's resignation made me think about this. All that talk about what he has done to raise standards rings hollow for local authority-based adult educators. Twelve inspections in six years hardly added up to a strategy for inspection-driven quality improvement.

While the chief inspector inherited few resources to meet his statutory duty to assure quality in LEA-secured adult learning, he never asked for more. Yet, as his annual lecture this year made clear, the slender evidence base on which Ofsted could draw was no inhibition to sweeping judgments about lifelong learning.

Perhaps now, with the new system just about to get into gear, we can look forward to a less adversarial relationship with inspectors. For me, at least, their qualities as creative advisers make a far more effective contribution to quality improvement than their role as auditors. Both matter, doubtless, but the silent art of encouragement takes a lot of beating.

And so to Bryan Sanderson. He spoke at a conference of voluntary and community organisations working with adult learners earlier this month, and impressed me with his warmth, wit and willingness to learn. If the Learning & Skills Council he chairs can maintain those qualities, the future may after all be better than the past.

15 December 2000

Deprived estates won't change overnight

by Alan Tuckett
Section: FE Focus; Further Education; Opinion. Issue 4407, p38

DAMILOLA TAYLOR'S death in a Peckham stairwell highlights the challenge at the heart of the neighbourhood renewal strategy. On the one hand, the bleak pictures of uninterrupted urban flatland remind viewers that the landscape of metropolitan poverty is as stark as ever. On the other, the CCTV pictures of a boy hopping from stone to stone, or skipping along the lines marked in a public square, are pictures of hope and promise.

It is desperate to move so fast from that bubbly exuberance to death. And, as in the case of James Bulger almost a decade ago, desperate, too, that there seem to be cameras to police our every movement, except when it matters.

Not far down the road from North Peckham, the Aylesbury estate in Southwark presents many of the same features of flawed, large-scale social planning. Almost 20 years ago, the Inner London Education Authority sponsored a week-long action research project on the Aylesbury. Outreach workers from all over inner London worked together to try to identify what learning opportunities might make a difference to the lives of local people.

After the week, they continued to meet and to reflect on what they had learned and what their employers ought to do. The product of their work, the Aylesbury Report, was seen as sufficiently provocative for the ILEA to refuse the offer of publishing it. So it was published by Southwark Institute of Adult Education. For the last decade, copies of the report have been passed from hand to hand.

Finally, this week, it has been re-published with a new forward by Dan Taubman, NATFHE's assistant secretary. As a Southwark outreach worker, he was one of the moving spirits behind the project.

As he observes, the report has much to offer contemporary debates about how best to make an education system fit for all our communities. He describes the last 20 years as a dark age for progressive adult education, and the publication of *Aylesbury Revisited: Outreach in the 1980s* represents a determined attempt to stop the wheel needing to be reinvented all over again.

So, on the subject of what the government's Social Exclusion Unit report on skills calls "community champions", the report has this to say: "There are real 'resource' people in the community who can relate to their neighbours and teach them a thing or two. They may not have strictly bona fide recognised educational qualifications, though they may have considerable industrial/commercial service experience over a number of years, and skills which they can share with other people."

It is clear from the report that the tension between widening participation and raising standards is not new. Mike Cushman and Dan Taubman describe a long-running battle "around the issue of 'educational standards' put forward by the inspectorate as having universal application, but seen in the light of workers' experience to be only narrowly valid". And in a thought-provoking piece, Sally Nicholls and Evelyn Murray remark: "In our daily work we have been constantly trying to present adult education in terms that encouraged people to use it, and then having to present to Southwark Institute activities and demands that were not compatible with their terms of reference." It is unlikely that the Learning & Skills Council will escape without having to face that dilemma.

Outreach workers themselves can be gatekeepers with their own boundaries. Nicholls and Murray ask how, faced with a bewildering range of challenging social crises, so many outreach work initiatives focus on family learning initiatives, good as they are, and so few on the rehabilitation of drug offenders.

On the same day it published *Aylesbury Revisited*, the National Institute of Adult Continuing Education, where I work, published two other books on outreach work – one focusing on information and communications technology, the other, Veronica McGivney's impressive overview, *Recovering Outreach: Concepts, Issues and Practices*. Veronica's analysis reinforces the conclusions drawn in the neighbourhood renewal strategy, that it is only when people in the poorest communities feel empowered and supported in shaping the regeneration of their communities that significant change can happen. And effective outreach work, backed by enough patience and flexibility, can support the gains in confidence and agency for that transformation to happen.

But a system driven by audit finds it difficult to be patient enough. One local education outreach worker cited in McGivney comments: "You can talk to people and raise their awareness but it may be six weeks or six months before they come back."

Results take time. And there is the rub. We have a system impatient for results, and a world where catastrophe can happen at speed, but you cannot force the pace at which people choose to reshape their own experience.

19 January 2001

Countryside loses out in learning vision

by Alan Tuckett
Section: Further Education; Opinion. Issue 4412, p28

HOW ARE we doing on joined-up government? Three new policy documents give an opportunity to test how far the government's commitment to lifelong learning has spread from the heartland of education and employment policy.

First up is the urban white paper, *Our Towns and Cities: the Future – Delivering an Urban Renaissance*. It builds on the analysis in the Cabinet Office Social Exclusion Unit's reports on neighbourhood renewal, and shows a reasonably complex understanding of the complex of issues to be addressed to arrest urban decline.

The paper accepts that to make a difference, government, business and voluntary agencies will need to work together, across traditional boundaries. There are no explicit measures relating to adult community education in the paper, but there are plenty of opportunities for creative providers to demonstrate that community-based learning for adults has a key role to play in regeneration.

The paper has four key measures which should impact on adult learning. The core proposal, to create overarching Local Strategic Partnerships, may bring a groan to the lips of everyone struggling to make the existing jungle of local partnerships work effectively. Yet the role of the new partnerships – to develop a community strategy, to agree priorities for action and to co-ordinate the work of local partnerships, may yet hold out the prospect of a more coherent network of local links. Still, few overstretched voluntary-sector providers I have spoken to are holding their breath.

The role and budgets of regional development agencies in securing skills appropriate to the needs of industry are to be strengthened. Educators dedicated to widening participation for people who have had little or no learning opportunities since school, often forget that the workplace is a key site for learning opportunities. This is particularly true for semi-skilled and unskilled men, few of whom find their way over the threshold of conventional institutions of learning.

Skills in information and communications technology are given priority, notably through the development of UK Online centres. The paper makes an economic case for this, but strengthening skills will have a positive impact on confidence, citizenship, entrepreneurship and community involvement, as long as employers' needs are looked at alongside learners' aspirations.

The paper also recognises the valuable role higher education can play in regeneration, through involvement with communities and businesses. Then it goes on to endorse the findings of the Skills Policy Action Team report, and highlights the role local learning and skills councils can play in regeneration. All in all, then, a helpful paper.

By contrast, the rural white paper has almost nothing to say about learning, despite emerging from the same department, just a fortnight later. Does this suggest that learning is seen as an urban issue? In his foreword to *Our Countryside: The Future*, John Prescott comments: "How we live our lives is shaped by where we live our lives. But wherever that may be, people want the same basic things: jobs, homes, good public services, a safe and attractive environment and a society offering opportunity for all." And in a learning society, he might have added the means to enrich life and improve the chance of meaningful work, through access to learning opportunities.

Seriously useless learning

By a happy accident, the failure of the paper to look at the cluster of issues denying a fair chance to learn to poor people in rural communities was thrown into contrast by the publication on the same day of John Payne's *Rural Learning*, a practical guide to learning opportunities in the countryside.

Finally, the broadcasting white paper, a joint production of the Department for Trade & Industry and the Department for Culture, Media & Sport, recognises the importance of television and radio as 'public goods'. As the late Bridget Plowden observed, memorably: "Broadcasting is democratic, there are no reserved seats."

The white paper agrees: "With the growth of new technology, there is a real risk of a digital divide, which public service broadcasting can bridge, by offering new and interactive services of information and education, and ensuring the development of the Internet is not purely commercial."

All well and good. But the paper does not, alas, recognise the key role broadcasting can play in shaping attitudes towards learning. There is a proud record of effective campaigns promoting learning through broadcasting – from Channel 4's Brookie Basics to the BBC's Webwise.

Yet ITV will carry no obligation to promote learning, or to carry educational programming. So the risk is that the main channel diet will still leave learning at the margins of the schedule. Fine if you are a committed learner. But scarcely a help in achieving the vision of a learning society where everyone feels the right to join in.

All in all, then, a mixed picture – but as ever with adult learning, it looks as though it may pay to live in town.

16 February 2001

Finally, a grown-up approach to adult learning

by Alan Tuckett
Section: Opinion; Further Education. Issue 4416, p26

THE GOVERNMENT wants a fair wind for adult learning. It wants more learning in community settings to accompany the transfer of funds from local education authorities to the new Learning & Skills Council. The council has made the expansion of opportunities for adults one of four priorities for its first year.

Minister Malcolm Wicks' announcement of a 9% increase in the adult education budget, and the first ever capital grant for LEA adult education for 2002-3, suggest a real attempt to change the polices that squeezed adult education hard in the 1990s.

During this period, there is no doubt that authorities were quietly encouraged to raid their adult budgets to balance the books in schools. But what was the alternative? Adults never come out well when their case for funding is pitted directly against that of schools. Adults themselves all too often argue that young people must have first claim on the public purse.

The extraordinary thing is that so many authorities maintained or even increased provision for adults. They can now look forward to building on a strong base to improve opportunities for the least well-served adults in their areas.

Until the summer of 2003, provision for adults will be ringfenced, though LEAs will only receive the funding when their annual plans are approved by the local LSCs.

The ringfencing is welcome on two grounds. First, it will give time for LSC staff, who are largely from training and enterprise councils, to learn about the complexities of community-based adult learning; second, it will give time for services to collect better data about their stuudents. Because this area of work is underfunded, in many places it is hard to map students' "learning journeys", to use the BBC's attractive phrase.

At first sight it also looks as if the ringfencing of adult work will give the Learning & Skills Council breathing space to work out future fees for adults. Certainly, it has a lot to do for the system to function effectively in April. But the problem is not simple.

The Further Education Funding Council assumed that institutions would recover 25% of the cost of courses in fees. (Some institutions felt that it was sensible to waive the fees and live with a lower income.) In contrast, many local authorities recover the full cost of courses – especially those taken 'for pleasure' – to students. Most offer cheaper fees for low-income groups.

If the new council starts where the FEFC left off, and expects fees to cover a quarter of costs on every course, the effect in many places will be to reduce LEA provision.

Fees would drop, but so would the number of courses on offer, as public subsidy would get used up on a smaller body of work. As things stand, this is set to happen in 2003, when ringfencing ends and local authority courses are taken within the new council's funding framework.

However, it is not just an issue for LEAs. More adults learn in colleges than anywhere else. If, until 2003, colleges carry on recovering a quarter of costs through fees, whilst expanding courses of the type offered by local authorities, they will be using public subsidy to compete with LEA programmes. Hardly the level playing field to which the LSC is committed. So, the council needs to take an early view on fees to create a fair service offering a wide choice of courses to adults that excludes no one on the grounds of cost.

Colleges also need the new Adult Learning Inspectorate to undertake area inspections of adult provision whenever the Office for Standards in Education does its area inspections of 16-to-19 work.

Seriously useless learning

If area inspections are limited to young people, they will give a partial and lopsided view, and adults' needs risk being sidelined. If these issues can be sorted, we can all enjoy making creative use of the new funds arriving almost by the day. But unless they are sorted, they risk creating new barriers to access and successful participation.

16 March 2001

Colleges will flourish if leaders put down roots

by Alan Tuckett
Section: Further Education; Opinion. Issue 4420, p28

FOOT-AND-MOUTH made me stop and think. When you look at a map of the movement of animals, to market and to slaughter, it is easy to understand how the disease spread so fast. I recalled my childhood vists to my cousin's farm, when farmers went to the local market and lived their lives alongside their neighbours. This nurtured communal values. Too much movement weakens the links of community. Digging where you stand has a lot to be said for it.

Just before Christmas, I spent two days in colleges which have had stable leadership for well over a decade. The benefits were palpable. In Nuneaton, students showed pride in the place. Tutors talked with passion about their work, and senior managers debated with gusto how learners' aspirations, and the needs of the community, could be met within funding constraints.

In Accrington, the learners' awards evening demonstrated a college in touch with the full range of communities in its area. Posh frock days always inspire. But this was different. Through creative detective work the college had unlocked defunct grammar-school endowments to reward attendance, improvement and effort, as well as conventional success. It was a spellbinding evening – formal, yet sharing the intimacy of the weekly farmers' market.

If you leave a wood alone, species proliferate. The same is true of well-led institutions. Creativity grows in the spaces made by secure structures. By contrast, too much instability weakens the capacity of learners to shape the system to their needs.

I am in favour of the reforms the government is introducing. The Learning & Skills Council does provide a chance to create a system where the same kind of work attracts the same level of support – where all the different learning contexts, from workplace to village hall, can share the task of widening participation, raising achievement and fostering a learning culture.

But if that is to happen, we need a period for the new structures to bed down. I am particularly worried about the threat to colleges' work with adult learners, as entitlement is limited to the youngest students and inspection resources are weighted in favour of the same age group.

Multi-purpose colleges, meeting the needs of young people and adults, are the heart of the new system, as of the old. They are certainly the major provider of adult learning opportunities. This is not to decry the achievements of sixth form colleges, or adult education services, or the value of strengthening vocational education, far from it. However, without enough commitment to multi-purpose colleges, learning for adults will be impoverished. The danger is that general colleges look untidy and I have a sense they do not always make the best case for themselves. But like 'bog-standard' comprehensives, we cannot do without them.

This is not a supply-side argument. Of course, we need to stimulate demand and meet it in new ways. The use of new technologies and the development of workplace, voluntary and community-based learning are critical.

Even individual learning accounts have a role to play, at least in combination with other measures – like the union learning fund or work with credit unions. Yet at the heart of a community learning strategy must lie people's palaces of learning – with a rich curriculum, high-quality teaching, learning and learner support, and real skills in consulting learners and potential learners alike. Many of those palaces will be colleges.

One last thought for David Blunkett, if, as seems likely, Labour wins the next election. If colleges benefit from stable, confident leadership, so too would education in England.

13 April 2001

Adult learners deserve all our support

by Alan Tuckett
Section: Further Education; Opinion. Issue 4424, p26

FOR TEN years now, people have been telling me that Adult Learners' Week is a good thing. They go on to say there is just one thing wrong – the date. When we ask for advice on when it would be better, it emerges that May is the least bad date for most people. Although many say September would be helpful, most are too busy enrolling to organise celebration events. And, anyway, many of last year's students are no longer about. And the whole point of Adult Learners' Week is to celebrate their achievements in all their diversity as a stimulus to others to join in.

The main argument for May is that it is the only month when we can secure coverage on all the terrestrial television channels – squeezed in before Wimbledon gobbles up the air time on the BBC, and test matches do the same on Channel 4. But in 1997, another advantage was that it fell just over

Seriously useless learning

a fortnight into the life of the new government and provided David Blunkett with a platform to make his first public policy speech as secretary of state.

He announced the government's intention to make lifelong learning and widening participation for excluded communities a key policy priority. The Learning & Skills Act, the creation of the LSC and major new investment are all testament to that aim.

I thought Adult Learners' Week was similarly well-timed this year, before the foot-and-mouth crisis and the abandonment of May 3 as election day. If the general election is called for June 7, the Week will fall during the period when Parliament is prorogued and ministers will be unable to take part, unless new cross-party arrangements can be put in place.

Does this matter? Well, over the last decade, the Week has provided a clear slot in the diary for politicians to meet inspiring adult learners, and also to make policy speeches. We have tried to make sure these are on emerging policy priorities to accelerate initiatives benefiting adult learners. This year's conference is on promoting and stimulating demand.

The LSC has a statutory duty to promote learning and the University for Industry has a clear remit for promotion, too. How far this is a marketing task and how far promotion is an integral part of the curriculum of adult learning will be keenly debated. Bartle Bogle and Heggarty's famous family literacy adverts for the BBC shocked adult literacy specialists by using storylines that moved outside the gentle supportiveness of most earlier campaigns. But it was a spectacular success.

On the other hand, the normal market segmentation studies all too often condemn those most excluded from learning to last place in the queue for attention. It may be efficient to concentrate on the cohort of potential learners who are easiest to recruit, but it won't do much for the learning divide.

Another feature of Adult Learners' Week is the encouragement every unemployed person receives with their Giro cheque to ring learndirect (0800 100 900), the free telephone advice service run by UFI.

It is highly effective. For the fortnight in May there is a major surge in enquiries, and a third of those people take up courses.

I hope that during the life of the next government we can see a parallel initiative to encourage people to ring the helpline in the pension book and the family allowance book. The LSC initiative to support bite-sized courses this summer, funding two-hour courses targeting groups new to structured learning, should also make a difference.

Providers should think outside of the normal curriculum limits and make fresh connections. Then there may well be a measurable impact on the national participation target for adults – which I hope the LSC will re-adopt in its corporate plan.

11 May 2001

A world where qualifications are less dominant

by Alan Tuckett
Section: Opinion; Further Education. Issue 4428, p30

I READ regularly that financial markets move on sentiment. Articles galore suggest that, at last, the market has turned – and that punters should once again part with hard-earned savings in the hope of making money. The failure of events to match the forecasts never seems to faze the writers of such pieces.

It is rather like the people who have calculated the exact date of the end of the world. Neither the purveyors of millennial doom nor the financial-page journalists pause for a moment. They move quickly to recalculate in time for the next deadline, or the next movement in the constellations. The literary critic Frank Kermode described this state of permanent expectation, permanently thwarted, as immanence.

I have spent much of my professional life looking for signs that things might be about to improve for adult learners. From time to time, I have felt confident that the moment has come, only to find out that new cuts or reorganisations set us back a few years. As I have got older, I should have developed a proper sense of caution, but I haven't. The imminence of the general election brings risks that the landscape may change for the worse again. Yet, I find myself convinced that we may be on the cusp of cultural change.

I think the overwhelming hegemony of qualifications in post-school education may be on the wane. The first prompt to this renegade idea was the lecture that Dick Smethurst, provost of Worcester College, Oxford, and the National Institute of Adult Continuing Education's president, gave to our annual conference. In it, he explored the limitations of the value of metaphor in policy-making, focusing on how the language of industrial production had come to shape thinking and decision-making about education, and how an excessive audit culture had grown up as a result.

He captured the dangers of an over-reliance on metaphor in a wry passage in which he pointed out that, unlike widgets, the outputs of the educational production line had a disturbing habit of running back to the beginning of the line and jumping on again.

Qualifications are invaluable in an audit culture – since they provide a proxy for the quality and complexity of learning undertaken. They also provide a useful sifting mechanism for public support. Courses leading to qualifications attract better levels of funding – whatever the motivation or circumstances of learners.

Yet, there is plenty of evidence that the range of qualifications on offer

Seriously useless learning

bewilders all but the most assiduous bean counters. I learned this early when my father explained that he couldn't see any reason why I shouldn't get a first-class degree since I had passed my 11-plus. After the 11-plus, all tests blurred into one for him. I think the unswerving popularity of A-levels are the result of people knowing broadly what they mean.

The second prompt was Alwena Lamping's presentation of the findings of the Nuffield Inquiry into Languages to the Adult Learning Committee of the Learning & Skills Council. She described a real mismatch between the pattern of course offers to adults wanting to learn languages, and their retention patterns. Many learners, voting with their feet, made the case for bite-sized learning opportunities. Providers are too often trapped by funding structures and custom and practice into offering less flexible provision. One organiser's drop-out becomes another's flexible learner in a better-geared system.

The third prompt was Geoff Mulgan's description of the Performance Improvement Unit's review of workforce development. Are qualifications quite as central to the development of a skilled workforce as we have assumed these past 20 or 30 years? As an employer myself, I want to answer yes and no. For my colleagues, qualifications formally recognise their talents and achievements, giving them mobility in the labour market. Yet, often I find I don't quite know what I can ask of them that is different as a result of all that hard work. By contrast, the learning gained and reflected on at work is often easier to identify and make use of, and I am convinced we must foster curiosity and learning as an integral part of the work, whether that learning is accredited or not.

A world where qualifications are less dominant has its own challenges. How are learners to have a secure measure of the learning journeys they have undertaken? How can we benchmark good practice? How can we secure progression?

They are key questions for a funding system that can support NVQs, uncertificated French and teamworking skills, but they have long been central concerns for adult education. NIACE is working with the Learning & Skills Development Agency to capture the assessment of achievement in non-accredited courses. But I have a sneaking feeling it is work that may imminently impact across the whole terrain.

8 June 2001

Uncivilised restrictions on asylum-seekers

by Alan Tuckett

Section: Further Education; Opinion. Issue 4432, p38

IN ONE of Bertolt Brecht's plays, he suggests that we can measure the quality of a society by its treatment of its most vulnerable people. The recent street disturbances in Oldham make clear that, by that measure, we are not very civilised in Britain. They reminded me of Salman Rushdie's analysis that when Britain could no longer export an empire, it imported a new colony to carry on the same social and economic relations with black people. Writing at the time of the 1980s riots, he concluded: "The members of the new colony have only one real problem. That problem is white people. Racism, of course, is not their problem. It is yours. We simply suffer the effects of your problem."

The television images from Oldham showed a physical environment steeped in poverty – in stark contrast to the prosperity of suburban Britain, but reminiscent of Toxteth, St Paul's and Brixton 20 years ago. Where are the parks, the community centres, trees on the street, the pavement cafes? People need public spaces to make culture and communities which work.

Lee Jasper, who advises Ken Livingstone on policing in London, writing in the *Guardian*, described his own experience growing up in Oldham, and the repetitive patterns of how poverty and exclusion feed racism. Most depressing was his account of the role teachers played in his school in reinforcing the racism encountered outside. And even if there has been a total transformation in Oldham's educational institutions since then, it is not surprising if people so totally failed by schooling, and by other state agencies, have little hope that giving the system a second chance will make an impact on their chances in life.

I was depressed, too, by the debates about asylum-seekers during the general election campaign. You would think that Britain was sinking under a tide of people desperate to move here. But we are not. Numbers of applications for asylum dropped last month.

It has been a curious feature of Tory policy of the past 20 years that a party in other respects besotted with the American example should fail to recognise the contribution to American prosperity made by their migrant communities. Entry for highly-skilled migrants, economic or political, is regulated, but by British standards it is relatively open. Less formally skilled migrants take a riskier route to navigate entry, just like here. The contrast lies in the treatment people get on arrival. There, high levels of investment in public education offer migrants the chance to gain qualifications and bring

Seriously useless learning

their skills to the economy. At the same time, mechanisms are in place to recognise and accredit overseas qualifications and experience. Neither is available here, despite developments over the past four years.

Yet, there is evidence in abundance that over-restrictive policies are short-sighted, and work against our economic and cultural interests. I live in Leicester, a city whose prosperity has benefited significantly from the creative and entrepreneurial people displaced from Idi Amin's Uganda.

The lessons of its experience, though, have been slow to spread. Geoffrey Howe's panic to avert the arrival of large numbers of Hong Kong's population at the time the colony was handed back to China is replicated regularly. More recently, Jack Straw's Home Office has obliged asylum-seekers to live below the poverty line, and to use vouchers instead of cash.

The National Institute of Adult Continuing Education has just finished a modest but important piece of work, interviewing asylum-seekers to match their skills and experience to job opportunities in the local economy. Asylum-seekers bring talents aplenty, and want to contribute while they wait and wait for decisions on their future. Our rules stop them from taking a job for the first six months, but an enlightened Home Office would use that time to strengthen skills in English, and vocational skills. As Gandhi said when asked what he thought of Western civilisation: "I think it would be a good idea."

13 July 2001

Polish tale shows power of combined thought

by Alan Tuckett
Section: Further Education. Issue 4437, p38

I HAVE always been attracted to stories which involve an imaginative reworking of the scenery. A good illustration was offered at the further education chaplains' conference in York. The event opened with a blessing, a prayer and an inspiring story – we were told about a group of Quakers doing relief work in some villages in rural Poland at the end of the first world war.

The food distributed by the Quakers was critical to the survival of the starving villagers, whose conditions were desperate. One of the relief workers caught typhoid and died. Local by-laws prohibited burial of anyone other than a Catholic in the local cemetery and, despite popular protest, it proved necessary for the worker to be buried outside the cemetery, because the official interpretation of the by-laws proved inflexible.

At the request of the local villagers, the worker was buried just next to the cemetery, as a mark of respect. On the day after the funeral, the relief workers found that their friend's grave was now in the cemetery, since the villagers had, overnight, repositioned the fence to include him.

After the chaplains' event, I drove to Taplow where the Learning & Skills Development Agency were hosting an international seminar on stimulating demand. Sofia Valdivieso Gomez from the Canary Islands, joint director of Unesco's adult participation study, gave a paper entitled *Just when we understand the rules they change them*. It reminded us that the forces that change the rules are not always benign and learning friendly.

The current policy context offers plenty of opportunities for imaginative reworking of dominant themes. You can see it in the way the government's adult basic skills strategy has built on the work of the Moser Committee. It has subtly reworked Moser's agenda, to include provision for adults who speak English as a second or subsequent language, and adults with learning difficulties. Of course, we still have national tests and the target numbers that make the Treasury comfortable. But there is a gathering recognition that literacy, and particularly numeracy, will only be strengthened for many thousands of adults if they are embedded in context for people pursuing other studies.

That will involve different roles for specialist literacy and numeracy staff, who will need to combine specialist teaching with learning support for tutors and students across the curriculum. It will also involve everyone who teaches adults acquiring a basic understanding of how to support learners trying to strengthen literacy and numeracy. The teacher's portfolio of skills will need to include basic skills as a competence, just as they all need to understand how to foster equal opportunities, and how to secure health and safety at work.

Moser had little or nothing to say about writing, but it seems to me that a focus on learning literacy through writing would reconnect the basic skills curriculum to wider adult studies. My experience of the literacy campaign of the 1970s and early 1980s is that the intellectual ferment and sense of shared achievement was fostered by powerful student voices. Revitalising student writing is one curriculum focus the new Learning & Skills Council might usefully explore.

The Learning & Skills Council will need to reframe existing ways of doing things if it is to make learning accessible to those whose exclusion was so clearly described in the Social Exclusion Unit's Skills Policy Action Team report. Reframe, but not too quickly, since institutions need enough security to be able to respond to new challenges.

Given the scale of the task facing the council – nationally and locally – I have, so far, been impressed with its pragmatism and openness. I am delighted that work is being done to identify sound data sources to enable the council to adopt an adult participation target. The National Institute of

Seriously useless learning

Adult Continuing Education expects to work with the council, the Department for Education & Skills and others to make sure the measures adopted are fit for this purpose.

There is a long way to go, however. One of the hardest challenges facing a funding system focused on individual achievement is to develop mechanisms which will recognise that what groups of people learn together is greater than the sum of what they learn alone.

This is, of course, at the heart of community learning. Developing the capacity to solve problems together – the confidence and imagination to move the cemetery fence overnight – produces outcomes easy for us to see. But how can we assess the process of learning that went into them? That is a real challenge for the next 12 months.

10 August 2001

Swedish model shows success doesn't come cheap

by Alan Tuckett
Section: Further Education. Issue 4441, p26

THE NATIONAL adult basic skills strategy has made some early gains. There have been marked strides towards a national curriculum framework and a co-ordinated approach to strengthening the skills of staff working in literacy and numeracy. Adults with learning difficulties, people learning English as a second or additional language, and adults with dyslexia have all been included in national development work. Literacy and numeracy are being embedded in other learning. The first evidence from national pilot projects suggests that nine in ten students are prepared to take the national tests that have been developed. And all this effort is fuelled by co-operative endeavour by a wide range of agencies overseen by an impressive, cross-government Cabinet committee.

Claus Moser's report, with its headline finding that 7m adults in the UK lack basic skills, and the work that followed, persuaded the Treasury to release unprecedented sums of money, and Labour promised to achieve targets for strengthening basic skills for 700,000 adults.

Yet, while experienced literacy and numeracy workers have welcomed the extra attention and funding, they have expressed some hesitations over the targets and some of the detailed measures proposed.

Take the headline numbers. The 7m figure derives from the International Adult Literacy Survey – undertaken in the mid-1990s. France famously dropped out half-way through, apparently disquieted at its poor performance.

From the beginning, the survey's methodology was questioned, but its impact cannot be denied. In countries such as the UK – which did poorly with 23% of adults having difficulties – this was, perhaps, unsurprising.

But in Sweden, which came top by a long way, with just 7% of adults having difficulties, a new measure was introduced, offering an entitlement to everyone without school-leaving qualifications to a year's full-time study on full pay, with the state picking up the bill.

At a UK-Sweden conference I attended, the Swedish education minister explained that the issue was a civil rights concern. "If the survey had shown there was only a thousand, a hundred or just ten adults needing help, it would be just as much a priority," he explained.

Now, the debate about the IALS numbers has flared up again. Tom Sticht, the American literacy expert, suggests in the *Washington Post* that the American survey may have got the numbers wrong, and there might be only half as many people with literacy and numeracy problems as it suggested. Ensuing debate in our press shows it clearly depends where you draw the line, and what constitutes basic skills. Mary Hamilton and her colleagues at Lancaster University have shown how people have different levels of competence in different contexts. And as you aggregate up for the population as a whole from the number of young people leaving education without qualifications, you quickly arrive at 6.5 to 7m.

None of this removes the imperative for Treasury funding. Even if the overall numbers were revised downwards, millions would still need high-quality education in literacy, numeracy and the other skills underpinning broad-based national targets. And, as the Swedish strategy suggests, success does not come cheap.

Far too much basic skills work in the UK is limited to two or four hours a week. To make substantial progress needs allowing more time. We knew this 25 years ago when the Manpower Services Commission funded up to 36 weeks' Training Opportunities Scheme courses. They worked. Learners prospered and had significantly different life chances at the end of it. Then the MSC confused throughput with output. Courses were shortened and their success compromised. In time, they were dropped.

Tests, too, have limitations. They risk leading us to separate off literacy and numeracy from the contexts in which they are applied – and it is learning, not scores, that really matter.

One final concern with the strategy is the risk that we hold the victims responsible for the system's failings. The proposal to withhold benefit from people choosing not to strengthen their basic skills surely derives from authoritarian social policy that has no place here. Literacy and numeracy are rights, not obligations. Where the state has failed to secure them for its citizens, the onus must be on the government, through encouragement, support and incentives to persuade people to try again.

Seriously useless learning

21 September 2001

Strangers who bring gifts of cultural diversity

by Alan Tuckett
Section: Further Education; Opinion. Issue 4447, p34

IN THE mid-1980s, my friend Adnan visited Britain for the first time. His great ambition was to see the British Museum. I met him for a drink after his first visit. He came in, awestruck: "You have more of Egypt here than they have in Cairo, Englishman," he said.

Adnan has spent his whole adult life in the Palestinian camps in Damascus working with adult learners – overwhelmingly literacy students – and pre-schoolchildren, struggling to share a sense of Palestinian identity within the constraints of a national curriculum, and an embargo on a return home.

Palestinian adult education is developed in the spaces allowed in 15 to 20 different host national adult education systems – and, of course, within major financial constraints on the West Bank and Gaza. He sensed that here in Britain we were able not only to define ourselves but the experiences of others too.

I was reminded of him last week when the annual Adult Tutors' Awards ceremony was held in the new conference centre underneath the glorious new Great Court of the museum. John Healey, minister for adult skills, was chief guest.

All of us who attended the event saw afresh the rich resources for learning on offer as we made our way to and from the ceremony. It reminded us that museums are powerful contributors to informal learning for young people and adults.

But the collections come from all over the globe and Greek visitors will often feel that the Elgin marbles might better be returned to Athens, or West Africans that the Benin mask is out of place in London.

The complexities of global mobility and its consequences were shown too in the experience of Mongay Lek-Lek Bapindikwa, a Congolese refugee who was short-listed for an award.

He arrived in Britain nine months ago speaking little or no English and is now a successful and inspiring teacher, sharing his new skills with other refugees and asylum seekers. Skilled, motivated and infused with an affection for the space afforded in liberal democracies, he represented a powerful case for recognising the merits of permeable borders.

A second national event was held on Saturday, September 8, to mark International Literacy Day, and the Sign Up Now campaign co-ordinated annually by the National Institute of Adult Continuing Education at the Victoria & Albert Museum.

The event was a family learning day which explored how the galleries and exhibits might be used as springboards for inter-generational learning. Again, a colleague of mine was surprised to discover that her family surname was shared with a south-Asian royal dynasty and a collection in South Kensington.

Shared experiences are not always uncontested, though. This summer, at Ocho Rios on the north coast of Jamaica surrounded by dripping white sand beaches, the International Council for Adult Education held its first world conference for eight years. There was marked agreement among adult educators from all over the world about priorities in stimulating demand, improving advocacy, seeking entitlements for adult learners and in sharing experience across national boundaries.

In the margins of the conference, a meeting of Commonwealth adult educators looked at future co-operation. The meeting agreed that there was enough to merit a continued dialogue – if only because there are few viable networks for north-south discussion – and because the learning histories of families in all our countries cross national boundaries.

I came back to the debate in Britain about the introduction of a language proficiency test as a pre-condition for citizenship. To many this seemed an intrusion, and I read one piece which suggested that Kurdish refugees, escaping the suppression of their language, would see such an obligation as an affront.

I strongly disagree. As long as the state provides access to education for all asylum seekers, refugees or domiciled speakers of other languages, it seems a reasonable demand. It guarantees that all who share responsibility in a democracy for shaping it have access to the learning necessary to do so in an informed way.

But any such measure should be accompanied by greater opportunities. Countries that invest in new arrivals reap rich rewards in the economy and civil society. No bad goal for us this year – to recognise the rich treasures that migrants bring.

19 October 2001

The fight goes on to widen access to learning

by Alan Tuckett
Section: Opinion; Further Education. Issue 4451, p28

JUST BACK from a decadent weekend. Altogether too much good wine and food at my friend Helen's 60th birthday celebrations in the Loire valley, and a chance to debate the place of life histories in social policy and education, albeit in my execrable French, with Alex and Denise in Poit-

Seriously useless learning

iers. Amazing what a cheap flight from Stansted makes possible. And a reminder that travel can enrich the mind, and a change of scenery is a rich incentive to fresh insights.

In Chinon we passed a group of pensioners, concentrating on the story of Richard Coeur de Lion as they drifted round the town. A great advert, surely, for Saga and its sister organisations that offer learning journeys.

Nearer to home, *Time to Learn*, now published by City & Guilds, offers an extraordinary variety of short courses – each offering a combination of a good place to be and new things to think about. No bad thing in the present context.

Short-term residential colleges have been all but invisible to policy-makers for the past 40 years. Indeed their strongest advocate, Richard Livingstone, made his case for them during the long years of the second world war.

Yet every year, people make their way to Little Benslow Hills for music, to West Dean College for silversmithing, to Dillington in Somerset for landscape painting, and to The Hill in Abergavenny for any number of things.

Livingstone argued that it was necessary to get away from the rhythm of your ordinary life to see the world afresh. For many working class students, going away to study was, for many years, the only option. The residential experience can be intense and it can change lives. That is what deputy prime minister John Prescott captured so movingly in his obituary of Raph Samuel, the historian who inspired generations of Ruskin students.

More recently, the growth of access courses has offered learners the chance to study at home, without the disruption that a year away at college means for many adults. It is hard to remember, now that such courses are a major route to higher education for adults, just how hard the fight was to get them accepted – first by individual institutions for individual courses; later as a nationally-recognised standard.

Last week, a leading champion of that fight, Maggie Woodrow, died suddenly. I knew her, and often argued with her, for 20 years, and was proud that she served on the National Institute of Adult & Continuing Education's executive. Nowhere was there a more persuasive advocate for high-quality, properly-resourced opportunities for adults wanting to prepare for a course of study in HE.

Like the late Philip Jones, whose tenacity created and protected the mechanism for recognising access courses, Maggie Woodrow's great strength was her willingness to be awkward on behalf of learners seeking a second chance.

Such awkwardness can be a good thing. Helena Kennedy provided a splendid example, at the Parliamentary bash for the Kennedy Awards scheme. She was scandalised that an award winner was unable to continue her studies to university, just because she is 54. Fifty-four is, of course, the witching age. Up till then the Treasury thinks it has got time to recover your student loan. After that, no chance. Even people prepared to mortgage their homes are unable to call on a state loan. For too many, this means that the new challenges and fresh impetus to life a higher education offer is denied them, just when they can squeeze the time to study seriously.

Yet we know that learning, like exercise, prolongs active citizenship, delays morbidity, and saves the health and social services money. I have no doubt that Helena's energy will make sure that this daft anomaly is addressed in the new review on student finance that higher education minister Margaret Hodge has announced.

Talking of announcements, none is awaited as eagerly as the Learning & Skills Council's proposals for the new funding system. Will they offer incentives to widen participation? Will they punish institutions for having learners with interrupted attendance patterns? As ever, the demons of anxiety, fuelled by half-heard rumours, make everyone nervous. They are only likely to be quelled once the paper is in the public domain.

Another document about to appear – if a little delayed by the war – is the Performance & Innovation Unit's policy paper on workforce development. I hope it develops on chancellor Gordon Brown's conference suggestion, that the time has come to move on from mere voluntary measures. Jim Sutherland's work for the Fryer Committee suggested a mechanism for introducing codes of agreement between employers and workers in all sizes of firms – to ensure that training was on the agenda of every workplace in the country.

If it contains that, it will have been worth waiting for.

16 November 2001

Profit by exploring the many routes into work

by Alan Tuckett
Section: Further Education; Opinion. Issue 4455, p32

CHRIS HUGHES, the chief executive of the Learning & Skills Development Agency, argues, persuasively, that further education colleges should focus on their core mission of vocational education. If they spread themselves too thin, so the reasoning goes, they can lose clarity of purpose.

Learning related to the world of work is distinctively the responsibility of FE colleges. No other publicly-funded institutions will supply enough joiners, programmers and engineers to the labour market. He is right, too, to suggest that colleges that lose sight of the needs of their local economies pay a high price when employers turn to the private sector to meet their needs.

The argument makes me nervous, though. I have no disagreement with a central focus on the vocational, but what does that mean for everything else? Years of work with adult learners has taught me to be cautious of tidy missions. You could see the notorious schedule 2 of the 1990s – which divided post-school education into well-funded, certificated work and poorly-funded, uncertificated courses – as just such a tidy-up initiative. It failed because you cannot tell the purpose of a student from the title of a course, and learners pursue their own logic in their learning journeys.

For communities most excluded from the labour market, it is essential that colleges and other community-learning agencies recognise the need for opportunities that start from where the learners start, and involve them in the shaping and managing of their learning. That is a key lesson of the Adult & Community Learning Fund, which is just about to launch its sixth round of bids.

Another lesson is that many people have forgotten the skills of outreach and negotiation necessary to such work. As the Social Exclusion Unit report on skills recognised, many of the poorest communities have little contact with any institutions. Such work is some way from the labour market, but it is vital if the twin goals of economic engagement and social inclusion are to work.

At the further education/higher education interface, a focus on vocational education would, of course, let foundation degrees and access courses in nursing and accountancy through.

But what would it mean for those broader access programmes in the humanities and social sciences. Large numbers of my colleagues have found that studying history, literature and sociology were perfectly effective foundations for successful working lives.

Their experience also points up the problem with what counts as vocational. In a world where today's job-specific skills have a shelf life of five or ten years, the really important skills are in learning and in transferring lessons from one context to another.

For adults with learning difficulties, further education colleges share with other providers a wider responsibility – to secure for people as full a life as possible, access to the skills of participation in civil society, including work, but not narrowly focused on it. Indeed, you could re-read the Tomlinson report on inclusive learning as the case for embedding vocational education in a wider, richer concept of a learning institution. Tomlinson is, of course, worth revisiting – and I look forward to a Learning & Skills Council review of its lessons for the new enlarged sector.

Then there are all those vocations which relate to, but are distinct from, the paid labour market. The bulk of carers in the UK work without pay, yet without their effort there would be a huge increase in the demands on public finance. How far is the role of FE limited to the work carers do, and how far to their broader needs? I know if I were dependent on a single person for my contact with the world, I'd want him or her to be as widely educated, stimulated and enriched as possible.

The same is true of family learning. We recognise the value in training professional staff who work with younger children, but we are only now seeing the richness offered by the family as a site of learning. The Pre-School Learning Alliance has a powerful record in helping parents enrich their own learning as well as their children's. The same goes for many primary schools. Surely there is work for colleges in this field.

We should cast the vocational mission in a rich soup of other engagements with employers, unions and the wider society – much as colleges now do. There is an uncomplicated and uncontested solidity in the role of community colleges in the United States. They offer something for everyone. It would be good if we could recognise that our own colleges do just the same thing.

14 December 2001

You've got to laugh in lifelong learning

by Alan Tuckett
Section: Further Education; Opinion. Issue 4459, p44

GLOBALISATION UNSETTLES everyone. Three weeks ago I was in Singapore for its second Manpower Learning Festival. The city state has an impressive economic record, with 8.5% growth rate year-on-year for almost two decades. Yet the American economy's downturn, and the shift of manufacturing production to cheaper sites elsewhere in Asia, left Singapore confronting very similar challenges in helping adult workers adapt to new forms of work.

To date, the overwhelming focus of post-compulsory education in Singapore has been vocational. Yet here was the Ministry of Manpower hosting an event focused entirely on culture and creativity – partly because they have a larger part to play in design-rich, knowledge-centred economies, but also because motivating and training workers displaced by economic restructuring involves a different set of skills. Their learning symposium opened with a session in which the 1,000 participants sat in among the members of the Singapore Symphony Orchestra, while Roger Nierenberg explored with them and us how innovation, co-operation and communication worked in an orchestra, and in other learning organisations. Some members of the audience got to direct the orchestra, the players had passages where no one was given authority to set the tempo.

It was a convincing demonstration of the value of clear, flexible and responsive leadership. But mostly it was an exhilarating reworking of a familiar experience. The next morning, Tony Buzan wove his distinctive brand of mind magic; an American philosopher tried to link Kant and Confucius to the contemporary company; and there were a variety of community and arts-based presentations.

The pièce de résistance came at the end, when Dr Madan Kataria led a practical session in Learning Through Laughter. Dr Kataria was impressed by studies that show that laughter improves your immune system, reduces stress and makes us more flexible in responding to change – and by evidence that the way we live now means we spend less time laughing. All but abandoning his general practice work in Bombay, Dr Kataria has established Laughter Clubs International – developing clubs in parks and workplaces where people laugh together for a period at the beginning of the day.

Laughter exercises help people explore conflict through laughing – hard to feel quite so cross when you have wagged your finger in someone's face and roared with laughter at them, while tears stream down their face as they laugh back at you. I know it all seems daft, but Madan reduced a thousand deeply-serious people to helpless laughter within a few minutes as he taught us some basic strategies. Like other forms of lifelong learning, laughing is good for your health and for the mind. Hard to see how it would fit in schedule 2 of the 1992 Act, of course, but perhaps the time has now come for learning through laughter to find its way into neighbourhood renewal strategies.

I was not too surprised to see no reference to having a laugh together in the Performance & Innovation Unit's paper on workforce development. It was quietly released on the same day as Gordon Brown's pre-budget statement, and Stephen Byers' release of minutes of a meeting with Railtrack. Curious that the criticism attracted by Byers' timing was not equally applied to the Cabinet Office for failing to secure wider attention for the paper. Perhaps this is because, while most PIU papers are issued as government policy, this one makes clear that it isn't. More widespread inter-departmental consultation leading to a second paper next summer, suggests that this area is still some way short of settled policy.

The Skills Task Force was unequivocal in advising that adults should have an entitlement to learning up to level 2. The logic of the PIU report underpins that, but it sounds as though Treasury nervousness has intervened – an impression reinforced by the pre-budget statement itself, where an even tighter schedule 2 seems to have been reinvented in the narrowness of vocational focus for the new money in prospect. The PIU report says that introducing a requirement to train would be a big change, not to be undertaken lightly.

Surely, if we want a learning society, and a learning-rich economy, investment in the workforce should be a precondition of being allowed to trade, just as the obligation to secure a safe working environment is now. It is worth noting in passing that Singapore does have a training levy on all employers.

The Learning & Skills Council strategy for workforce development cannot surely wait until the summer. I think it needs a sharp and clearly-focused programme that works for existing and emerging areas of the economy; that does something to strengthen management and leadership training; develops measures to address skills gaps; keeps a consistent focus on what the CBI used to call the "long tail of underachievement"; and at the same time leaves room for a bit of a laugh.

11 January 2002

A message for lifelong learning, not Christmas

by Alan Tuckett
Section: Further Education; Opinion. Issue 4463, p31

HAPPY NEW year: at the last moment I was spared a visit to the Christmas pantomime in Bradford, where they were doing *Snow White and the Seven Dwarfs*, so I sloped off to catch a movie at the National Photographic Museum instead. I heard all about the play afterwards, of course, taking delight in my son, Lewis's enjoyment of the belly laughs. For the next 24 hours, "Oh yes you did", "Oh, no I didn't", punctuated all our conversations.

Perhaps I should have gone. It would have been good practice for getting back to work after a six-week sabbatical. This was brought home to me by the Learning & Skills Council's Christmas card. Few cards generate such intense debate as this one has. Its cover message is clear and bold, but alas misleading: "The saddest thing about this Christmas card is that seven million people in this country couldn't read it if they tried." Key words are picked out in tabloid red. Inside it says: "The best thing about this Christmas is that we will be working to change that" followed by season's greetings from the council. Of course, no one can object to the centrality of the core message – literacy matters, and it is reassuring that it is a top priority for the council.

I cringed when I received the card. Certainly, there are millions of people who need help with basic skills. But the architect of the International Adult Literacy Survey, on which our seven million number is based, has pointed out that 70% of those with the lowest scores in the American sample read a newspaper once a week or more. The same is likely to be true here. To overstate the exclusion of people with reading, or spelling problems, does not help. I felt like calling on the pantomime dame's help to say to the council: "Oh yes they could, or at least a fair number of them could, and do."

And then there is the tone of the card. Who is the audience? I felt it was unlikely to include many of the seven million. This is not a small point.

Seriously useless learning

If we are going to crack the literacy problem in Britain, we need to make strengthening reading, writing, spelling and maths a normal, adult activity.

We need to move away rapidly from seeing people who need to strengthen skills as inadequate, and start to capture and include their voices in the shaping of the services made for them. As one of the first literacy students, I was involved with in the 1970s, Roger Weedon said about his concerns about studying: "I'm not reading *Andy Pandy* – that's a racing certainty."

Now, I know it was only a Christmas card. And the council is right to recognise the importance of its mission in basic education.

Fortunately, it also has a remit for listening to learners. As that work gets into full swing, issues like tone will surely be fine-tuned.

Back in Bradford, I found that having narrowly escaped one sort of in-service training I had let myself in for another. The movie I caught was Jean-Luc Godard's *L'Eloge d'Amour*. Early on, the auteur figure at the heart of its rather fractured narrative asks: "What is the definition of an adult?" He reflects that while everyone knows what youngsters are – so that we define them by their youth, by what they share in common with other young people – and while everyone recognises older people's distinctiveness, it is immensely difficult to sum up what constitutes an adult. Is it a common set of experiences, or evasions?

I think some version of the same uncertainty affects public policy-makers, when considering the needs of adult learners. Too often, the world over, 'adult' gets narrowed to 'labour market participant', with the result that the curriculum of adult learning is similarly narrowed to those things employers recognise as useful; and the planners of the system often have little experience outside the vocational. But as the Godard film demonstrates eloquently, it is elsewhere that the largest questions about the meanings of our lives, the nature of our relationships, and our ability to learn from experience are played out. The complexity and diversity of adults' experiences, challenges in life and curiosities make for a rich arena for learning. That complexity brings with it a bewildering variety of forms for learning, often brilliantly fit for purpose. It happens in reading groups, libraries, cinemas and pantomimes, as well as colleges and workplaces. But, currently, only a small proportion receives public funding, and with it public scrutiny. For learners, that may be a mixed blessing – but for planners, the challenge is to know enough about what works outside the limits of publicly-funded provision to support different and innovative work where they meet need.

8 February 2002

Two steps forward, two steps back, now twizzle

by Alan Tuckett
Section: Further Education; Opinion. Issue 4467, p34

I USED to go folk dancing in Cornwall in the 1960s – I liked folk song, and folk culture there had not yet split apart. You might go to an event to hear John the Fish and Brenda Wootton, but once you were there, there was no escaping the Cumberland Square Eight and the rest of the repertoire. All the dances offered a semblance of intimacy, and a curious logic which separated you from your partner as soon as the dance got under way. Quite a good metaphor for early adolescence as a whole.

However, I was reminded of a different feature of folk dance when discussing the tension between meritocracy and democracy in lifelong learning policy in England the other day. Lots of the dances involve two steps forward, two steps back and twizzling your partner on the spot. Yet somehow you progressed down the line. That seems to me to be the way we make progress in lifelong learning.

The National Health Service University clearly represents two steps forward for the democratic dynamic in government. It aspires to be the largest corporate university outside China. It has recruited Bob Fryer as chief executive; its target is to involve everyone working for the NHS – all 1,200,000 of them. Its budget, £2bn, will amount to a third of that dispensed by the Learning & Skills Council. Like lots of New Labour initiatives, it comes hard on the heels of other measures with overlapping concerns – all of which will need to be carried into creative partnership.

A great deal of its budget is spoken for in existing commitments. But the decision that everyone means everyone holds out real prospects for those people at the bottom of the NHS feeding chain. There will be a recognition that everyone contributes to patient care, a focus on communication and values, and a skills escalator where staff can transform career opportunities by getting credit for what they have learned. It will be exciting to watch it grow.

The news on the basic skills national tests, though, is less encouraging. The Moser committee all but failed to agree a common report over the proposal that national tests should be an obligatory part of publicly-funded literacy and numeracy work. The happy compromise the committee agreed was that tests would be developed alongside other equivalent measures of progress. This approach was fleshed out by hard-working task groups, which met following the publication of the report to address implementation issues. Now we hear that only those learners who have signed up on

Seriously useless learning

courses, and sat and passed an approved qualification in basic skills, will count towards the national target of 750,000.

The Adult Basic Skills Strategy Unit is clear that funding will not be limited to provision leading directly to the test. But providers are often confused. The assumption is that perhaps a half of all those who sign up for basic skills will follow through to take the test. There is also quite encouraging news that large numbers of learners are willing to sign up.

However, when the Adult Learning Committee of the Learning & Skills Council discussed the target, I was keen that they should adopt a wider measure of learner achievement. In part, my concerns about the test are borne of years of experience, albeit earlier in my working life, with learners who had been failed by education where teaching had been narrowly focused on preparing them to pass tests.

When that approach does not work, and you fail the test, you tend to blame yourself. But even if times have changed for many, there is still the technical problem that the UK's basic skills crisis relates to the application of literacy and numeracy skills in the widest range of contexts – literacies and numeracies difficult to capture in a 'one-size-fits-all' testing model.

We risk letting a tool to measure progress distort what is taught and learned. Targets galvanise systems into action, and that is a good thing. But when they are allied to too narrow a system of audit, they can get in the way. What we need is for every course in the workplace, in colleges and communities, to offer basic skills support and for people to take confidence from the skills they gain. That will need different measures. The narrowing of the measures towards the target feels like two steps back.

Every reversal for the democratic dynamic ends up reinforcing privilege. In this case, everyone is trying their hardest to do their best for people failed by the system. But we should trust good tutors to tell us the balance needed to measure the progress we are all committed to secure.

Persistence pays

FIVE YEARS into a New Labour government, Tuckett mused: "But where is the strategy which commits every institution to widening participation for adults as well as the young?" The target for getting half of the 18-to-30 age group into HE, while welcome, could make life difficult for older people wanting the same, he wrote. And for 14-to-19s, adults, FE and HE, Chris Hughes, chief executive of the Learning & Skills Development Agency, education minister Margaret Hodge and the LSC were all supporting largely vocational specialisation.

He remained unconvinced and was still hoping the Downing Street Performance & Innovation Unit, Gordon Brown's spending review and LSC workforce strategy, would bring about level 2 entitlement "because voluntary participation of employers still neglects the most needy and vulnerable workers. Community-based adult education was in better health than usual, but the decision to hand control of adult and community funds to local LSCs was not good because many failed to recognise the importance of wider adult learning to their social and economic agenda. "Five years on, we still have a long way to go." And then there is the voluntary sector, the new-look individual learning accounts and the new broadcasting legislation. "There are opportunities – and real risks – for adult learners, with every ladder matched by serpents' tails."

It was also five years since David Blunkett used Adult Learners' Week to give his first speech as secretary of state, announcing the creation of an advisory group to shape lifelong learning. "The decade to mid-90s saw a dismal time for adult learning, with a quarter of an already small cohort dropping out by the mid-1990s." In opposition in 1992, Labour said it would introduce an entitlement for all over 50, but in power it subsumed them in broader commitments.

Tuckett's frustrations really come through in his column of June 2002, when he says that for all of the education secretary Estelle Morris's support for adult learning and despite 80% of FE learners being adults, her speech to the LSDA conference was devoid of reference.

"She came with some new money, a consultation paper and a number

of challenges – and the audience recognised extra resources the government was committing. Everyone recognised that low morale and pay in FE needed tackling if aspirations in the consultation paper Success for All were to be met. But where were local education author-ity and voluntary-sector adult education services? There was a mention of adults' right to learn for leisure – but that scarcely captures the rich mix of purposes that the government's lifelong learning policy and the remit of the LSC recognise: where was learning for active citizenship, community regeneration, prolonging active citizenship, passion and curiosity, let alone spirituality?"

Despite bold long-term spending plans in the Comprehensive Spending Review to 2006 and to 2010 for adult level 2 targets and basic skills, and fine words from Estelle Morris that "too many adults have been failed by the system", there was nothing in the review to show it as anything but low prior-ity – exactly what the lifelong learning policy was supposed to overcome, Tuckett noted. Government officials said the implications of the review for FE would become clear in the autumn.

Meanwhile, he pointed out there's nothing on closing the 6% pay gap with schools, on how lifelong learning could overcome social exclusion or on adult community learning. Measures in the LSC equality and diver-sity announcements also mounted to "sins of omission", with little beyond much-needed support for the Commission on Black Staff in FE and guide-lines and local initiatives; "poor compared with FEFC in early 1990s, which commissioned Tomlinson on social exclusion and Kennedy on widening participation".

In his September column, he voiced what was a general frustration in the sector. "Spending review priorities in the UK have become a top-level dialogue behind closed doors rather than a democratic dialogue – weigh-ing up the priorities." It's the sort of thing you might expect, he suggests, in impoverished parts of Brazil, rather than in the UK – a new primary class-room or better street lighting? It augers the resurfacing of a silo mentality with the key question being whether "ministers, like champions returning from a medieval joust, have secured victory or defeat". That said, he is far from negative about the year's achievements. The year brought good news about adult learners' successes: a 40% reduction in working-age adults who lack level 2 and a doubling of the basic skills target for 2007.

"However, the language has shifted from the first term of the Labour government. Then, social and economic prosperity were twin goals. Now attention is much more clearly focused on the relationship between learning and work."

While the CSR, he said, exhorted everyone to "provide incentives to employers to train" and "widen participation in learning by the low-skilled", they were goals not targets and there was no mention of the other side – learning for later life, family learning, regenerating neglected communities. While Tuckett saw the obsession with targets as anathema, they could not be avoided since they followed the money. Moreover, he observed the following month, *Success for All* made too little use of, and put too little emphasis on, the role of local authorities and voluntary groups in adult learning. For example, there was "the launch of the 'golden hellos' for recruits to FE in shortage subjects – which schools had had – but not for local authority and voluntary sector adult education services facing the same shortages". This was not special pleading.

> *"There is a risk that in seeking to solve one problem, the government will create another. Big fish, the schools, eat first. Once their appetite for shortage subject teachers is slaked, colleges, which are less politically visible and therefore medium-sized fish, can eat. And when will the minnows in the adult and community sector get to the table? Involving them last sells adults sort, despite evidence of DFES-sponsored Wider Benefits of Learning Research Centre which links adult participation to good health and reduced crime ... and heed the warning of the squeeze on the labour markets as the baby boomers retire."*

As the end of the year neared, he reflected on the highs and lows of Labour policy:

> *"For adult learners, The Learning Age, the last comprehensive spending review and the Learning & Skills Council remit letter, were all highs. The narrowness of the remit of the skills review, and the exclusion of adults over 30 from the higher education target, were both lows."*

New Year 2003 brought a note of optimism, or at least pressure from high-profile sources to boost adult learning in the widest sense. Tuckett saw several challenges around the need to maintain high quality learning for adults as all the financial and other incentives for colleges focused on success and retention of younger learners; for example, with 50% HE participation target to age 30, what happens to the other half? he asked. Also, the decision to treat institutions differently would create disincentives: golden hellos and a fully qualified teaching force for FE but not for local authority adult and community learning (ACL).

Nevertheless, significant and supportive reports were emerging, including *The Learning Curve* from the Economist Intelligence Unit and *In Demand*

Seriously useless learning

2 by the Strategy Unit. Both stressed the need to improve the skills of poor communities and recognised that revitalised ACL has a key role to play. They also suggested that the level of support for education was more important than the money spent. If old arguments had been forgotten, there was new evidence that "what the CBI called 'the long tail of under-achievement' called for policies which addressed economic prosperity and social inclusion at one and the same time," he said. "This was the rationale behind the Delors' European white paper on competitiveness in the 1990s, and behind this government's impressive lifelong learning policy, spelled out in *The Learning Age* and the legislation that flowed from it." Jacques Delors' paper, *Growth, Competitiveness, Employment* "argued that lifelong learning policies needed to focus on social inclusion as well as economic modernisation, and to treat education and training as one system".

But Tuckett warned there was a danger of being in too much of a rush. The sector was in a position to benefit from the changes. "Meanwhile, the initiatives rain down remorselessly. *Success for All*, the latest skills strategy, the review of adult funding, workforce development, new ideas for higher education – all good, in part at least. But all would benefit from time to improve policies and build consensus rather than a mad dash to implementation.

> *"The prospects look gloomy, though, as paper after paper lays out a truncated timeline, where the need to act fast puts creative and reflective policymakers under unproductive pressure. It takes time and space for things to grow, and for quieter voices to be heard."*

By March and he was writing of a fairly new idea on the policy block. Professor Richard Layard of the Centre for Economic Performance proposed a happiness index. The thesis, Tuckett wrote, was that "getting richer does not make you happier, unless everyone around you is doing broadly as well as you are". Evidence emerged, for example, by contrasting Scandinavia with the US; in countries such as the US, where the gap between rich and poor was greatest, both enjoyed poorer health. The same appeared to be true for the gap in educational attainment. Meanwhile, evidence from the Centre for Research on Wider Benefits of Learning showed learning had a positive effect on health and longevity. At the same time, Ivan Lewis, recently-appointed junior minister for education and employment, was touring the country saying that "the vocational qualifications system is not fit for purpose". He also made clear his commitment to learning for its own sake alongside with a key role for the voluntary sector.

Tuckett called for the Kennedy widening participation agenda to be revisited, with wider tutorial support system for adult learners (similar to that introduced for A-level students) and suggested the LSC build happiness measures alongside student satisfaction surveys. "Up and down the country, key officials feel the pressure to achieve the LSC's headline targets, and too many believe that uncertificated learning is a luxury they cannot afford. With a happiness measure and participation target alongside the headline Public Service Agreement targets, it might be easier for planners locally to include the enrichment of the lives of pensioners in their thinking."

But what chance did such policies have with Ed Balls, chief adviser to Treasury, threatening to impose a requirement on employers to train people? Balls had little support from either Charles Clarke, secretary of state for education and skills, or his junior minister Ivan Lewis, who insisted courses must reflect employer need before any regulation could be introduced. Tuckett suggested that the Treasury was simply out of touch with the needs of the most disadvantaged.

"What can the strategy do for, say, a cleaner, bringing up a family and working for three or four employers, none of whom sees her development as their responsibility?"

When all seemed lost and Parliament was in recess, as in a Greek drama (or Hollywood melodrama), along came a hero to rescue at least part of the day in the form of Ivan Lewis, junior minister for education and skills. On publication of the White Paper, *21st Century Skills: Realising Our Potential*, he secured a guarantee that would last well into the Coalition government a decade later safeguarding a wide range of learning opportunities for pensioners, including leisure-based learning which was accessed by many older people. Older people will also benefit from the new entitlement, announced in the white paper, to free learning for all those studying for their first full level 2 qualification (five GCSEs or a similar vocational qualification) as a skills foundation for employability. And even though the latter commitment would be diluted in future years, Lewis told the *TES* at the time that the decision was in no small measure "due to the persistence of Alan Tuckett". The safeguard was set at 3% of the LSC budget – £300m, declining to £210m as budgets shrank.

Welcome though the safeguarding was, there were still developments to watch with the latest skills strategy, he said. Also, new 'formula funding' was coming as spending guarantees under the Learning & Skills Act were coming to an end. Dedicated funds for local authorities were going and the new skills strategy would direct adult and community cash to poorer areas. All well and good, he said, but "what will happen to less affluent pensioners in middle class areas?" How soon would the LSC develop a strategy to improve provision? What would the adult entitlement to level 2 qualification mean for college budgets and the curriculum? There was still a long way to

Seriously useless learning

go to meet Kennedy's vision for widening participation, and a review of how the voluntary sector could assist in this was long overdue despite "exciting developments" in local LSCs, such as Birmingham and Solihull linking colleges with voluntary bodies.

Tuckett also sensed too much of a rush for results in the government's new skills strategy, despite the new LSC boss, Mark Haysom, "making all the right noises" following the launch of the new Skills Alliance, the body charged, along with the LSC, with hitting the new skills target of 2m new level 2 qualifications by 2010. "There is a danger that it will go for quick wins – those needing few skills – rather than the slow, expensive journey of engaging the hardest to reach," Tuckett wrote. "The LSC slithered away from original WP target as too many targets would be a burden, and now says it will introduce a 'measure'; fine if it serves the purpose." In December, he returned to the theme.

"The danger is that in pursuit of level 2 qualification targets, we will neglect those who lack confidence to gain a whole level 2. Again, quick wins not hard cases who need a range of bite-sized chunks."

And as the year ends, he asks:

"Is it too much to hope for an early review of one controversial pilot scheme? Seeking to make participation in basic skills provision compulsory for benefit claimants who do not want to lose a proportion of a tiny weekly pay-out does not seem fair. It smacks of one rule for the affluent and another for the poor."

Commentaries
5 April 2002 to 5 December 2003

The last resort is a good place for adult learners

by Alan Tuckett
Section: Further Education; Opinion. Issue 4475, p38

FOR THE last few days I have woken up with Marvin Gaye's *What's Going On?* playing in my head. Not surprising really when you look at what is happening to adult learning opportunities across the board. There is evidence of a lot of activity but little consistency and shape to it all. It is clearly welcome that the government has put such a premium on widening participation in higher education. Pressures to include more working class people in HE will tend to strengthen further education too, as the principal route to HE for adults from under-represented communities.

Less good is the way this commitment to widened participation is expressed as a government target. The pressure to get 50% of 18 to 30-year-olds into some form of HE by 2010 will make life more difficult for adults over 30 seeking the same type of education.

After all, funding is finite and expansion of chances for young adults risks squeezing those for older people. Of course, having more people with early experience of HE is, in principle, a good thing.

But Britain is ageing fast. And it is not only in the Thames Valley where employers are trying to entice experienced early retirers back to the labour force – with offers of updating programmes – because of the shortage of young people. HE badly needs a new initiative to help it serve the interests of older adults. We need loans and grants beyond the mid-50s. If targets are to drive everything, a little target for the other end of the age spectrum might limit the damage that the current, well-intentioned target risks creating.

In FE, the biggest danger is the search for tidiness. Chris Hughes, chief executive of the Learning & Skills Development Agency, has developed his thinking about the missions of FE colleges, and makes a persuasive case for them to specialise in the things they are best at – whether that is 16-to-19 work, adult access or work at the FE-HE boundary. The risk otherwise, he argues, is that colleges will be seen as institutions of last resort.

Margaret Hodge, too, is reported to value specialisation. And the Learning & Skills Council's Centres of Vocational Excellence initiative tells the same story. I am not convinced. I worry about people who found education unrewarding the first time but want to put their toes back into the water. The advantage of the cosmopolitan college is the range and variety it offers, and its flexibility in meeting the needs of individuals. Unlike Chris, I believe that an ideal mission statement for colleges at the heart of communities is that they are "institutions of first and last resort".

The same pressures that privilege the young in current HE policies are there in the 14-to-19 policy. We already have area inspections for young people but not for adults, who comprise most of the college population. The inequalities in opportunities and outcomes highlighted in Helena Kennedy's 1997 report persist.

But where is the strategy which commits every institution to widening participation for adults as well as the young? Five years on, we still have a long way to go. Perhaps the Downing Street Performance & Innovation Unit's second report, the chancellor's spending review, and the LSC strategy for workforce development will help, with a level 2 entitlement for adults that will open doors to paid educational leave. I hope so because workforce development, with voluntary participation by employers, continues to neglect the least skilled and most vulnerable workers.

At first sight, community-based adult education is in better health than usual. New buildings, capital grants, rising investment and a degree of enthusiasm in many local LSCs all augur well. Even here, though, there are clouds on the horizon. The rationale for taking funding for adult and community learning into the LSC was to secure a reasonable offer for all, wherever they lived. Yet decisions about the volume, range and focus of adult and community learning provision are to be decentralised to local LSCs.

Initial plans suggest that few recognise the importance of the work to the council's social and economic agenda. It is just one more dimension of the council's challenge to be locally responsive and guarantee a minimum reasonable offer to all. But to get that balance right there needs to be more capacity in the middle so that good practice can be effectively shared and policy developed. And then there is the voluntary sector, the new-look individual learning accounts and the new broadcasting legislation. There are opportunities – and real risks – for adult learners, with every ladder matched by serpents' tails.

19 April 2002
It's no small feat to harness the world's energy

by Alan Tuckett
Section: Opinion; Further Education. Issue 4477, p34

"ANOTHER WORLD is possible." Swept up in the opening festival, it was easy to agree with the assertion in the title of the second World Social

Forum. Fifty thousand people surged through the streets of Porto Alegre in Brazil, making music, shouting slogans, laughing, arguing, banging sauce-pans, and waving banners – loosely allied by a shared concern that there must be better ways of doing things.

Just over the border, the Argentinian economy was in a state of collapse. But there was optimism in facing the challenge of a debt crisis, where the wealthy countries are subsidised by the debt-servicing repayments of the poorest. The World Bank's structural readjustment programmes involve the same poor countries in cutting the very education programmes which offer them the hope of learning their way back to financial health. And there is an international trade in street children's organs.

I was reminded of the energies of the Anti-Nazi League rallies at the end of the Seventies in Britain; of the ferment of history workshop conferences; the easy communality of rock festivals; the theatre of carnival. The scale of the task – in creating viable alternatives to a world where the largest companies operate in a global market substantially unmediated by global civil society – is immense. But so, too, was the agenda of the 800 workshops, 150 large seminars and 50 conferences that constituted the forum.

A young people's forum attracted 10,000 participants; the World Parlia-mentary Forum and the World Congress of local authorities worked in different ways from the global alliance of indigenous peoples. Noam Chomsky drew an audience of 4,500 – late bookings for the forum were accommodated up to 80 miles away and bussed in daily.

Despite the scale and the cornucopia of choices available, it was surpris-ing how many people wove similar journeys through the week's programme. Surprising, too, that such effective planning could be sustained by the loose coalition of interests that constitute the forum.

As with the Greater London Council in the Eighties, we benefited from the support of local government agencies committed to popular democracy. Porto Alegre and the regional government of Rio Grande de Sul engage annually in popular budget-making processes, involving hundreds of thou-sands of people in deciding priorities for local government investments. Support for the forum grew from that.

Unsurprisingly, the forum attracted less press attention than the World Economic Forum taking place at the same time in New York. Southern Brazil is a long way from the centres of the global media. English took its place as just one of the languages of communication; and there was no single closing communique drafted in advance by a leadership. No formal organisation, no formal leadership, and no single mechanism for evaluating the strengths and weaknesses of the occasion.

There were few participants from Britain or other northern European coun-tries, yet thousands from France, Italy and Spain. Doubtless a similar event in Africa would have seen more people from Britain – given our old colonial ties. Yet the forum exposed gaps in our public debate and lifelong learning agenda that I do not think we can lightly ignore. How best to forge an informed sense of our mutual dependence with the peoples of the south? What kind of global democracy can we create to counterbalance the emergence of a global economy? How can the voice and energies of young people contribute to revitalising democratic forms? In short, what is the place and form for political education for us now?

Paul Belanger, the distinguished Canadian adult educator, argued passionately that the only route to "another possible world" was through the engagement of the creativity, imagination and learning of all the peoples of the world.

But all means everybody – a global version of the challenge facing lifelong learning here, and one no easier to confront.

The forum was the largest adult learning event I have participated in – but there was little paperwork; there were open and permissive arrangements for participation. No one inspected – but there were lots of people to get advice from. I might find it hard to elaborate precise learning outcomes from my trip – except for the hard-learned lesson that it is a mistake to leave your trousers on the beach in Rio – yet everyone I spoke to was inspired by the richness of the experience and the challenge of the agenda.

The third forum meets in the same place next year. It will be a good place to sharpen energies and to remake the world.

`10 May 2002`
Older, but not wiser enough
by Alan Tuckett
Section: Further Education; Issue 4480, p38

IT IS ten years since the government of the day brought forward the final stages of the 1992 Further & Higher Education Act to avoid a clash with the first Adult Learners' Week. And it is five years since David Blunkett used the week to give his first speech as secretary of state, announcing the creation of an advisory group to shape lifelong learning.

More people are learning overall now. In 1991, just 36% of adults said they had engaged in learning over the past three years. By 1996 that number had risen to 40%, and this year's survey shows 42%, slipping back from 46% in 2001.

Growth has not been even though. Over the decade, participation among top professional and managerial groups rose from 50 to 60%. Among the poorest, by contrast, growth was just 2 percentage points – from 23 to 25%. Last year's figures showed a more optimistic picture. This year's survey suggests that the struggle to create a learning society is a major one, and that the learning divide persists.

But there have been important changes. There was a 4% gap in men's and women's participation rates in 1991. In 2002 the gap has closed.

The major losers over the decade have been older learners. In 1991, 15% of adults over 65 said they were learning formally or informally. After a quarter of the already small cohort of older learners dropped out in the mid 1990s, their participation rate has crept back to 16%. This despite the success of the University of the Third Age and the commitment to Better Government for Older People.

In its 1992 election manifesto, Labour said it would introduce an education entitlement for adults over 50. Andrew Smith, the then opposition spokesman for further and higher education and now chief secretary at the Treasury, argued the case eloquently. But by 1997, that policy was lost, subsumed by broader commitments.

Older adults were also the big losers when changes derived from the 1992 legislation kicked in. Courses that were not accredited failed to get funds and community-based learning suffered successive cuts. Things have improved since the Learning & Skills Act triggered modest growth – at least until next year.

Participation dropped during the 1990s, though research shows that learning is good for your health and prolongs your active citizenship. The population is also ageing, which means that the economic value of older people must be more widely recognised.

Tom Schuller, architect of the proposals in 1992 for older learners' entitlement, has dusted off the idea and adapted it for this decade, in a provocative report for the Institute for Public Policy Research. It could be just the thing to correct the imbalance in policies dominated now – just as they were a decade ago – by the youth agenda.

You could see this in John Harwood's impressive presentation to the All Party Parliamentary Group for Further & Adult Education, on the day of the FE lobby of Parliament. The case he made for investment in the sector, and for decent pay for staff, was powerful and persuasive. Yet apart from his opening sentence, all the evidence he cited on the achievements was about 16 to 19-year-olds. This is hardly surprising when area inspections are limited to that age group, when 14-to-19 policy and the prime minister's target for HE all focus on young people.

But the great success of colleges in the 1990s was to open themselves up to tens of thousands of adult learners. Adult participation is the main business of many colleges. And, overwhelmingly, they do it well. That work needs the nurture of regular scrutiny and celebration.

I thought colleges had good reason to take heart from the MPs' report on

ILAs. The picture that emerged was of a scheme well served by publicly funded bodies, and by established private-sector training providers – damaged by the failure to secure minimum standards among new entrants, and to guard against fraud.

And the moral of all this? Simple: value adults as well as young people, trust the public sector more, and celebrate achievement. There is clearly still a need for Adult Learners' Week each year.

31 May 2002

Let adults share the whole learning experience

by Alan Tuckett
Section: Further Education. Issue 4483, p30

DID YOU know that yellow is the last colour in the palette to be recognised by people developing Alzheimer's disease? And that red is the second last? I learned it during Adult Learners' Week, when the older learners' project at Brockenhurst College received an award for its work with social services and a group of residential homes.

Those in the project showed great patience, care and imagination in building a curriculum fit for their students, whose ages ranged from 75 to 106. Exercises in the project's art classes focus on yellows and reds, rather than the sludgy browns and English greys that Alzheimer's sufferers let go first.

Working with adult learners always involves three overlapping disciplines, well illustrated by Brockenhurst. The first, of course, is the discipline of the subject – the accumulated understanding of everyone who has struggled with a body of ideas, or a set of practical challenges.

The second is the discipline involved in teaching that subject to adults. It involves the recognition that adults have a wealth of experience to bring to their learning, negative as well as positive, and that any effective learning involves a dialogue that draws on that experience.

The third discipline relates to context. You cannot teach art to the cosmopolitan communities of south London without locating the different aesthetic traditions that shape the cultural heritage the capital draws on. You cannot drape the walls of a dressmaking class with stereotypical images of young white women without contributing to the invisibility of everyone else. This third discipline is the central focus of much equal opportunities work. And the Brockenhurst example highlights the professionalism tutors bring to the task of turning the slogans of widening participation into a lived practice.

In a magical inaugural lecture at Leicester University, in which she asked what Dickens would make of vocational education and training now, Lorna Unwin reminded us that medieval university students were awarded master of arts for completing an apprenticeship in "the crafts of the free person". The craft needed to offer the Brockenhurst learners access to the stimulus of learning, and its associated freedoms, is not acquired quickly, and to be applied needs patient co-operation by people working across policy silos. Not surprising, then, that the real costs of successful widening participation are one-and-a-half times the cost of conventional participants in further education, and one-and-a-third times the cost of the better-funded participants in higher education.

My son had his ninth birthday on the Saturday of Adult Learners' Week and I found I could not easily switch off thinking about the less formal learning we rely on to make sense of our lives. Lewis and his friends had a football party in a local indoor warehouse, which hosts 120 indoor football league matches each week. The coach who organised the games was experienced at crowd control and at the rhythm of individual and group-focused skills needed to keep boisterous nine-year-old boys, and the odd five-year-old girl, contented. Where did he learn them? Mainly on the job, swapping experiences with other people, noticing what works, he said.

Later in the day, the awards ceremony for Nirvana football club was held in the African Caribbean Centre in Highfields, Leicester. The club runs teams for under-eights through to under-15s in local leagues, and this evening of celebration noted the highest goalscorer, the most-improved player, the players' player, and the manager's player, for each of the 12 teams supported by the club. Then we highlighted the achievements of the managers, volunteers and the women who wash the kit. In events like this, people practise the skills of active citizenship, managing the surplus energies of boisterous kids, the shyness of adults unused to the limelight – sharing values, skills, energy. Nirvana is living proof of the benefits that derive from an open society. The club draws on the full range of Leicester's cultural mix – but we also noted the improvement of results due to the arrival of refugees from Afghanistan and Somalia. Voluntary agencies provide spaces for people to build new relationships and they are a rich source of mutual learning. No one spoke about formal learning all evening, but I am in no doubt that the people who give up time to make the club work have a rich vein of understanding of the crafts of a free person.

Now what has all this to do with workforce development on which the LSC is currently consulting? Everything and nothing. Lorna Unwin held out a vision in which vocational learning enriches the whole person – just like Lewis's football club. We should seek nothing less.

Seriously useless learning

28 June 2002

Adults have needs – but not on paper

by Alan Tuckett
Section: Opinion; Further Education. Issue 4487, p34

THE LEARNING & Skills Development Agency's summer conference was quite an event. For the first time, it seemed to me that a distinctive cadence emerged in which a newly-defined sector spoke a common and inclusive language, explored some tough challenges, with enough trust and enough recognition of common purpose to hold out warm hopes for the future.

In the myriad seminars on the afternoon of the first day, it was, time and again, difficult to predict where contributors worked, since each framed what they had to say in terms of a common project. Learning & Skills Council staff engaged with the crisis faced by an underpaid sector; private-sector providers and publicly-funded colleges vied to address the quality agenda.

Not bad, when you think how quickly the ground has been travelled, from the establishment of the LSC, and its 47 local arms. Council staff exuded a new assurance – that after all the confusions of the early months, when it was often unclear who had the authority to make a decision, they now had a grip on the agenda.

There was a healthy mix of senior and middle managers from colleges, a sprinkling of private-sector providers and a small cohort of adult education services. Estelle Morris came with some new money, a consultation paper and a number of challenges. As ever, she was engagingly open, warm and celebratory, and she was tough on the need to agree the grounds for dialogue. She encouraged frankness, direct speaking, and some recognition on the part of practitioners of the real additional resources the government is committing.

Of course, some of the dialogue was not two way. Comprehensive spending reviews seem now to last forever. Everyone in the field agrees that the twin crises of low morale and inadequate pay in the further education sector must be cracked, if the proposals in *Success for All* (the purple consultation paper) are to bear fruit. Roll on the summer and a chance to renew that part of the debate after the review.

Meanwhile, in the spirit of openness and mutual respect, I had a different concern with Estelle's presentation and the language of the policy paper.

She is without doubt a politician with conviction and we are lucky to have her. Despite recognising that 80% of college learners are adults, the focus of the speech was, overwhelmingly, on FE meeting young people's needs. Adult learners' experiences were all but invisible. If you scratch the surface of *Success for All*, you find that adult education services are covered. It was right to recognise the gains in the coming together of the Further Education Funding Council, training and enterprise councils and school sixth-forms.

But where were local education authority and voluntary-sector adult education services? There was a mention of adults' right to learn for leisure – but that scarcely captures the rich mix of purposes that the government's life-long learning policy and the remit of the LSC recognise: where was learning for active citizenship, community regeneration, prolonging active citizenship, passion and curiosity, let alone spirituality?

Now, I know that the bulk of ministers' speeches are drafted and redrafted by civil servants, and I also know from the sensitivity and empathy the secretary of state showed at the launch of Adult Learners' Week that she brings all her experience as a teacher to bear on her work, and understands intuitively the struggles many adults overcome to return successfully to learning. But it is worrying if the government is not yet mirroring in the language of official papers, the gains in understanding across the patch that the conference demonstrated. It needs to match LSC chief executive John Harwood's recognition in his speech to the conference that the sector has twin duties, each life-wide in scope, for adult as well as young people's learning.

The detailed language of a speech and a policy paper would not be such a concern if there were not already real imbalances in the policy portfolio – for example, in the target to get 50% of 18 to 30s into higher education by 2010.

No one designed that policy with the intention of reducing the volume or range of adults' access to HE. But that surely will be the effect, if substantial new resources are not found, since that target is one for which the Department for Education & Skills will be accountable to the prime minister's Delivery Unit.

Targets have their uses, but not at the expense of the policies they are meant to encapsulate. And the great trick for all of us in making sense of the new sector, is to use a language and illustrations that make clear that success for all means all.

26 July 2002
Missing pieces leave us puzzling over future
by Alan Tuckett
Section: Further Education. Issue 4491, p26

THERE WAS good news for post-school education in the recent public spending review, which sets all state spending for the next three years. Good news especially on adult level 2 targets for 2006 and 2010, and the revised basic skills targets. I was pleased to see Estelle Morris quoted in a

Seriously useless learning

Whitehall press release saying: "Too many adults have been failed by the system ... and many have not reached their potential." Even better, she was reported as adding: "We've got to develop the skills of these adults, both for their own quality of life and if we are going to close the productivity gap with countries such as the US, France and Germany."

Just what we wanted to hear, except that in her actual speech, Estelle failed to say anything significant about FE. This leaves an overwhelming impression that it does not matter, or is a low priority. Exactly the problem the lifelong learning policy was supposed to overcome.

But look carefully and you notice the things not said in the review announcements. Nothing on closing the gap on pay between school and college teachers. And, given a 6% increase in education funding overall, a 1% rise for colleges committed to reform does not sound enought to maintain, let alone narrow the pay gap with schools. And where was the role lifelong learning can play in overcoming exclusion and helping poor people too old to get education maintenance allowances? Where, too was adult community learning?

What the review actually means for FE will become clearer in the autumn, once departments have finished internal debates about priorities. Meanwhile, morale is fragile, despite welcome injections of cash. And that is where the symbolic importance of politicians' speeches comes in. If FE, let alone lifelong learning, is ever to lose its Cinderella status, it must be talked about, not relegated to the press release.

We find similar problems in the Learning & Skills Council's approach to equality and diversity. Like the spending review, its sins seem to me to be ones of omission – and not just because the latest (and second) meeting of the LSC equality and diversity advisory body fell victim to the London tube strike.

What the LSC has done is laudable enough: supporting the work of the Commission on Black Staff in FE, producing equality and diversity guidelines and lots of impressive local initiatives. But its early record compares poorly with the start made in the early 90s by the Further Education Funding Council. It commissioned John Tomlinson to lead an inquiry, which led to the ground-breaking Inclusive Learning report. Later it commissioned Helena Kennedy to lead a comparable inquiry into widening participation. These provided an agenda for the LSC to apply to its much broader range of providers.

The LSC's record seems all the poorer because, unlike the FEFC, it has an explicit planning remit. Since April last year, there have been civil disturbances in Oldham, Burnley and Bradford; the new race legislation and the 2001 Special Educational Needs & Disability Act is coming into effect.

But where is the authoritative voice of the LSC on these matters? How regularly does it consider equality issues? Where is the equality dimension in its draft workforce development strategy? And how well is it serving the needs of people with learning difficulties?

One problem is the structure the LSC has for dealing with discrimination. At a time when plans to merge the different national equality commissions are under consideration, it seems odd that the LSC keeps the management of work with adults with learning difficulties separate from broader equality and diversity work. It seems odd, too, to me at least, that the equalities work is limited to the quality arm of the national council. I think it should be based in the chief executive's office, acting with his authority. Cultures form early, and if equality work at the council starts off as a low priority, the risk is that that is where it will stay.

I believe the LSC needs to establish a wide ranging equality and diversity commission, with an authoritative, external chair. Its report would sharpen thinking and practice throughout the LSC and its providers, and help with the wider debate about what post-16 education can do to make our society worth living in.

7 September 2002

Piper needs more than mere ministerial music

by Alan Tuckett
Section: Opinion; Further Education. Issue 4500, p38

WHAT IS the best way to set spending priorities? Britain's comprehensive spending review process has sharpened minds. Work is now under way to produce evidence for the next round. Interested groups can and do make submissions, but the exercise is essentially a private dialogue behind government doors. Occasionally there are exceptions – such as when televised promises shape the outcomes, recently to the benefit of the health budget.

The British way is in stark contrast to budget-making in Rio Grande de Sul in Brazil. There officials prepare detailed spending priorities, highlighting implications for communities. A quarter of a million people then meet to weigh up the options – a new primary classroom or better street lighting or pooling resources with neighbouring communities to pay for a health clinic. Representatives from these meetings then help to select options until a budget with wide popular support is produced. The Popular Planning Programme that flowered and died with the Greater London Council had the same idea. As a result, in Brazil we find support for substantial public investment, and a recognition that this involves taxation ... and 250,000 people each year learn active citizenship.

Seriously useless learning

Here, we wait anxiously to hear if the case for significantly greater invest-ment in colleges has succeeded and whether departmental ministers, like champions returning from a medieval joust, have secured victory or defeat.

This year's review was good for adult learners. The adoption of the new public service agreement target, aiming to secure a 40% reduction among adults of working age who lack level 2 qualifications or their equivalent, and the doubling of the basic skills target to 2007, were both welcome. However, the language has shifted from the first term of the Labour government. Then, social and economic prosperity were twin goals. Now attention is much more clearly focused on the relationship between learning and work.

The spending review charges the Department for Education & Skills "to undertake a review of the current arrangements for funding for adult learning post-19, including how the government's various support mechanisms for learning could be more effectively applied".

So far, so good, but the review adds "to provide incentives to employers to engage in training; cause institutions to be responsive to employer needs, building their capacity to work with employers; widen participation in learn-ing by the low-skilled; and enable regional development agencies to play their full and effective role in developing and implementing regional skills strategies". No one can object to the value of those goals. But what about the other sides to adult learning? Where is money to be spent to revitalise democratic engagement? Where is learning for later life? Family learning? Learning to develop the capacity to regenerate neglected communities?

Beyond the headlines these issues are apparently covered by the review – which will stretch from community-based learning to employer-provided training. But who would know from the remit? Ministers and the key civil serv-ants who will work on the review certainly. But what about junior staff, new to the patch, who may be misled by the headline?

One local Learning & Skills Council interpreted policy priorities by issuing contracts to local education authorities with the maximum number of people over 60 fundable under the contract, explicitly laid down. The figure was drawn from the proportion in the whole population (including 0s to 16s who are outside the LSC remit). Fortunately, the contracts were withdrawn and reissued without such crude rationing. But the lesson is clear: language, and especially the headline targets, shape perceptions among over-pressed and busy folk.

This is where the mood music of ministerial speeches makes a big differ-ence. They can reassure partners in the field, and check over-enthusiastic pursuit of the major priorities at the expense of the others.

Adult skills minister Ivan Lewis made just such a welcome intervention in a speech to the Local Government Association in July when he recognised the role of local authorities, and the broad remit of adult learning. Estelle Morris's speech to the TUC had the same effect. But unless we can develop popular budget-making in Britain in the near future, we shall need plenty more such speeches to keep the breadth of government's concerns in the public (and the policy-makers') eye.

25 October 2002

Look out for the smaller fish in the big pond

by Alan Tuckett
Section: Opinion; Further Education. Issue 4504, p34

JANE WILLIAMS, the new post-16 standards tsar, got off to a flying start at the launch of the new Department for Education & Skills' teaching and learning initiative in post-school education. The event had a reassuring tone of enquiry and exploration, and civil servants were evidently in listening mode. Jane Williams's strengths lie in emphasising that the work she will lead needs to be developed as a collaborative task, with practitioners and managers as well as policy-makers shaping and refining the work.

She demystified the role of mandarin, telling us her own professional journey, and communicating a passion for learning and for the importance of learners' perspectives. She showed a refreshing awareness that change will not be achieved all at once.

It was a long way from the smack of firm government and truncated timetables for implementation that seemed for so long to frame debate.

The focus on teaching and learning in the consultation paper *Success for All* is really welcome, but it will still be hard to secure the time to get things right.

Politicians are keen to make a difference, within the attention span of the electorate. Yet some things do not benefit from being rushed. Adults bring such a diversity of experience to their studies, and have such a wide range of goals, that they will never have the full range of their learning needs captured by a national curriculum put together at speed, and with the schools' model in mind.

We need time to build a culture in the learning and skills sector where every teacher and mentor is a confident, reflective practitioner, engaged in real dialogue with learners about their journeys. Of course, the recent public panic over A-levels highlights the risks of rushing too quickly at change, so perhaps there are real grounds for optimism.

One minor quibble about the set-piece presentations, though. You could have listened all morning without realising that adult education services in local authorities and the voluntary sector were part of the remit of the *Success for All* agenda.

Seriously useless learning

It can be demoralising for colleagues to have their serious, professional work systematically ignored. This was, of course, exactly the point David Gibson, chief executive of the Association of Colleges, made at the Conservative party conference when he pointed out the Tories' failure to call for excellent colleges as well as excellent schools and universities.

Silence too frequently leads to neglect. This was brought home to me the next day, when the DfES announced the welcome 'golden hello' initiatives for new recruits in shortage subjects in colleges. This was a necessary balance to the measures taken to boost school recruitment. Alas, it did not extend apparently to adult education services, many of which have full-time and fractional posts in exactly these shortage areas.

There is a risk that in seeking to solve one problem, the government will create another. Big fish, the schools, eat first. Once their appetite for shortage subject teachers is slaked, colleges, which are less politically visible and therefore medium-sized fish, can eat. And when will the minnows in the adult and community sector get to the table?

The same systemic Darwinism is at play over capital expenditure, investment in mapping the occupational competences of staff, investment in staff development and learner support. Yet local authority and voluntary sector providers play a key role in extending the reach of the system, and do a good job at meeting the expectations of their learners. Involving them last in all these investments sells these learners short. What, then, is to be done? A more strident lobby for the less formal parts of the system might work – but risks squabbles among the sectors, just when co-operative ways of working are back on the agenda.

The findings of the DfES-sponsored Wider Benefits of Learning Research Centre may help, too. Its work is beginning to firm up the links between participation and good health, engagement in learning and likelihood to commit crime.

Alternatively, adult educators could opt for patience. The census showed that there are already more people over 60 than under 16 in Britain. Demography will undoubtedly lead to a review of policy goals as we seek to squeeze more years of labour market activity out of the baby boomers, and as we realise that learning is cheaper than visits from the doctor or the social worker. We need to work convivially on teaching and learning, and to complain together until we get the system that supports all providers across the sector and beyond.

22 November 2002

Seesaw of learning won't shake off adults

by Alan Tuckett
Section: Further Education. Issue 4508, p36

WORKING IN the voluntary sector often felt like being the child at one end of a seesaw – as the partner with the weight, money and time to attend meetings (the adult) bounced about at the other end, trying to be equal – but there were the occasional spills and it was seldom the senior partner who fell off.

It is tempting to see the policy arena as a whole like that. For adult learners *The Learning Age*, the last comprehensive spending review and the Learning & Skills Council remit letter were all highs. The narrowness of the remit of the skills review, and the exclusion of adults over 30 from the higher education target were both lows.

But where are we now? Seeking the Views of Learners, the LSC's learner-satisfaction survey, is a definite high, and one of the first clear demonstrations of the gains to be had from the creation of a sector for further education, work-based training and community-based provision for adults.

More than 90% of the learners interviewed expressed satisfaction with education and training, and learners in local education authority adult education expressed the highest levels of satisfaction of all.

In a week when another survey suggested that half the children at school are bored, the finding that almost nine in ten of the post-school participants who had left school with negative attitudes to learning felt that taking part in college, adult education centre or workplace training had changed their minds about learning. Overall, older people feel more positively about the education and training on offer than 16- to 18-year-olds.

I used to have a colleague who revelled in the HE statistics which showed that the percentage of good graduates (defined in the research as holders of 2:1 or 1st class degrees) rose with every extra year in the age at graduation. The percentage of 22-year-old finalists securing good degrees is better (or rather was better since the research is a decade old) than the 21-year-olds; 27-year-olds did better than 26-year-olds, and so on, up to the age of 41, when the results drifted down gently, resting at the same level as those finalists in their mid 20s. But no one did as badly as the cohort that went straight from school to university. My colleague suggested that this showed that education is wasted on the young – and the satisfaction survey suggests that many young learners agree.

On the down side, another survey published in the last week reminds us that a major cohort of school-leavers remain convinced that the system has little to offer them. *Adult Learning and Social Division – a Persistent Pattern*, the full report of the National Institute of Adult Continuing Education 2002 participation survey, maps the continuing strength of the learning divide. The links between current social class, family background and early education are as powerful as ever. But it throws up new connections, too, as John Field, professor of lifelong learning at Stirling University, highlighted at the launch. The survey findings show a strong link between sociability and learning. If you like to go to the pub, join societies, visit the cinema, or take part in faith activities, you are also likely to be an active learner. People whose leisure is spent quietly indoors are much less attracted to learning.

ELWa, the Welsh funding council, funded a booster sample to create a Welsh cohort large enough for further analysis. The findings were of considerable interest to the Welsh Assembly committee beginning work on the school of the future. I was privileged to be part of a NIACE Dysgu Cymru delegation giving evidence to the committee on the role schools can play in fostering lifelong learning. I was impressed by the quality of the debate and the energy to make a difference that characterised the work of the Assembly, and by Wales's inspiring education minister, Jane Davidson. I came away convinced again that schooling is a key site for creating a culture of lifelong learning. To that end, they can only benefit from being open to the enthusiasm for learning that adults bring. As Judith Summers' new policy discussion paper for NIACE says, *Schools are for Adults Too!* – and, judging by the surveys, they should be.

3 January 2003

Five challenges that will test ministers this year

by Alan Tuckett
Section: Opinion; Further Education. Issue 4513, p28

CAN WE really develop an education system that keeps the learner at its centre, and offers success for all? Despite its considerable strengths, I'm afraid it is likely to be harder once the measures in the government policy paper *Success for All* are implemented. I see five immediate challenges to overcome. The first relates to the recent proposal to reward successful colleges with 5% extra money. The first paper, published in the summer, was warmly received for its commitment to making learning and teaching central to the post-school system. We looked forward to a shift away from the obsessive attention needed to make institutions viable during the Nineties. But it said nothing of the proposal to reward better colleges. As a result, there was little debate about how this will affect learners in less successful institutions.

Bertolt Brecht argued that the measure of a civilisation was its treatment of its most vulnerable members. So, the question to ask about the higher education 50% target is what impact it is likely to have on the other half of the 18-to-30 age cohort. For colleges, how will standards and services be improved by only rewarding better performers? Is there evidence that the best providers are the best people to share good practice. Will they use extra money to consolidate their elite position?

A second challenge also arises from this plan. If retention and achievement have a dramatic impact on rewards for institutions, won't they be tempted to narrow participation to guarantee success? Chris Hughes, of the Learning & Skills Development Agency, reminded me that the postcode factor added just 8,000 learners to colleges after the Kennedy report.

I replied that when the widening participation factor was just one of many affecting funding it was insufficient to force change. I said asking colleges to outline successes in widening participation, when allocating core budgets, was more likely to succeed. But it won't work if the incentives ignore the issue of participation altogether.

A third challenge lies in the decision to treat individual providers differently. We already have golden hellos for college staff, but not in adult education. We have welcome and necessary increases in budgets, but no guarantee that learners in local authority services will get the same volume, range and quality of provision as those in colleges next year.

Learners in FE can look forward to a fully-qualified teaching force by 2006, but their counterparts in work or the community have no such assurance. Mobility of students between colleges and community may get worse before it gets better. How can we avoid uneven development?

A fourth challenge arises from the determination to construct a distinctive 16-to-19 focus in institutions that educate students of all ages. Can that be done without weakening services to older learners? And where is the evidence that teenagers do better when they are taught separately? In this, at least, Jane Davidson is leading Wales in a different direction to the one Andrew Adonis seems to be taking England.

Finally, education secretary Charles Clarke has made an impressive challenge to colleges to raise their game with employers. The challenge will be to free colleges to meet employers' needs, while keeping track of the plethora of targets.

Employers want bite-size, just-in-time training and prefer to invest in learning on the job. It will do no good to offer mass solutions. To meet their expectations we will need qualifications reform, better processes for assessing prior learning, and a more relaxed approach to what counts towards qualifications.

A separate dynamic is at work in the neighbourhood renewal strategy. *The*

Seriously useless learning

Learning Curve highlights the need to improve the skills of poor communities. The Strategy Unit report, *In Demand 2*, recognised a revitalised adult and community learning service had a key role to play. Alas, the Learning & Skills Council workforce development paper did not mention this.

But adult educators in local authorities were comforted by minister Ivan Lewis's clarification of the role of adult education: to improve skills, and foster cultural and citizenship education. It bodes well that he recognises complexity and the need for diversity.

To make this work for all learners is no small task. But with luck policymakers will be so busy working out what to do that we may enjoy an initiative-free New Year. Well, January is a time for dreaming!

24 January 2003

Time and space for the benefits to flow

by Alan Tuckett

Section: Further Education; Opinion. Issue 4516, p38

THIS IS a column in praise of slowing down. Zhou en Lai, when asked whether he thought the French Revolution had been a good thing, retorted famously: "Too early to say." Contrast that with the haste with which we now invent policies with targets, timelines and benchmarks; and then move on to shake up some other dusty corner of the public services. Before you know where you are, the whirligig of policy-making is back: shuffling the organisational arrangements, refining or replacing targets, identifying new imperatives. Six years into the life of a government with an itch to do different, there is a risk that we may lose sight of the good things done in response to the day before yesterday's policy priorities. I wholly applaud the government's aspirations to make a post-school education and training system that supports the creation of a vibrant economy, where people can find jobs which are rewarding in themselves, make use of the skills people bring to their work, and develop new ones. People who benefited least from schooling are more likely to get the chance to learn at work than elsewhere.

Yet, we have developed systems of workplace and work-based learning in which part-time and temporary workers and the least skilled are offered much less of a chance than their educationally-privileged colleagues.

Giving the least skilled a chance – addressing what the CBI called "the long tail of under-achievement" – necessitates policies which address economic prosperity and social inclusion at one and the same time.

This was the rationale behind the Delors' European white paper on competitiveness in the 1990s, and behind this government's impressive lifelong learning policy, spelled out in *The Learning Age* and the legislation that flowed from it. The government, wisely in my view, took its time to settle on the policy and the structures needed to implement it. Partners were consulted extensively and involved in thinking through the balance of national strategy and local responsiveness the system needed.

There was nuance, and a sense of the complexities and differentiation needed to create a vocationally dynamic and socially inclusive system, where everyone could find a place – whether their aspirations were to consolidate professional development, to appreciate Miles Davis, or to learn collective solutions to a community's shared problems.

When the Learning & Skills Act passed through Parliament, there was considerable bipartisan agreement on many of the measures. I thought at the time that this was the product of the time taken to identify the challenges and work on the maximum level of agreement. But then, the pace changed. The embryonic Learning & Skills Council was given half as long for setting-up time as the less complex Further Education Funding Council had been given a decade before.

The chief executive had a miniscule team to manage the transition until the date the training and enterprise councils were abolished. Then, all of a sudden, thousands of people were in place needing to be managed.

There was, it seems, no time for a cool analysis of the skills sets needed to support the breathtaking range of provision the 47 local councils were responsible for. As a result, the vast bulk of staff with job entitlements transferred straight from the TECs to the new councils. This produced a challenge for the new council's staff to develop competence and sensitivity about all areas, while delivering the new system from day one.

All in all, it is impressive that the transition was managed without major mishap. The council gave proper priority to securing stability for existing providers. Decision-makers impatient for evidence of change had to wait while the new structures bedded down; and, inevitably, some of the nuances of the council's first remit letter were marginalised when the prime minister's Delivery Unit boiled the task down to hitting the headline targets.

My sense is that we are now in a position to benefit from all that change, if only we could leave space for the benefits to flow. Effective change takes time. Meanwhile, the initiatives rain down remorselessly. *Success for All*, the latest skills strategy, the review of adult funding, workforce development, new ideas for higher education – all good, in part at least. But all would benefit from time, to improve policies and build consensus rather than a mad dash to implementation.

The prospects look gloomy, though, as paper after paper lays out a truncated timeline, where the need to act fast puts creative and reflective policy makers under unproductive pressure. It takes time and space for things to grow, and for quieter voices to be heard.

Seriously useless learning

21 February 2003

Don't leave the referee on the sidelines

by Alan Tuckett
Section: Opinion; Further Education. Issue 4520, p28

PICTURE THE scene. Welford Road, Leicester, half-time on Saturday afternoon, with the crowd in high dudgeon. Martin Johnson has yet again been sent to the sin-bin, a harsh decision in our view. There is the usual interval celebration of successful primary school teams; streams of thirsty fans make an optimistic dash for the bars.

All of a sudden the announcer asks us to put our hands together for all the stadium stewards. All 84 of them have completed an NVQ2 in safety control, through Telford College. Four stewards come to the pitch to pick up certificates (the others are hard at work). The announcer suggests it is a pity that there isn't an NVQ in referee control.

Sixteen thousand fans applaud the achievements of the stewards, and I think that leaves only 999,916 to go by 2006 for the new level 2 target to be achieved. The powerful message of the occasion was that it is normal to get qualified; that good employers such as Leicester Tigers rugby team help their part-time as well as full-time staff achieve qualifications relevant to their work. A few more occasions like that and the thousands in the crowd will be asking whether structured learning is needed in their own working lives.

This was promotion at its best – positive, inspiring and not a gremlin or a hint of barbed wire in sight.

The incident showed, too, that qualifications and sports and cultural events mix well. The cultural industries are a serious site of lifelong learning, as the Department of Culture, Media & Sport recognises. Media studies graduates are markedly more likely to land work in the media than law graduates to get jobs in the law. Yet, few law students suffer the easy jibes about Mickey Mouse degrees that seem to be the daily lot of media students.

I was telling this story to a colleague at work. "Unfair," he said. What's unfair? "Slighting referees in that way." I pointed out that the referee had been too quick to judge. But he persevered, to point out that, in soccer at least, there may not be NVQs in refereeing, but every referee was scrupulously supervised and commented on by their peers. Only the successful progressed up the leagues.

Every Saturday on the hundreds of pitches on Hackney marshes, and in parks and school fields up and down the country, there is an invisible college in skills-building among referees. We are not yet brilliant at capturing it, when we reflect on the skills of the British labour force, but competence acquired in one setting transfers easily to others.

Refereeing, running a charity shop, governing a college, organising the school run, all develop the skills of active citizenship. That is one huge strength of the voluntary sector. Its reach among the most excluded communities is another, and a third lies in the fact that it is voluntary, not reliant on an Act of Parliament, but on the will of people freely given.

Bryan Sanderson has made a welcome commitment to strengthening the Learning & Skills Council's engagement with the voluntary sector, building on the exhortation in the grant letter for the council to take account of the voluntary sector compact adopted across government.

There is a big mountain to climb. Both the National Institute of Adult Continuing Education and other groups in the voluntary sector have reported real frustration among the agencies they work with since the council was established. Communication has been poor, and the threshold requirements on new providers is high. The priority has been to secure a stable transition to the new order. However, the failure of the council to establish a national unit for dealing with voluntary-sector providers to parallel its national business unit is surely a continuing mistake.

There is a long history of education having a weak relationship with the voluntary sector. A 1990 Home Office study highlighted the then Department of Education & Science as one of the weakest in Whitehall in this respect. Yet, the sector has much to offer to the council and the department in pursuing equality and diversity, in successfully widening participation and achievement, and the building capacity to listen to learners.

I was disappointed to see no mention of the higher education sector's role alongside voluntary bodies: higher education's obligations to defend unpopular opinion, and to inform communities on the ethical, political and social issues arising from the work of academia. Yet, surely that role is the reason for protecting higher education's distinctive academic freedom.

The white paper had little to say about adults, how HE might work with the voluntary sector, the place of part-time learners, or the funding of pensioner students. All clearly await the second part of the strategy, *Higher Education – The Adult Experience*. It should be in the shops and on the web any day now.

21 March 2003

Skills strategy and the pursuit of happiness

by Alan Tuckett
Section: Furthur Education; Opinion. Issue 4524, p34

RICHARD LAYARD'S London University lectures on the pursuit of happiness as a goal of public policy have opened up an important vein of debate, of relevance to everyone who works with learners who participate of their own free will.

The thesis of the LSE's professor of economics is that everyone is able to tell social enquirers how happy they are, and that getting richer does not make you happier, unless everyone around you is doing broadly as well as you are. This chimes nicely with the evidence that the healthiest societies are those with narrow differentials between the affluent and the least well off.

By contrast with Scandinavia, the rich and the poor in the United States enjoy poorer health. The lesson seems to be that other people's misery is bad for you.

Meanwhile, the lessons from the Wider Benefits of Learning research centre show that learning has a positive effect on your health and longevity.

Going to class keeps your brain active, gives you a sense of purpose and a spring in your step. And, for most people, makes you happier, too.

This celebration of social capital is directly relevant to the skills strategy the government expects to publish in June. So far, the focus of much of the debate has been on how best we can adapt the system to achieve the new Public Sector Agreement target to reduce by 40% the number of people without level 2 qualifications.

The National Institute of Adult Continuing Education has argued that this offers a useful opportunity to revisit Helena Kennedy's proposal, in *Learning Works*, for the creation of a New Learning Pathway – offering people pursuing level 2 qualifications the package of tutorial and learner support that make such a difference to young people on A-level programmes, and adults pursuing Access courses. It would, I think, be money well spent – and would lead quickly to soaring retention and achievement rates.

As part of the skills strategy work, the learning and skills minister, Ivan Lewis, toured the country listening to employers talking about their experience and expectations of the formal system. The message he heard was consistent and powerful: our current national vocational qualifications system is not fit for purpose. The packages are too big. As a result, we can hope for a more coherent and inclusive qualifications framework to emerge from the joint work of the Qualifications & Curriculum Authority, the Learning & Skills Council and the Sector Skills Development Agency, which have been given the job of reviewing the structure at speed.

There is a good case, too, for making sure that every area has coherent outreach programmes; for selective introduction of regulation to make sure all employers take their responsibilities for the development of their workforce seriously; and for a package of guidance activity that values barefoot as well as specialist guidance services. But it was not until I read Richard Layard's argument that I saw the case for an ancillary measure for the skills strategy. A happiness measure could build on the LSC's very useful learner satisfaction survey, and explore with learners the impact of their studies on the quality of their life at work, and outside of it. It would remind planners that the route to improved productivity is a complex one and that there is more to learning than supporting economic growth.

It might re-secure a balance in the thinking about the role of adult and community learning, as we now call it. Ivan Lewis has made clear his commitment to the place of learning for its own sake alongside first steps learning. And the national policies of the LSC underpin that commitment through the guidance offered to local councils.

But up and down the country, key officials feel the pressure to achieve the LSC's headline targets, and too many believe that uncertificated learning is a luxury they cannot afford. With a happiness measure, and a participation target alongside the headline Public Service Agreement targets, it might be easier for planners locally to include the enrichment of the lives of pensioners in their thinking.

To support this line of thinking, NIACE has made a case to ministers for the funding review to include the clear expectation that local councils should commit at least 3% of their budgets for culture, community and citizenship. That is modestly more than the inherited and ring-fenced local authority budget for uncertificated work and the new initiatives in family learning and capital development the LSC now spends. It would take account of the valuable work in community-based adult learning that many colleges undertake, and it would enable those areas with thin provision to catch up.

Taken alongside the active 'first steps' investment in neighbourhood centres, guidance and outreach, it should provide the rich mix needed to underpin a skilled and happy society.

16 May 2003

Bonkers Brit regime needs to be changed

by Alan Tuckett
Section: Further Education. Issue 4532, p40

GREECE IS a beautiful country, especially in spring. Some say the combination of light, olive groves, twinkling blue seas and oodles of ouzo tempt people away from learning. Whatever the reason, adult participation in Greece is modest and principally in vocational education.

It was something of a surprise, then, when the first European Union conference on adult education was hosted under the Greek Presidency in 1994.

Similar conferences followed across Europe as policy-makers and practitioners sought to understand what they could learn from each other, and to hammer out common policy frameworks. In part, they were responding to

Seriously useless learning

the challenge of the 1993 Delors European white paper, *Growth, Competitiveness, Employment*, which argued that lifelong learning policies needed to focus on social inclusion as well as economic modernisation, and to treat education and training as one system.

The impetus to develop coherent policies was boosted during the European Year of Lifelong Learning in 1996, leading to the adoption by all countries of a commitment to developing lifelong learning.

Now, once again, Greece holds the presidency of the EU, and again has broken new ground in convening this weekend a meeting of those in charge of adult education in member states – to review progress in developing lifelong learning.

This is bad timing for the UK representative, since the policy review of the funding of adult learning and the skills strategy will not be unveiled until next month. On higher education the government can say more, but its recent white paper neglected to say much about adults over 30 in higher education.

But the smoke should have cleared in time for the UK's contribution to the second of this year's international reviews of adult learning policy. This one, called by Unesco, takes place in Bangkok in September. The 167 member states signed up to an agenda for action at the 5th World Assembly on Adult Learning in Hamburg in 1997, and will be invited to report on progress. To complement their accounts, the International Council for the Education of Adults has prepared a 20-country report on progress towards commitments, areas including workplace training in adult literacy and the education of women and older people.

Progress will not be as good as was hoped: Unesco recognises the six years since 1997 have been difficult ones for adult learning worldwide.

However, the UK will be able to report some areas of progress. In expansion of investment, in workplace training, in institutional reform, in the Skills for Life strategy there is much to celebrate. At the Hamburg meeting, Kim Howells, fresh into his post as minister for lifelong learning, proposed a Unesco international adult learners' week. Six years later, more than 40 countries are running it and sharing best practice with each other. That too, is cause for celebration.

But the meeting ought to be an uncomfortable reminder that the job is not yet done. For older people especially, the policy isn't working well. Tory MP Boris Johnson illustrated this graphically in an hilarious but perfectly serious Commons adjournment debate on All Fools Day.

Boris told the story of Andrea, a keep-fit tutor in Wallingford, Oxford, with a class of 50 women, aged 40 to 80, who has given up teaching. She had been defeated by the 300 forms needed for just one class:

"I spoke earlier of the forms that Andrea had to fill in when assessing the progress of women who are often aged 80 or over in achieving fitness. She said that the forms were rather depressing. The minister is beaming, but it is sometimes difficult to put a positive gloss on attempts to improve the fitness of women aged 80 or over, or to say that their general stamina and co-ordination are improving, even with the ministrations of Andrea in Wallingford.

"She said that she found it taxing and dispiriting to fill in forms intended to record the progress of her charges, when some of them had, quite frankly, made no progress. In a word, the process was completely and utterly pointless, and it was driving her bonkers."

Behind the levity, Boris makes a serious case for a more appropriate audit and quality assurance regime, and for trusting learners' judgments in courses that make modest calls on the public purse.

No other European country is as obsessed with audit as we are. There is more trust and better-quality courses. It might be useful for our representatives in Athens and Bangkok to ask international colleagues how they manage with a lighter touch approach, and to emulate the best practices they find.

13 June 2003
Seize chance to make learning adult-friendly
by Alan Tuckett
Section: Further Education. Issue 4536, p40

I FIRST met Manish Jain at the launch of an exciting Unesco initiative on Learning Without Frontiers. Manish stood out for the clarity of his thinking and his belief that Unesco's bureaucracy should not get in the way of experiences that transform the lives of learners young and old. Alas, the initiative was still-born, and Manish gave up on Unesco, returning to work in a south Indian community project.

Manish has been an important contributor to a debate sparked by Sir John Daniel, assistant director for education at Unesco. John had written in praise of globalisation, and the associated "commodification". In this context, commodification means preparing courses for standardised global marketing – like baked beans, with all cultural specificity squeezed out.

But in this 'McDonaldisation' of learning, who gets to decide what is worth commodifying? The responses of Manish and his colleagues are vivid in defence of learning not just as a product but as a way of enhancing dignity, choice, cultural diversity. He also argues in defence of learners determining what they study themselves.

All this is relevant to developments in the UK. I was cheered up last week, at the annual parliamentary reception for the Pre-School Learning Alliance, when the politicians spoke so powerfully in favour of the idea that learning should be fun. There was also a recognition of the vital role the voluntary sector plays in revitalising poor communities, and of the importance of engaging parents as partners in education.

If we can bring the same spirit of imagination and inclusiveness to the skills strategy, and avoid too much 'McDonaldisation' we shall, I think, be doing well. There are signs that elements of an effective policy are being put in place.

The government's review of vocational qualifications offers the best chance for a generation to create an adult-friendly qualifications system, where larger qualifications are supported by a more fine-tuned and inclusive credit system – so small chunks of work can be recognised and counted.

But will the review come too late for much of the work currently supported as 'other' FE (courses not specifically related to the national qualifications framework) as local planners seek to hit headline targets? An early test of the new skills strategy is what it does for the tens of thousands of adults who will need to take the 'other' FE route.

A second test will be how the strategy supports the development and funding of basic skills embedded in other courses. If the skills strategy is to work for most adults needing some help with writing, spelling and reading, it will surely be woven into the studies they pursue.

A third test concerns what will be offered to workers in firms unconvinced of the economic case for investing in training.

Ed Balls, chief adviser at the Treasury, has hinted at pressuring firms to train with talk of the government's move towards a "post-voluntary" approach to learning at work. But Charles Clarke and Ivan Lewis have said emphatically that we need to make sure courses better reflect what employers need before any moves to regulation are introduced. So what can the strategy do for, say, a cleaner, bringing up a family and working for three or four employers, none of whom sees her development as their responsibility?

There are positive signs that the government does intend to make a difference to social exclusion through education – talk of entitlements to a first level 2 (GCSE equivalent), which would take the explicit costs out of returning to learn; and of a new type of individual learning account being targeted at new learners who do not have any qualifications.

Statutory endorsement of trade union learning representatives is welcome, as are the Employer Training Pilots. But much of this will be put at risk if the effects of new targets for FE encourage colleges to shy away from widening participation, where there is a high risk of not meeting targets.

So the fourth test of the strategy is how much emphasis it gives to reaching out to the diverse groups who do not participate in learning.

Finally, the strategy must respond to the needs of older learners, and of those who share Manish Jain's view that learning is for delight, and the transformation of our lot in life. Clearly the strategy won't give us everything we need. But let's hope it avoids the pitfall of making things worse.

11 July 2003

Darkest hour is waiting for paper to arrive

by Alan Tuckett
Section: Further Education. Issue 4540, p44

WHEN I was young, I used to work on the pea vines –12 hours a day seven days a week, lifting lorry loads of vines onto the shredders that separated the peas. Bird's Eye's contractors were best. The work was hard, but it came in spasms. Thirty minutes on the grab, and then there was time for a cup of tea, to sit and read the paper in the shed, while the next lorry arrived and dumped its load.

The same job on nights for Ross Foods was different. There were fewer peas, for one thing. Often the work was effectively over by about 3am. No chance to sit down, though. If you wanted to be paid, you had to look busy and brush the bits of vine on the yard floor from one side of the room to the other, until the end of the shift. I didn't last a week. It was a useful learning experience – people work better when they have some agency over what they do.

Drafting a column the week before the publication of the new *Skills for Life* white paper, knowing it will appear after many readers have seen its contents, feels a bit like the hour before dawn at Ross's. Energy flags.

There is nothing else to be done before dawn, except to wait, discover what it says and prepare to respond. I am feeling optimistic. I think the government does well in building the maximum degree of consensus in the shaping of its policies – the next trick is to get enough time for implementation.

The debates leading up to the publication of any white paper are a little like stately square dances. If you want to influence the out-turn, you must first advance the case you have to make. Then the counter arguments are made, and you feel sure that things may turn out worse than they have ever been. Consultative committees rehearse old themes afresh; the pattern repeats. Eventually a date is set for the end of the dance. The paper is published. A new dance starts when it is taken through Parliament. You propose amendments in one house, then the other. After Parliament, everyone works out what to do to put the policy into practice.

Even if you lose the vote in committee, the quality of the argument can affect what happens when the legislation is implemented – so in the 1992 Act, the government of the day resisted fiercely legislative amendments that would allow adult education services to be funded directly by the Further Education Funding Council – only for the council to accept the practicality of exactly that arrangement from the day it began work.

While waiting for the new white paper to appear, I went to Bangor for Bob Fryer's Raymond Williams memorial lecture. It was characteristically broad in sweep, erudite and challenging. One of his many strengths is the choice of telling quotes. Two he cited offer benchmarks to test the new policies against. First, Jacques Delors' demand of education systems, in *Learning: The Treasure Within*: "None of the talents which are hidden like buried treasure in every person must be left untapped – memory, reasoning power, imagination, physical ability, aesthetic sense, the aptitude to communicate with others and the natural charisma of the group leader, which again goes to improve the need for greater self-knowledge." Can the post-school policy secure that generosity and inclusiveness of vision?

The second challenge is sharper. Zygmunt Bauman's analysis in *Postmodernity and its Discontents* is bleak: "No jobs are guaranteed, no positions are foolproof, no skills are of lasting utility, experience and know-how turn into a liability as soon as they become assets. Livelihood, social position, acknowledgment of usefulness and the entitlement to self-dignity may all vanish together, overnight and without notice." He continues: "The switch from the project of community as the guardian of the universal right to decent and dignified life to the promotion of the market as the sufficient guarantee of the universal chance of self-enrichment, deepens the suffering of the new poor -adding insult to their injury, glossing poverty with humiliation and with the denial of consumer freedom, now identified with humanity." That is more or less the analysis that informs the government's social exclusion policy. How far the white paper can address the challenge facing the 'new poor' will be one test of its aspiration to combine the economic and the social justice imperatives of education policy.

Beyond this white paper, one challenge is to find resources to meet the burgeoning demands on budgets for English as a second language teaching. Apart from the demands made by people settled in Britain, there are those from people seeking citizenship under the new nationality provision; from refugees, asylum-seekers, and those with exceptional leave; those on work permits, and on managed migration permits. Then there is a raft of new European directives affecting the rights of migrant labour, and the extension of the European Union to ten more states. A case for Skills for Life 2, perhaps?

5 September 2003

New waves yet to display their style

by Alan Tuckett

Section: Analysis; Viewpoint; Opinion; Further Education. Issue 4548, p4

WE HAVE a busy autumn in prospect as waves of policy initiatives come on board. One example is local authorities that maintain discrete adult education services: the Learning & Skills Act funding guarantee is coming to an end, and the move to formula-funded budgets will necessitate adjustments.

Last year's *Success for All* strategy was welcomed for focusing on the learner, though some of its measures are yet to affect LEA services. It is a little early for the backwash of this summer's skills strategy, but intentions are clear. Budgets for adult education, for personal and community development, will be secured, but there is an intention to redistribute towards the poorest areas.

What will this mean for less affluent pensioners studying in middle England? Will local providers concentrate more on 'first steps' courses, which are linked to the progression routes the strategy encourages? Or to a significantly higher fees recovery policy? Providers will await the detailed proposals with concern.

LEAs will also be looking for the roll out of the Learning & Skills Council information and communications technology strategy. They will want to learn the lessons of the early round of inspections of adult education services – to strengthen quality assurance processes and make the case to the Adult Learning Inspectorate for inspections fit for purpose. Like everyone else in post-school education they will hope to speed up moves towards a sector skills council for lifelong learning. They will want more details on occupational competences and training and development needs of staff in this diverse sector.

People working with adult learners have parallel concerns. How quickly will the Learning & Skills Council move to a coherent planning mechanism for adult learning that recognises that other college provision may enrich communities and create the network of progression routes that will make the achievement of the strategy's key goals possible? What will the entitlement to free study offered to adults without a first level 2 qualification mean for institutions' budgets and curriculum focus? How soon will new arrangements for credit, and distinct adult assessment regimes be available? Ken Boston's arrival at the Qualifications & Curriculum Authority brought a change in thinking. But is everyone in the QCA converted yet? The key to successful policy change will be in the detail. It is encouraging that the Learning & Skills Council is establishing a high-level committee to focus on credit.

Other LSC developments should impact on practice everywhere. The widening participation strategy has taken time to evolve, but must renew focus on the role the system has in contesting disadvantage and exclusion. The college sector has many proud stories to tell in this work: however, there is still a long way to go before Helena Kennedy's vision of widening participation becomes embedded in the system. Meanwhile, a head of steam is building around the Higher Education Funding Council for England's widening participation work – much of it likely to affect colleges working with younger adults at the FE-HE interface.

Shirley Cramer of the national council is leading a new, if overdue, look at how the LSC relates to the voluntary and community sector. This should help the widening participation strategy, of course, since many voluntary and community organisations have the confidence of communities currently under-represented in the system. Her committee will need, urgently, to sort out effective arrangements for national voluntary bodies, and to improve the dialogue between funders and the sector.

There are exciting practices to map – not least Birmingham & Solihull LSC's initiative to link colleges and voluntary bodies, to share good practice on quality enhancement, and to try to recruit a more diverse workforce. Business as usual then – masses to react to and more coming over the horizon. But will it all be coherent? And will adults be better served as a result? Let's hope so.

`10 October 2003`

Skills report has jumped the gun
by Alan Tuckett
Section: Viewpoint; Opinion; Analysis; Further Education. Issue 4553, p4

WHEN CHRIS Woodhead stepped down as chief inspector of schools, there was a welcome retreat from polemic in the statements emerging from the Office for Standards in Education. Until the past week, that is. Suddenly a press release questions the progress in literacy, numeracy and language education for adults, highlighting the risk that thousands of learners may fail due to poor teaching.

This issue is nothing new. Consistently, the Further Education Funding Council inspectorate found that literacy and numeracy had a higher concentration of poor teaching than other areas of FE provision. But now is not the time to undermine confidence in the national strategy. In the past two years, national standards have been identified for literacy, numeracy and language teaching to adults, and major national training programmes have been developed. Tutors working above a threshold of hours have been through training, but that does not mean that all people teaching literacy and numeracy in the sector have been trained. And the period covered by the

Ofsted thematic review straddled much of the time when tutors were undergoing training. So the effect of the programme on quality might be expected to come later. Classes taught by trained tutors apparently met quality thresholds. So where is the problem?

The challenge seems to lie in the success of the *Skills for Life* strategy in encouraging new forms of provision – where quality systems can lag behind the enthusiasm to get started. No one wants to justify poor teaching – especially for adults who have been failed by the education system once already. I think it is excellent that Ofsted is monitoring quality. I hope the government takes two key messages from the report. First, that we must redouble investment in staff development, since the journey to universally available high quality basic education is a long one. Second, that developmental work in new contexts, and where literacy, numeracy and language support are embedded in other studies needs significant learning and learner support.

My difficulty with the report lies partly in the rush to public judgment characteristic of an audit culture. I can't help feeling that a public report would have been more welcome in a year or two, when the provision has bedded down, when training has had an impact on tutor confidence and quality, and when certain curriculum development initiatives come to fruition. Meanwhile, inspectors might help practitioners overcome weakness by giving priority to disseminating the good practice they find. Arriving now, it risks generating a knee-jerk rush to narrow the contexts in which adults can expect support with reading, maths and language, or at the very least an argument – again about standards.

There is an old frustration at work here. The Learning & Skills Act created one funding regime spanning sixth-forms to community based learning and the workplace. It then gave us two inspectorates. I thought it was wrong then – and for all the excellence of colleagues in the Adult Learning Inspectorate and Ofsted, I think the benefit to adult learners is less than the sum of their endeavours. Neither seems to be as sensitive to context as you could expect from HMI before the 1992 legislation. Hasn't the time come now for the two inspection regimes to be reunited? It works well in Wales, where Estyn is in a position to comment on all school and post-school provision. Why not in England, too?

I remember with gratitude the advice and support for development which HMIs offered my colleagues and me on their visits, and I recall how quickly that led into practice in classrooms. HMIs' time was spent 80% on development visits and supportive monitoring, and 20% on inspection. Inspectorate summer schools were a key site of professional development, and inspectors were respected as leaders in the field.

Shifting the regime to spend more time on inspections and formal reporting helps funders to identify weakness. It provides good headlines and heated debate. But does it give enough support to raise standards and to nurture excellent practice?

October 31, 2003

Rise to learning culture challenge

by Alan Tuckett

Section: Viewpoint; Opinion; Further Education. Issue 4556, p4

MARK HAYSOM has quite a job. He has taken over the Learning & Skills Council and must strike a judicious balance between coherence, encouragement of solutions for local councils, and at the same time oversee the work of the new meetings of the Skills Alliance.

But it is good that his role in the alliance will remind him that achieving a change of learning culture in the UK needs the creative partnership of a range of agencies.

I have been impressed with his openness so far, but it will not be easy to resist pressures to concentrate almost exclusively on managing the complexities of the LSC. Just how much importance the government attaches to the alliance was seen when five ministers attended its launch meeting. But the key challenges lie with the Council and the Sector Skills Development Agency.

The council's widening participation strategy captures the challenge neatly. Six and a half years on from Baroness Helena Kennedy's *Learning Works* report there is still a way to go to achieve her vision of consistent and equitable access to learning for adults. The LSC recognises this.

It has adopted a welcome definition: "For the purpose of the strategy, widening participation is defined as a process where education and training providers successfully adapt their programmes and ways of working to meet the learning needs and aspirations of individuals and groups whose experiences or circumstances inhibit participation."

The difficulty is that those adaptations will have to go ahead while targets are achieved. There are bound to be temptations for local offices to focus spending on quick wins – topping up skills for those with short learning journeys to achieve qualifications, rather than the slow, expensive and uncertain investment needed to engage the hardest to reach and keep.

That was why, when the LSC was created, the National Institute of Adult Continuing Education argued strongly, and apparently successfully, for the adoption of a participation target backed by surveys so that under-represented groups could be easily identified, and supported in local LSC areas.

Three years on, the target promised in the first two corporate plans has slithered from sight as the council seeks to avoid being bogged down with an overload of targets. The talk is now of "a measure". Whatever it is called, it must be a key tool in identifying those people the system needs to adapt itself to, if the widening participation strategy and the skills target are to be achieved.

The council will need to change, too. Take the voluntary sector – regarded as a key partner in extending the reach of the system. A sign of serious intent would be to end the long-term resistance to creating a national voluntary sector unit, to parallel the national business unit. Bodies like the Pre-School Learning Alliance, or the Salvation Army, need a single point of expertise and experience in the LSC, capable of exploiting the potential of the sector.

There are challenges, too, for providers. We are not likely to see investment on this scale again in those people failed by the system, if every effort is not made to make the strategy a success.

In colleges, there will need to be determination to keep other further education courses in place, until they are blessed with recognition under Ken Boston's qualifications reform. And local LSCs should be encouraged to ease up on draconian measures to cut back such work – since it caters for the very learners who need support to progress to level 2 GCSE-equivalent qualifications.

Most daunting of all is the task facing Christopher Duff of the Sector Skills Development Agency this year. Not only must he put in place a full suite of sector skills councils – with the lifelong learning council puffing along at the rear of the pack – but to develop credible programmes with real reach.

A good start has been made, at least for all those working on major constructors' sites. But to reach each small self-employed carpenter or plumber, Christopher will need your help and mine – to turn the loft conversion trade from a price-sensitive to a qualifications-sensitive business. Almost certain to make conversions dearer, but safer. And we will be doing our bit for the strategy.

3 December 2003
Counting the cost of qualifications
by Alan Tuckett
Section: Viewpoint; Further Education; Opinion. Issue 4561, p4

EVIDENCE-BASED policy is a good thing, and despite the government's commitment to it in principle, it is surprising where it is and where it is not applied. Take 'other provision' in further education – that pot-pourri of provision that does not quite fit the qualifications framework.

What do we know of how it is used by businesses, looking for ways of making use of the system to meet their own skills needs? Or of how individuals have woven learning journeys, en route to formal qualification? What do we know of learners' sensitivity to price changes? Or of how learners use credits from open colleges in mapping their way through the system? How much of the work fits exactly the 'first steps' provision lauded in this summer's white paper?

My sense of it is that we know too little of the scope and impact of this work, to be confident in cutting it back. Yet local learning and skills councils are under pressure not to increase such work – whatever the manifestation of local demand. Meanwhile, as *FE Focus* has reported, the Qualifications & Curriculum Authority is reviewing the size, nature and rules of combination needed for adult qualifications.

The most encouraging thing I heard at the first meeting of the Skills Alliance delivery partners was Mary Curnock Cook from QCA saying that the system needed to produce more flexible qualifications and also to value meaningful learning that stops short of qualification. That seems to me to be right.

We urgently need a credit-based system underpinning our qualifications. When we have got one, we risk finding that we may have abolished many of the building blocks of the system in 'other provision' in FE by prioritising what gets supported without a good enough evidence base.

Clearly there is a need for a short, sharp study on the size, scope and characteristics of 'other provision'. The danger is that the welcome focus on level 2 qualifications will cut out the range of preliminary studies that give people confidence to gain a whole level 2.

Mind you, I am also waiting with bated breath to see what the level 2 entitlement will mean in practice. How small a bite-sized chunk will you be able to study and still claim public support? How long will you be able to take to complete your studies? What if your purposes change along the way? Here my worst fears are that we shall find that policy-makers will yet again find part-time learners difficult to deal with, and go for quick wins with learners willing to get a qualification quickly.

This piloting of adult study grants for full-time learners is an excellent development, however modest the funding. But how long will it take before part-time students have the chance to benefit?

I do not envy the Learning & Skills Council its task in securing three million new level 2 qualifications by 2010, with the pretty clear remit to do it with no additional resources. There will, of course, be welcome quick wins – like the decision of the large employers in construction to require a licence to practise for everyone working on their sites. For many, the qualification will be a confirmation of already-existing skills; for others a modest top-up will suffice. For the LSC this will hold out the prospect of a lower unit cost for a completed level 2 qualification.

But the council must both achieve its goals for equality and diversity, and offer real access to qualifications to people experiencing multiple deprivation and low skills levels. That will not come cheap. A key feature of the skills strategy is the determination of ministers to secure coherent policy-making across the piece.

Given the commitment to a voluntary approach to employer engagement, where carrots are preferred to sticks, is it too much to hope for an early review of one controversial pilot scheme? Seeking to make participation in basic skills provision compulsory for benefit claimants who do not want to lose a proportion of a tiny weekly pay-out does not seem fair. It smacks of one rule for the affluent and another for the poor.

Finally losing the plot

GOVERNMENT MINISTERS may be very supportive of ACL but the Treasury makes the decisions. Anything in the public realm that cannot be measured and fixed to targets is invariably seen as 'expenditure', and only rarely as 'investment'. Professional judgments from the world of education about the long-term social and economic benefits of 'other' learning seldom count, even when supported by evidence. In the Treasury's view, these are qualitative judgments and 'quality' has to be achieved cheaply and quickly – not always possible.

Ivan Lewis was a minister who understood that ACL, or 'other' learning, was the seed-corn of future prosperity and wellbeing for a swathe of disadvantaged people, as well as an essential support for getting a foot on that skills ladder. He knew because his route to Parliament had been through the voluntary sector. Indeed, along the way, he created his own successful not-for-profit social enterprise, Contact Community Care Group, a learning disabilities support agency for which he also did outreach work. His success in securing the £300m safeguarding for adult and community learning was based on sound judgment.

Without being disparaging, however, what impact could the 3% for ACL have over the 97% of expenditure, driven increasingly by utilitarianism and private sector rules? The 3% could go much further with the multiplier effect of empowered local authorities, voluntary groups and community organisations. Unfortunately, there had been too little sign of a willingness to see this through in the deluge of recent consultation and legislation emerging from the Commons.

Tuckett talked through such scenarios with the *TES* on many occasions at this time and, notwithstanding the optimism and enthusiasm that always bubbled through, the spring of 2004 saw the turning point, where he finally acknowledged that Labour had lost the plot; targets were everything. In March 2004, he wrote:

> *"It is hard to feel cheerful in adult education right now. Everywhere you look, funding pressures are leading to narrower courses for adults. Closures, cuts and rumours of cuts abound. From the distinguished*

bastions of university adult education to the modest provision in a rural village, the smack of firm government is felt. Does this work contribute to our targets? No? What use is it then?"

A NIACE discussion paper, *Testing, Testing: One, Two, Three*, by Peter Lavender, Jay Derrick and Barry Brooks, "concludes that tests and targets are no simple proxy for the learning that really matters. Targets have their uses in concentrating the minds of providers on public priorities, and in squeezing cash from the Treasury. And the last thing we want at the time of a spending review when money is tight is a loss of visibility for language, literacy and numeracy."

But for thousands of people taking English for speakers of other languages (ESOL), the point was to become fluent in oral communication not to be thinking of a written test; they wanted numeracy lessons to deal with money worries before worrying about the piece of paper, he wrote. "Targets distort what providers do and tempt government to miss the real strength of the achievement."

Utilitarianism and the constant pressure to hit targets were skewing the way people and their institutions behaved, he observed. For example, he was dismayed at reports from the Adult Learning Inspectorate (ALI) which suggested large-scale weaknesses in the Workers' Educational Association (WEA) and in the quality of leadership in adult and community learning organisations. The problem is not with ALI's criticisms but with the consequences:

"I worry that the inspectorate's tools of judgment need refinement for adult education if we are not to be driven to abandon much of the neighbourhood provision so valued by learners. But my larger concern is that funding constraints, area review processes and inspections are producing a risk-averse profession. One price of that is shrinking opportunities for adult education to engage with the big issues of the day."

By early summer, we see a revival of Tuckett's more sanguine side. Ivan Lewis at a national conference had reminded FE of what had been achieved in seven years. The government's union learning fund was blossoming and the NHS University (NHSU) promised success, being targeted at all who'd had no training and development opportunities, including cleaners and porters. And Tuckett was encouraged by Lewis urging employers to meet a bigger share of the costs:

"All reports of the evaluation of the employer training pilots suggest

*that they do motivate employers and staff alike to get involved in
education and training, tailored to meet their needs. But it is costly,
and to roll out the state-funded pilots as a national programme in their
present form would surely break the bank."*

But again there were caveats: where was the 'learning pathway', a wrap-
around of guidance, support and planning for family learning promised in
1997? "It sank without trace and needs reviving since the skills support
strategy must mean help for those not ready for it to take 'first steps'." By
July, with continued optimism, he was writing about the first industry training
consensus for 50 years with the CBI and TUC announcing a shared strategy
for work. Patricia Hewitt, trade and industry secretary, said the strategy was
fuelling work-related learning: ICT for mothers returning to work and midnight
classes in workplaces for shift staff.

*"She highlighted the gender gap in apprenticeship take-up in higher
paid industries; the challenge in engaging black and ethnic-minority
groups in skills building. Here was the government's policy aspiration
– that economic modernisation and social inclusion, competitiveness
and equal opportunity go hand in hand – made credible through practical example. The same message is there in the opening passages of
the skills strategy report."*

The autumn, too, saw cause for further optimism. In October Tuckett wrote:

*"The new union learning academy, to draw together various initiatives,
is likened by Gordon Brown to a 'workers' university'. Ufl was built on
an idea in Motorola's corporate university and showed huge demand
for modest learning packages. Then there's NHSU; its chief executive
Bob Fryer points out that an institution serving the largest workforce
outside the Chinese army and the Indian railways has the potential to
become the largest corporate university in the world."*

But there is a wider debate to have, he said, returning to his notions that
true lifelong learning is about raising all boats.

*"How can we create institutions which command the respect our
universities enjoy, but which cater for people whose learning journeys
are more modest? Tertiary legislation, the Ufl and NHSU all draw on a
single idea, that a learning society needs a continuum of study from
literacy and numeracy to continuing professional development for
consultants, engineers and orchestral soloists, and that it is best to*

think about them all together. Common sense, really, but hard to bring about."

In the end, little of the Brown vision would remain, just as his end of 'boom and bust' in the world of finance proved wildly over-optimistic.

BY NOVEMBER, Tuckett was expressing concerns about even modest ambitions for outreach and other work needed due to lack of resources. And, by December, his concern was about the distorting effects of the basic literacy tests. "Apart from 750,000 who passed the tests, another 1.5m benefited without taking them and we simply need adequate schemes to assess them."

Of course, using narrow criteria based on targets, this success is no success at all.

Then in January 2005, it was clear that demographic changes, which the government had either ignored or failed to prepare for, had put a huge spanner in the works; education secretary Ruth Kelly was forced to admit she could not square the government's ambitions for lifelong learning with the cash available. As Tuckett wrote in his column, more adults were available to take jobs.

"But immediate pressures to fund the rising 14-to-19 cohort grows, putting more pressure on adult funding. So, just when we need to stimulate demand for adult learning more than ever, cash from the public sector will be tighter than ever since government came to power."

Worse still, previously optimistic evidence of successful employer training pilots was proving to be a false dawn since employers were found to be unwilling to pay. "Of course," he wrote, NIACE argues that employers should pay more and those individuals who could afford it." The problem was that previous policies encouraged colleges to offer low or no fees to employers and individuals alike.

"It takes time to change but evidence of employer training pilots is that they won't or can't pay and take up is by big firms and multinationals. The Skills for Life strategy attracted 2.4m people and the level 2 skills target needs the same approach. But those who can't do level 2 and need first steps are at risk because of LSC planning and because tight budgets are leading colleges to narrow their offer to those who are easiest to reach."

In response, there appeared to be some ministerial redirection over ACL;

Seriously useless learning

but was it too late? Ministers found extra cash for FE and exhorted the LSC and others not to neglect "other further education" outside the National Qualifications Framework (NQF). But still colleges cut basics in order to meet the level 2 targets and older IT students saw courses rise from £40 to £110. "Fine for the well-heeled but not for the struggling pensioner. Extra cash gives breathing space but this is still the most challenging year for a decade, particularly with the 16-to-19 population bulge."

Little new money could be expected and adults would suffer most, despite the fact that two-in-three jobs would have to be filled by adults already out of school. Also, there was much to gain from adults as volunteers and carers in the light of new childcare and mental health strategies. "The adult learning agenda can ill-afford cuts," he said. But even at this late stage, Tuckett was not expecting the state to foot the complete bill. "Employers and individuals spend less in the UK than almost any other leading nation." But with the extent to which employers had become dependent on state benefits for their training needs, he said, "changes will have to be modest in the short term if we are not to destabilise the system".

By April, the government's strategic intentions were made clearer than ever. A skills white paper called for a realignment of post-school education and training to meet employers' needs. It included a section renewing commitment to personal and community learning but, at its heart, it was a utilitarian focus on workforce skills. The utilitarianism contrasted sharply with observations in Professor Layard's new book, *Happiness: lessons from a new science*, published at the same time as the white paper, in which people demonstrate that wealth (income) is relative but leisure (holidays) is an absolute good. So, he asks, why do we organise policy so obsessively around increased overall prosperity? Layard suggests our work-life balance is out of kilter.

Tuckett used the study to reinforce his argument for a broad adult curriculum. But he found that politicians were not in a hearing mood. "While you can take parenting, language and drawing classes, the emphasis is increasingly on the vocational; witness the LSC trying to rebalance beacons of liberal education excellence such as City Lit and the WEA to get greater commitment towards government targets. Learning for fulfilment is no longer seen as a valid claim on the public purse, and we have already seen a 7% decline in pensioner learners and it will get worse."

In May, the 2005 general election win for Labour came with howls against spending cuts to adult learning. Despite a promised 5% increase in January, there are widespread reports of college cuts as LSCs pressed for it to be directed towards 16 to 19s.

"Already, LSC figures show a 3% drop in adult numbers with over-60s

in college down 7%. So much for the promise of a transitional year with preserved budgets."

The cause of the decline was clear, he argued. The crisis arose because of the LSC's single target driven pursuit of *Skills for Life* and the national Employer Training Programme (for 'full' level 2). Moreover, evidence was emerging of dead weight – employers using state cash for training they would otherwise have paid for; effectively pocketing the profits. "Those losing out are from the less affluent and less skilled groups."

As if things were not bad enough, new skills priorities would make things worse and in effect reinstate the iniquitous schedule 2 of 1992 FHE Act. Tuckett explained that when the Tories had refused to fund uncertificated courses, vulnerable LEAs moved speedily to certificate such courses through OCN (the Open College Network) and qualify languages, art, fashion and other such programmes for FEFC money.

"Labour swept away the ridiculous divide with the Learning & Skills Act 2000; so, where LEAs qualified for old FEFC money they got it from the FE pot. In addition, adult and community budgets were ring-fenced for three years from LSC."

But then, in 2005, adult and community learning was protected but LSCs decided to cut old 'schedule 2' work in the face of a cash crisis and white paper skills priorities. "As a result, language courses leading to OCN accreditation and effectively first step on the skills ladder are at risk, while holiday Spanish is safe. It's ridiculous, surely, when the skills strategy is aimed at increasing international competitiveness." Well-heeled LSCs such as Birmingham and London thrived with the support of local area partnerships. But they were the exception. Targets were all well and good provided there was the cash to pay for them. "There is more adult language and literacy, and of high quality, than a decade ago," he said. But cash shortages meant free tuition was only available for those taking qualifications equivalent to five GCSEs, but not for studies leading to it. "Not much point having a ladder for skills where the rungs begin just out of reach over your head."

Spending cuts were now really taking a toll with 1.5m adult learning places predicted to go in the coming year with a hike in fees. Chris Hughes, chair of the national inquiry into adult education said "those outside level 2 and *Skills for Life* are not low priority, they are no priority". Casualties included ESOL, signing and courses for absolute beginners. Yet evidence of benefits continued to mount: the National Mental Health Strategy, the Home Office's Citizenship Strategy, the FSA report on financial education for young and old alike and the Department for Culture, Media & Sport's learning for pleasure

Seriously useless learning

and personal enrichment all highlighted community learning as essential to social and economic health. "Yet in adult learning, you almost feel the need to apologise for enjoying what you learn," wrote Tuckett.

By December, it seemed to him that adult education was being written out of the script entirely. He challenged Sir Andrew Foster's report of his review of the future of FE colleges, *Realising the Potential*, for failing even to address the role of colleges in adult learning.

> "The report focuses heavily on 16-to-19 despite the fact that this group will decline in colleges by 500,000 over two years and that adults already out of education need training for the new labour market jobs."

Tuckett pointed out that Foster was the only report that failed to address adult learning, while earlier Turner on pensions, Leitch on skills and the national mental health strategy all recognised the importance of adult education.

By February 2006, the government was waking up – in some quarters – to the costly backlash on the UK of restrictions put on the working rights of migrants and gains were being made. "Effective education and training strategies to help migrants and refugees into work are emerging from the NIACE-led development programme, Progress GB, launched last June. Good practice has been identified, which can now be shared. It shows common needs and challenges among the different groups – not least the need for good guidance for learners, employers and intermediary agencies. But overall a national strategy is needed, with cash to back it."

Home Office ministers agreed. "Tony McNulty, minister of state for immigration and citizenship, has highlighted the gap between current priorities for ESOL support and the practical help workers need, with the loss of skills essential to the UK economy."

But, as would be seen in the dying years of Labour's third term in office, the years would be characterised by crises around key skills areas such as the of provision of ESOL and mounting accusations of spending ever greater sums on 'dead weight' training for which employers should have been paying.

Commentaries
26 March 2004 to 17 February 2006

26 March 2004

Targets aren't the be-all and end-all

by Alan Tuckett
Section: Viewpoint; Opinion; Further Education. Issue 4576, p4

IT IS hard to feel cheerful in adult education right now. Everywhere you look, funding pressures are leading to narrower courses for adults. Closures, cuts and rumours of cuts abound. From the distinguished bastions of university adult education to the modest provision in a rural village, the smack of firm government is felt. Does this work contribute to our targets? No? What use is it then? Oh, the pleasure of a clean crisp target – it clarifies the mind and purifies the spirit. And for those learners who don't want a qualification? Better, surely, to steer them to what is good for them. You see it in the valiant struggles of the Learning & Skills Council to meet the basic skills target: 750,000 passing tests by 2007.

The trouble is that, despite the impressive successes to date, many learners are backsliding. The aim was that for every 2.7 adults joining a course or programme, one would take a qualification that counted towards the target. Alas, three years in, and the ratio is slipping. This year it is 2.8:1. Unless there is clarity, who knows what may follow? That way anarchy lies. To see it off, local councils put more pressure on providers to ensure enough people get GCSEs, key skills qualifications, or the higher stages of literacy qualifications to pronounce the policy a success.

Yet the target is a proxy. It helps us to focus on whether the system is meeting adults' aspirations. For so many learners, though, the target is not the primary goal. For thousands of students queuing for scarce places on English as a second language courses, written comprehension – the basis of the national tests – must surely come second to fluent oral communication. Yet we find it difficult to measure talk on a scale of one to ten. For people with numeracy needs, allied to money problems, the pressing need is often to sort out the finances before worrying about the piece of paper.

This is no criticism of the role the Basic Skills Strategy Unit has played in creating more opportunities for adults seeking to increase their skills in literacy, numeracy and language. The problem is that targets can distort what providers do, and tempt government to miss the real strengths of its achievement. If only one in three literacy, language and numeracy students takes a test that counts towards the national target, it might mean that recalcitrant and ideologically-motivated tutors are preventing their students from gaining public recognition for all the learning they have done.

It is more likely, however, that adult learners are using the system to meet their own real needs, rather than those predicted by target-setters.

Typical examples of this group are people seeking to strengthen skills in maths and English along the way to a qualification in catering, or law or nursing. Their key motivation is to get better at making food, clarifying and resolving disputes, or caring for people too vulnerable or poorly to look after themselves. Getting better at writing, or estimation can help immensely with those aims. But how can the state see any improvement in the basic skills without tests?

The National Institute of Adult Continuing Education has just published a policy discussion paper on these matters. *Testing, Testing: One, Two Three*, by Peter Lavender, Jay Derrick and Barry Brooks, concludes that tests and targets are no simple proxy for the learning that really matters. Targets have their uses in concentrating the minds of providers on public priorities, and in squeezing cash from the Treasury. And the last thing we want at the time of a spending review when money is tight is a loss of visibility for language, literacy and numeracy. We need to work on measures that capture the richness and variety of learners' achievements. We also need a mature policy debate about the lessons learned from major initiatives such as the Skills for Life programme. The aim should be to use the target as a measure, to examine where predicted outcomes need modification in the light of experience. That would provide the basis for the evidence-based policy the government wants.

23 April 2004
Lessons from the coal face
by Alan Tuckett
Section: Viewpoint; Further Education. Issue 4580, p4

END OF term brings fresh insights into old problems. The heritage industry can offer a romanticised version of a genteel past – all elegant gardens and country-house gift shops – where no one apart from the servants seemed to have to work for a living.

At its best, though, it offers a window on the forces that have shaped the lives we live now. We spent a day at the Black Country Living Museum in Dudley – heritage culture with grit – learning that formal education had an ambivalent role in the emancipation of the spirit or the improvement of the material circumstances of working class people in Victorian Britain.

A half-hour participating in a vivid reconstruction of a primary school class, complete with slate and pencil, rote learning and the cane for misbehaviour, provided a vivid reminder that schooling is about control, discipline and, in this case, knowing your place.

There was something comforting about the structure, but little or no chance for creativity, individual expression or divergent thinking. Much the same thing could be said of work down the mine, where a moment's individual rashness could put the lives of hundreds at risk. Yet, there, the message was subtly different.

Children progressed from opening and closing doors to circulate air in the mine at the age of 12, to leading the horses drawing loaded coal, to working the seam. At each stage, there was a critical need to learn what worked, to read the different seams, how far to stand back from a collapsing wall of coal – all learned from more experienced workers.

The pit might have been a more conducive learning environment, but the work itself, or the dust you breathed day and night, killed you: few miners working in the Black Country survived past 40.

The fish and chip shop and the pub had their lessons, too. An hour in the slow-moving queue at the chippie led people to talk to one another as they passed the sweet shop, the baker's and the chemist's – as things in the window unlocked memories of childhood, or stories passed down from parents and grandparents. By the time we were fed, we were hungry enough to appreciate the food, however narrow the choice.

No Coke or orange juice in the pub, but the first pint of mild I've seen in years. All this is excellent family learning, providing experiences that provoke conversations about the best way to learn, how far work shapes our lives and what makes life worth living.

Social class interacts differently with educational opportunity and wider life chances are different now than in Victorian Britain, but the ambivalent role of education in reinforcing social division, as well as offering emancipation for some individuals, is just as much a feature of working class experience today.

This was illustrated vividly in an analysis by Sir David Watson for an Anglo-American seminar on widening participation at Bradford University. He showed how much had been done to address unequal access to higher education for women, for most minority ethnic communities and for people with disabilities.

Class, however, is intractable, despite the evidence that nine in ten working class young people with two A-levels go on to university. The bulk don't stay that long, and working class adults are least likely to return to learning later on.

Since parents are the first and most powerful educators of children, adults' experiences of education help shape their children's expectations.

Active stimulus does make a difference. Working class adults do respond to effective initiatives that address their circumstances and aspirations, whether through union learning representatives, or employer training pilots, or in adult and family education.

As Tom Schuller, new head of education at the OECD notes in *The Benefits of Learning*, where family learning works well, trust levels improve to the mutual advantage of learners, their wider family networks and a wide range of institutions. Building that trust takes time and patience, and a willingness to support learning that speaks to participants' interests.

Without that patience and trust, we will continue to exclude many working class people from the benefits learning can offer.

`14 May 2004`

Maths: the missing link

We neglect numeracy at our peril, argues **Alan Tuckett**. *Research now shows that people lacking number skills suffer deprivation. The consequences are financial , social – and sometimes fatal*

Section: Skills For Life. Issue 4583, p2

REPORT AFTER report highlights the link between poor numeracy and poverty. The time has come to do more about it. The weaker you are at numbers, the more likely you are to get into debt. More than seven in ten prisoners have the lowest levels of numeracy. If you can't cost a round of drinks in the pub, you either lose face when it's your turn to pay or leave yourself short of cash for more pressing demands on your budget. If you can't estimate the cost of the weekly shop, you face the humiliation of putting things back if you spend too much. Compounded week after week, the lack of such skills will leave you in a mess.

At work, numbers are critical – patients suffer severely, even fatally, if measurements in their medicines are inaccurate. Think, too, of all the time wasted waiting in for people to deliver goods – in part because they can't forecast how long it takes to get from A to B. Then there is the snowstorm of financial choice and a blizzard of invitations to save, or spend – all calculated differently.

To make sense of political choices – on inflation, national debt, the ubiquitous national targets, global warming and so much else – it is necessary to have number skills. Understanding probability is essential when assessing the risk to a child of having a rubella vaccination.

You would think we would all be motivated to strengthen our skills with number. But the National Research & Development Centre (NRDC) for adult literacy and numeracy reports that many learners who don't study numeracy urgently need to because they use it in their everyday lives. The Department for Education & Skills' Survey of Need last October showed that two-thirds of adults with the poorest grasp of numbers mistakenly believed they were 'very' or 'fairly' good at numeracy. Only 2% thought their skills inhibited them at work. It is common, too, for people to boast, as someone did to me at a recent CBI dinner, that they are hopeless at maths. No one talks about poor literacy in the same vein.

The same DfES survey painted a devastating picture after measuring how poorly prepared adults are to undertake a range of tasks. It revealed that 15m 16 to 65-year-olds have number skills equal to or lower than 11-year-olds. Fewer than one in five (18%) achieved the equivalent of a good GCSE grade in both literacy and numeracy. One of the starkest revelations was that while only one in three men achieved GCSE level in numeracy, women did even worse, with just one in five making the grade. Women performed worse than men with maths at every stage of their lives.

Parents are a child's first and most important educators. Lack of confidence and skill with numbers is learned early – and building parents' skills can have a positive effect on their children's school performance. This has a real impact on a person's earnings for life. Just improving a person's skills from those of an 11-year-old to the equivalent of a low grade GCSE (D-G) produces a 9% productivity gain – higher wages and more in the national purse. No wonder the Treasury backs the Skills for Life strategy.

There is much to celebrate in that strategy. There are now national standards for work in literacy, language and numeracy; tutors are better trained; there are better teaching and learning materials and 2.3m people have improved skills in these areas. However, numeracy is the poor cousin within the strategy.

Three years in, literacy has been the focus of the strategy and public debate. Last October, a survey by Ofsted, the schools inspection watchdog, and the Adult Learning Inspectorate noted that "numeracy is taught less frequently than literacy although there are as many adults with poor numeracy skills as there are with poor literacy skills". The Smith report, *Making Mathematics Count*, published in February, showed a shortage of maths tutors and a failure of curriculum, assessment and qualifications in schools to meet the needs of learners, employers and higher education.

There was a lack of resources, infrastructure and continuing professional development to support teachers in schools, colleges and in the workplace. The NRDC concurs, arguing that numeracy isn't "embedded" or practical enough. There are, too, inadequate numbers of people available to develop a full range of programmes as the *TES*/NIACE survey shows.

The case for a focus on numeracy is clear. We are pleased to support this special *TES* supplement which aims to promote a bigger debate. It launches Adult Learners' Week, our annual festival to celebrate adult learners' achievements and encourage others to join in. This week is important because motivation – a sense that this is for the likes of me – is a vital element of the adult curriculum. This supplement – supported by NIACE, the DfES and the European Social Fund – appears as several big issues come to fruition.

First, the debate on how much new money education will get from the government's comprehensive spending review is intensifying. Second, the Financial Services Agency is gearing up for a big policy paper on the importance of financial education. Third, the key elements of the government's wider skills strategy – but not the money – are falling into place. Fourth, strategic area reviews by the Learning & Skills Council will establish local learning and skills priorities.

The following pages capture some of the really creative work being done to improve things – from numeracy energiser weekends to financial education websites – such as www.moneymatterstome.co.uk, which NIACE launched with sponsorship from Prudential, or the Basic Skills Agency's ground-breaking work in family numeracy. Overall, we hope it makes a powerful case that number matters, and we ignore it at our peril.

Real gains in numeracy will not come on the cheap. That is why NIACE submitted a £50m bid to the spending review for new initiatives in basic skills, which aim to strengthen adult participation in learning. NIACE supports the government's policy goals in the Skills Strategy and in Skills for Life, but is concerned that there is insufficient policy money to achieve them.

21 May 2004

Engagement is still a key word
by Alan Tuckett
Section: Viewpoint; Opinion; Further Education. Issue 4584, p4

COMMUNITY LIFE in Cumbria was devastated by the outbreak of foot-and-mouth disease in 2001. Farming families were quarantined and faced the end of their way of life. The Pentalk Network, winner of this year's New Learning Opportunities Award in Adult Learners' Week, was first founded to boost communication among farming families, issuing free computers for six months and training in web skills, finance and wider communication skills. Perhaps its finest achievement was to give hope and agency to a community in crisis.

The network lives on, with more than 1,700 learners on 1,220 farms. Half are men, and three in five are over 40. Farmers now act as Pentalk ambassadors, mentoring new participants. This is citizenship and community-building in action, and there is not enough of it about.

A major purpose of education is to secure engaged citizens, able to take part in democracy, secure justice, exercise freedom – and to encourage debate on the issues of the day. As the cultural critic Raymond Williams put it, people turn to learning at a time of social upheaval for three reasons – to understand change, to adapt to it, and to shape it.

It is worth reflecting on how the war in Iraq has stimulated reflection about democratic freedom, minority rights and the war's impact on inter-community relations in Britain. There is much discussion in shops and pubs, fuelled by horrific photography showing torture of Iraqi detainees by Western troops. But look at the taster courses and special events in Adult Learners' Week and there is little to suggest that issues of such moral weight absorb us.

Funding systems have put the squeeze on learning providers, forcing them to address narrow issues of skills and qualifications. Liberal adult education of the kind celebrated by Raymond Williams just about survives, but is unable to show significant revenue for cash-hungry institutions, and with its confidence battered after more than a decade of utilitarian policy-making. The responsibility for this frailty lies partly with adult education's organisers. Fewer of them are ready to push back the boundaries to include courses of study that are contentious.

The Workers' Educational Association has a proud record of democratic adult education. But last week, it was criticised in its latest inspection report. Despite encouraging judgments about Middlesbrough, Derbyshire and Doncaster, inspectors take a dim view of adult community learning overall.

Using tools honed in the inspection of larger institutions, they report large-scale weaknesses in adult community learning's leadership, management and quality assurance. By contrast, teaching and learning in adult services is judged much better, a message confirmed by surveys which show that students in adult education report the highest satisfaction rates of all.

Of course there are weaknesses, and inspectors from the Adult Learning Inspectorate are held in high regard in the sector. But how can poor leadership, management and quality assurance support the good teaching and learning which students have confidence in? Surely something must be going right.

In the case of the WEA, what are the consequences of taking seriously the educational and organisational challenges of putting learners at the centre of organising?

I worry that the inspectorate's tools of judgment need refinement for adult education if we are not to be driven to abandon much of the neighbourhood provision so valued by learners. But my larger concern is that funding constraints, area review processes and inspections are producing a risk-averse profession. One price of that is shrinking opportunities for adult education to engage with the big issues of the day.

Yet hundreds of thousands of people are still engaged with the challenge of creating a sustainable future in which more enlightened environmental

Seriously useless learning

policies might go hand in hand with freedom from want for the peoples of the world. Across the globe, the movement to find alternatives to the dominant forms of globalisation attracts millions of people's energy as they search for better ways for us all to co-exist. A healthy adult education system ignores their concerns at its peril.

18 June 2004

Passion and best practice

by Alan Tuckett

Section: Viewpoint; Analysis; Further Education. Issue 4588, p4

HELENA KENNEDY rouses the spirit, quickens the pulse, and generates passion and enthusiasm in the struggle to inspire more people to learn. It is seven years since her ground-breaking report, *Learning Works*, brought the idea of "widening participation" centre stage.

At a National Institute of Adult Continuing Education conference to review progress last week, Baroness Kennedy reminded us that a tough challenge remained and encouraged us all to generate a new national campaign to create a "learning country" – as called for in her original report.

In a confident and inspiring response, Ivan Lewis, the adult skills minister, reminded us how far things have come in seven years, and of the scale of the challenge ahead to reach disaffected and excluded people. The cycle of educational disadvantage, passed from parent to child, would not be broken by a quick fix but by serious and sustained hard work.

He encouraged colleges, adult learning centres and other providers – as partners in a shared enterprise – to stop talking further education down as a "Cinderella service". Take pleasure in what has been achieved, he said. But how do you remake an entire culture, so that everyone feels they have a stake in learning? It is best to start from where people are. Use trusted intermediaries – shop stewards, neighbours, pre-school organisers, religious advisers – who can open the door to participation.

Success of the government-backed union learning fund lies in building on and changing structures to make best use of existing resources. It is an approach that will also be the key to the sustained success of NHSU – the corporate university for the National Health Service.

The NHSU goal is to sign up everyone in the health and care workforce who has never been offered training and development. Even cursory attention to the complex work and domestic pressures on cleaners and porters in the health service reminds us that, for many, work is the only place where there is any meaningful chance for a return to learning.

In this respect, the Kennedy report and the government's skills strategy make a common cause. The workplace is clearly central to widening participation. All reports of the evaluation of the employer training pilots suggest that they do motivate employers and staff alike to get involved in education and training, tailored to meet their needs. But it is costly, and to roll out the state-funded pilots as a national programme in their present form would surely break the bank.

I was, therefore, encouraged to hear Ivan Lewis call for employers to meet a bigger share of the costs. Government can help by creating a framework for employers to take on that responsibility, just as it shapes the debate about the fees individuals should pay for different courses.

Outside the workplace, it is important to discover other structures that successfully widen participation. It is now recognised that the family can be a place that nurtures mutually beneficial learning and builds self-esteem and confidence in adults and children alike. Families can provide a 'system' for lifelong learning that meets the needs and wants of people of all ages. So can the community group, and even informal alliances forged on the allotment.

For adults returning to learn, the Kennedy report proposed a "new learning pathway", that could provide a necessary "wrap around" of guidance, learning support and effective planning to support progression and enrich the curriculum.

That idea sank without trace seven years ago. Now – heeding Lady Kennedy's call – it is surely time to look at that agenda again. Given the skills strategy target, it is imperative that we help people to make sense of what is provided on those 'first steps' back into learning, and to equip people for a sustained journey.

Mix in some passion, story telling, dancing and a sense of fun, season with staff development, and the sharing of best practice among supporters and intermediaries, and you have the core ingredients for a learning culture.

`16 July 2004`
Clouds spoil sunny view
by Alan Tuckett
Section: Viewpoint; Opinion. Issue 4592, p4

IT IS now a year since the publication of the skills strategy. The anniversary bash, hosted by education secretary Charles Clarke and skills minister Ivan Lewis, had several good things about it. Four stood out for me. The first was the announcement of just how far the Qualifications & Curriculum Authority and its partners, the Sector Skills Development Agency and the Learning & Skills Council, have progressed in creating a credit-based qualifications framework. When Ken Boston, head of the QCA, explained the proposals it was hard to remember why it has taken so many years to get this far.

Seriously useless learning

As the report, issued to coincide with the conference, made clear there is still a demanding timetable ahead and many knots to untangle. But this is a red-letter day for adult learners, and we have reason to be grateful to Australia for exporting Ken with all the chardonnay and shiraz that brighten up my life.

Just as impressive was the joint presentation by Brendan Barber, general secretary of the Trades Union Congress, Digby Jones of the Confederation of British Industry, and William Sargent of the Small Business Council. They announced a shared programme for development to achieve the goals of the strategy, to the evident delight of ministers. As they said, it is 50 years since such a consensus on priorities for public investment in skills existed across industry; and the dragon released by Mrs Thatcher, who ended any suggestion of a social compact between unions, management and government, is slain.

The third was the evidence that the new sector skills councils are finding their feet, and their voice. I was particularly impressed with the presentation of the e-skills passport. With a few slides we were shown how to use a simple online audit to identify strengths and weaknesses in a range of common and specialist computer applications, and to map these against organisational needs. I am going to sound out my 200 NIACE colleagues to see if we can use the passport.

The fourth good thing was the speech of Patricia Hewitt, the trade and industry secretary. She also celebrated the achievements of the strategy in fuelling new energies in work-related learning. But her speech was different – grounded in its effect on the lives of people previously excluded from education and training.

Taking her Leicester constituents as a frame of reference, she outlined measures to support women into information and communications technology jobs at De Montfort university. She described midnight classes at Sammworth Brothers' food processing factory provided by Leicester college.

She highlighted the gender gap in apprenticeship take-up in higher paid industries; the challenge in engaging black and ethnic minority groups in skills building. Here was the government's policy aspiration – that economic modernisation and social inclusion, competitiveness and equal opportunity go hand in hand – made credible through practical example. The same message is there in the opening passages of the skills strategy report.

By contrast to all this positive news, the five-year plan makes for a bleaker read. Any mention of the social inclusion dimensions of the skills strategy is missing from the plan's chapter on skills. The prospect of new school sixth forms and the return of inter-institutional competition, just when confidence in strategic area reviews is burgeoning, looks like bad policy to me.

All too often these statements of future purpose read as though they have been handed down from Downing Street, rather than grown from experience and best practice. Time after time Number 10's apparent passion for specialist academic provision for 16 to 19-year-olds seems to get in the way of rational local planning to meet the learning needs of all.

Despite this, employer training pilots, union learning fund initiatives, good access programmes and thousands of courses in colleges, communities and workplaces point to the way we can make the twin goals of the skills strategy work. It involves planning, co-operation flexible funding, learner and learning support, and a shared sense of direction – exactly the message of the conference. Shame about the five-year plan.

3 September 2004

Investment in adolescents

by Alan Tuckett
Section: Viewpoint; Opinion; Further Education. Issue 4599, p6

SUMMER SUN must be bad for the brain. One day I'm at the Edward Hopper exhibition – all sweat and elbows, making my way through the throng to pay obeisance to these masterpieces of American anomie. The next I'm sitting in the garden, drinking cold sauvignon blanc, playing the pictures back in my mind. And then – eureka! I realise that the three sad people in Nighthawks keeping the bartender from his bed have just failed to enrol for Spanish 3 at the Brasshouse in Birmingham. That bloke sitting in a singlet, looking out of the window over a bleak industrial landscape, was hoping to do an urban archaeology MA part-time in the evening at Birkbeck. But they have changed the night and he can't change his shift pattern.

The couple staring bleakly at the trees from the stoop of their house in the middle of the wood, can't agree whether he should take up orienteering, or she ornithology – nor who should stay at home to look after grandma.

The woman in her underwear, crouched over a text in an under-furnished room was luckier – though since we can't see her face we have to imagine her smile. She found a place on a Russian course, but is finding it hard to keep up with the homework, a full-time job, and regular visits in the evening from Willie Loman.

Adult education provokes strong passions – whether you get on to a course or whether you don't. You see this in the correspondence MPs report from the steady drip of adjournment debates that highlight the contribution to quality of life that the modest public investment in a yoga class secures.

No one has captured this passion better than Boris Johnson, the colourful editor of the *Spectator* and not quite convincing Tory MP. In a Parliamentary debate, he told the graphic story of the struggles of Alice, an 80-year-old

Seriously useless learning

student in a keep-fit class, who, try as she might, found that she was unable to demonstrate that she could do things better after a winter of inspired teaching and learning. The process of ageing thwarted her hopes to fulfil the learning contract laboriously written out at the beginning of the course.

Slowly, Johnson's gentle ridiculing of audit culture has created the conditions for lighter touch assurance processes in adult education. And not before time.

Back to the art galleries. This time, the Munch Museet in Oslo, just three days before its two most famous paintings were nicked at gunpoint.

The Scream brought the Hopper show to mind again. But this time there was no quietness in the despair. It reminded me how often people dealing with major trauma put their toes in the water of re-engagement with society through joining a class.

Perfect, really, in offering a low-risk chance to meet new people. And, despite the policymaker's concern with drop-out rates, it is not too much of a disaster if you can't bring yourself to attend a meeting or two.

I was in Norway to contribute to the International Council for Adult Education's three-week summer school for younger leaders in adult education. ICAE recognises the global challenge in giving experience and skills to younger educators, seeking to secure effective succession planning. The participants spent time looking at the impact of globalisation and the role of international agencies. And then they looked at practical strategies for making the case for adult learning.

It is a case to be made across the world – not least since the World Bank narrowed its educational support in many countries to measures which secure universal primary education.

The result of this in many countries of the South is that adult opportunities are shrivelling. Yet, all the research shows that learning takes root best where adults and children both have the chance to take part.

The Tomlinson agenda for 14-to-19s is welcome, and overdue, and will undoubtedly galvanise major new government investment in adolescents. That investment cannot be at the expense of opportunities for adults. But in my gloomier moments I think back to Munch's *The Scream*, and wonder if sense and proportion will prevail.

8 October 2004
All together now for union learning
by Alan Tuckett
Section: Viewpoint; Further Education. Issue 4604, p4

PLANS FOR a new Union Learning Academy have been put out for consultation by the Trades Union Congress. It aims to bring together best practice in the various union learning initiatives. For the past ten years, union learning has been a success, developing a new role for the movement alongside wage bargaining and the defence of working conditions and employment rights. Tens of thousands of working people have gained qualifications, and thousands more have become learning representatives – combining guidance with negotiating for the right to learn.

The academy must be warmly welcomed. From the Ford unions' early successes in negotiating the Employee Development & Assistance Programme (EDAP), which supported workers with any kind of learning other than explicit training, through Unison's Return to Learn programme and the recent flowering of learning initiatives across industrial sectors, there is much to build on. Indeed, the success of the union learning movement might be a useful benchmark by which to assess the employer-led Sector Skills Council's efforts to create a culture of learning at work.

Gordon Brown has described the academy as a "workers' university". The phrase has a ring to it, conjuring up the flowering of industrial democracy in the former Yugoslavia in the 1960s, or the 150-hour movement in Italy.

But recent experience also suggests that the term may be a distraction.

Look at UFL learndirect. The Labour manifesto in 1997 promised a University for Industry, building on the idea of a corporate university developed by Motorola, Unipart and a panoply of other transnational corporations. When Ufl arrived, university was heavily in inverted commas. No charter was awarded; no equivalence claimed with the educational institutions funded through the higher education funding councils. Indeed, early supporters of UFL argued that it was not a university, and that it was not just for industry. That has not stopped it demonstrating that there is a huge demand for modest packages of learning, and for information and advice on what is available.

The National Health Service University, or NHSU, was the next major initiative to stretch the definition of university. Its chief executive Bob Fryer points out that an institution serving the largest workforce outside the Chinese army and the Indian railways has the potential to become the largest corporate university in the world. What I most admire about the remit of NHSU is its focus on the people who work in the health service who have had little chance to engage in learning up to now. The NHS spends an impressive £4bn a year on developing its workforce, considerably more than the Learning & Skills Council has for post-19 education and training. Yet 46% of its workers get two days or less training a year. The NHSU holds out the prospect for real learning opportunities for porters, cleaners and care assistants.

If its early years are anything like UFL's, it will need resilience and clarity of purpose to keep on track. The Department of Health will want to exercise patience, too, to allow it to fulfil its potential. I just wonder if the "U" in NHSU

Seriously useless learning

makes that patience harder to achieve, as vested interests in HE express scepticism at such a broadly-conceived project acquiring university status.

To return to the Union Learning Academy, my advice is to avoid Gordon Brown's description for now. But there is a wider debate to have. How can we create institutions which command the respect our universities enjoy, but which cater for people whose learning journeys are more modest? This winter's legislation in Scotland, where proposals will be debated to create a single funding body for further and higher education, opens the way to the creation of a single tertiary system and a chance to engage with the arguments. Tertiary legislation, the UfI and NHSU all draw on a single idea, that a learning society needs a continuum of study from literacy and numeracy to continuing professional development for consultants, engineers and orchestral soloists, and that it is best to think about them all together. Common sense really, but hard to bring about.

5 November 2004
New look at the Big Apple's core values
by Alan Tuckett
Section: Viewpoint; Opinion; Further Education. Issue 4608, p4

GOING AWAY for a few days gives you a fresh perspective on things. Like everyone who works with adult learners, I have been worrying about how the daftest excesses can be avoided as new policies affecting adult learning get turned into practice. The broad lines of policy are fine. It is good that people get free tuition up to their first level 2 (GCSE-equivalent) qualification. Good, too, that local learning and skills councils are looking to reshape local provision via the strategic area reviews. And the proposals in the new LSC circular that aim to protect learning for personal and community development are very welcome, given the utilitarian, target-obsessed pressures in the system.

But it is hard to see how the various initiatives interlock, or assess the influence national policy advice now carries with local LSCs. Will opportunities for personal and community development be available to the full range of communities served by local LSCs? How fast can you close the gap when learners in Herefordshire get much less than their Gloucestershire neighbours, and without destabilising both services? I worry that as resources shift to new priorities, progression routes will narrow.

How will outreach and guidance services be paid for? Will good-quality provision survive for people with learning difficulties and those recovering from mental health problems? How can we support learners to strengthen literacy, language and numeracy skills while they pursue other studies? How do we support teachers to deal with change? The questions are legion.

Five days in New York gave me a fresh eye on all this. The first was that whatever you do, some kinds of adult learning will persist. In the subway, bright posters in several languages encourage you to enrol in English classes. Naomi Campbell adorns the cover of *The Learning Annex*, a free brochure about self-improvement classes, available on every street corner. It offers an "unforgettable" evening with the "supermodel and super-person".

Most people can only dream of such success – but "Naomi will show you how to achieve it – regardless of where you are in life". For $19.99, your life can be transformed. Among hundreds of courses you can find, "how to make the right man fall in love with you"; "open your own Laundromat – turn coins into cash"; and a course for writers, photographers and entrepreneurs: "How to be overpaid, well-fed, non-struggling, happy and working."

The market for quick-fix self-improvement, linking learning to people's dreams of changing their lives is alive and well in the United States – and there is no obvious parallel in the UK's portfolio. It points to a concern to develop the confidence of a can-do culture, if not to a curriculum in which most learners' aspirations are likely to be achieved at the end of the course. To my second conclusion: we need to do more – and more systematically – to foster learning for entrepreneurship.

Offers are everywhere in New York – the Gotham City writers' workshops; the Blue Note jazz club masterclasses. Every cultural institution offers programmes to extend your understanding of all you have seen and heard.

Such a private sector secures range, but for quality and depth, curriculum and staff development, the public system has no equal. The State University of New York and its community colleges, and the private universities, all make comprehensive and widely understood provision with clear progression routes. Innovation is at classroom level. Of course, it is not without problems – and even remedial classes at the local college need to be paid for.

Talking to a community college colleague, I envied the way she could take for granted the levels of stability in post-school learning, and how well-funded the public system is. Why can't we have it, too? Our debate is too much about structure, too little about learning.

Why can't we cherish teachers and trainers, and trust their judgement? Healthy forests thrive when the environment secures stability. The community colleges in the US remind us that the same is true for learning institutions.

Seriously useless learning

10 December 2004

Different learners, different needs

by Alan Tuckett

Section: Viewpoint; Opinion; Further Education. Issue 4613, p4

LOOKING BACK, Claus Moser's report on adult literacy and numeracy needs had a major impact. True, it omitted to look at English for speakers of other languages, or the literacy and numeracy needs of adults with learning difficulties. But those issues were picked up and included, with key skills, in the government's broader Skills for Life strategy.

The government's strategy set demanding targets: 750,000 to pass the national tests by 2004; 1,500,000 by 2007, and 2,250,000 by 2010. Enough money was pumped into the system to back the target and train teachers.

And, lest we forget, there is nothing inevitable about matching policy with resources, as the Skills Strategy shows. There we have a demanding target, widespread commitment to its achievement, but inadequate public or private investment for there to be a realistic chance of hitting it.

Since this year is the first benchmark of progress on the Skills for Life Target, you would think the time had arrived to celebrate the achievements of learners, teachers, institutions, and the creativity of the planners and funders who kick-started a major change of focus in the system. Time, too, to recognise that on top of the 750,000 and more who passed the tests, another million and a half adults have received help without taking national tests – in many cases, simply because we have yet to develop adequate schemes to measure what they have gained. Of course, not everything is perfect. We do need a more sophisticated assessment system, as Peter Lavender, Jay Derrick and Barry Brooks discussed in the book *Testing, Testing, 1, 2, 3* earlier this year. As always, there is a crisis in the supply of tutors and most notably in ESOL.

We have not yet developed a robust strategy for establishing literacy, language and numeracy work in other studies adults pursue, and the gremlins don't speak to the many thousands who say they have only a bit of a problem with spelling.

Overall, I feel that the success of the strategy to date bears witness to the resilience, determination and clear-sightedness of those people who have argued the case for a right to read since the launch of the campaign in the 1970s.

No one has done more than Alan Wells, director of the Basic Skills Agency, so, I was astonished to read his opinion piece here two weeks ago (*FE Focus*, November 19). Why would we want to distinguish between beginners and those en route to confidence and competence? His distinction read to me like the Victorian separation between the deserving and undeserving poor. Need is need, and the current strategy's breadth is surely part of its strength.

Down the years, estimates of the size of the population who might benefit have varied, from the million people claimed by the British Association of Settlements in 1974, through the two million the government identified in the late Seventies, to Moser's seven million, based on the International Adult Literacy Survey. Counting totals is hard, but the evidence of the link between poverty and poor numeracy is powerful, and difficulty with literacy, language and numeracy skills is not limited to those at entry level 1.

It is a long time since I taught literacy and numeracy myself, but my first students illustrate the point. The first was an absolute beginner – eloquent in argument, quick to learn but a new reader and writer. The second was an undergraduate, and then postgraduate at Sussex University, diagnosed as dyslexic and in need of tutorial support with spelling. Both had a technical need, but one would not have been included on any narrow targeting of focus on reading need. This, surely, is the basis of the current UK strategy: the recognition that the platform for confident and effective communication is different for differing contexts and different people.

I do not want to be cared for in hospital by a nurse who cannot manage volume accurately when giving me medicine. I don't want cleaners, or their supervisors, who have difficulties in interpreting instructions on the use of chemicals in confined spaces to be told their need is too sophisticated to count, or to lack a properly supported programme of study. Skills for Life is successful at engaging learners with a broad span of needs – and that is cause for celebration, not for carping.

7 January 2005

Robbing Peter to train Paul is no solution

by Alan Tuckett
Section: Viewpoint; Opinion; Further Education. Issue 4616, p4

RUTH KELLY faces a major challenge in squaring the government's ambitions for lifelong learning with the cash available. The economic and demographic logic, as the new education secretary will readily recognise, requires a significant expansion in investment in adult learning.

Since there are not enough young people to fill all the new and replacement jobs needed over the next decade, expanding adult skills is essential to the country's economic well-being. Yet the political logic concentrates the debate and demand for new resources on the education and training of the young.

The way the rules were written in the Learning & Skills Act 2000 means that the needs of 16-to-19s must be met, and adults get what is left. A rise in the size of the 16-to-19 cohort over the next half decade, and the government's success at engaging more of that age group in education and training, will squeeze the public budgets available for adult work. The way sixth forms are funded increases the pressure on LSC funds for adults, and Tomlinson's proposals to reform 14-to-19 education will also need to be paid for. The result is that just when we need to increase capacity to stimulate and satisfy adult learning, cash from the public sector will be tighter than at any time since this government came to power.

Of course, public funding is not the only source of money. The National Institute of Adult Continuing Education has long argued that employers have an obligation to develop their staff. We argue, too, that those individuals who can pay should pay a higher proportion of the costs, as long as concessions are readily available to those who need them, whatever they are studying. The difficulty is that over the last decade, funding streams have made it sensible for colleges to stimulate demand through low or no-fee offers to individuals and employers alike.

Of course, changing direction takes time. An active fees policy will open increased funding, but only after time. You do not need to persuade trans-national corporations of the value of investing in people. But many small and medium-sized firms do not spend scarce money on training and devel-opment. Nor do lots of self-employed people. The government's employer training pilots are designed to stimulate employer engagement – to use public funds to kick-start a learning culture at work by supporting staff to develop those skills employers identify as critical to future success.

But the early evidence of the pilots suggests that it is large multi-nationals who are quickest to respond to the opportunities of the pilots. There is still a need to persuade many small firms to join in and, once there, to pay more for training. The level 2 (GCSE-equivalent) entitlement currently being piloted in the north-east and south-east regions was another bold commitment to invest in those people who have done the least learning in the past. It complements the Skills for Life strategy the government adopted to support the learning of literacy, language and numeracy, and can usefully learn from that strategy.

The Skills for Life strategy has been impressive. The government's first target of 750,000 people passing a national test by 2004 has been achieved.

More importantly, 2.4m people have been helped to improve their skills, including many for whom the threshold of the national tests has been set too high. What impressed me about the strategy was the recognition that the tests would only engage a minority of the participants at any one time.

The level 2 target needs the same approach. There will be many, of course, who can sprint to the full qualification in a purposeful way. Others will take time to gain the confidence and sense of direction. For them, the maintenance of a range of 'first steps' provision is vital.

But again, evidence from the pilot areas suggests that first steps or other further education is at risk; if not from LSC planning decisions, then from the decisions of local institutions such as Sunderland or Bradford colleges. Tight budgets and tough targets lead to narrow curriculum offers, and a focus on those easier to reach.

These pressures do not make for easy judgments for providers, planners or ministers. We need the new initiatives in the Skills Strategy and the pre-budget report, but not at the expense of the infrastructure for lifelong learning patiently built over the last seven years.

The UK still spends less on post-16 learning than most of its competitors, when you add private to public investment. Given the economic need for more adult learning, the case for greater investment is overwhelming. And if the government remains wedded to voluntarism for employers, more needs to come from the public purse.

4 February 2005
Perils of ignoring adult learning
by Alan Tuckett
Section: Viewpoint; Further Education. Issue 4620, p4

WE FACE a dilemma. Ministers' unequivocal commitment to stable funding for post-school education budgets in 2005/6 is welcome. They found extra cash to add to the funds from the Learning & Skills Council. This ensures that money for adults overall can be sustained at the same level for that year. Ministers also made it clear that the LSC should not neglect "other further education" – all that work that falls outside the National Qualifications framework and the council's targets. With luck, providers will also temper any move to cut swathes of uncertificated work.

Despite this, depressing stories abound. For example, in one college, the local LSC recommends cutting the most basic courses in order to boost what can be offered at level 2 (equivalent GCSE grade A to C). What price widening participation and progression routes there, let alone student choice? Another sees fees for older IT students soaring from £40 to £110 – fine for well-educated and well-heeled folk, but hardly for adults struggling to get by on a pension just over the level where income support kicks in.

What the extra funding gives is a short breathing space with time for a rethink about what they offer. They will need to strengthen what they are offering by way of full courses at level 2 and above.

At the same time, they will need to maintain a broad curriculum that continues to meet the wider needs of the communities they serve. Also, of course, they need to balance their books. If 2005/6 offers a breathing space, 2006/7 looks like the most challenging year in a decade. This is partly the product of the post-16 sector's success in persuading more young people to stay on, coupled with the bulge in the population of 16 to 19-year-olds. The bulge will last until 2010, and then it will fall away dramatically.

Little new public money is likely to be available to address the overload in demand that we are set to see in the second half of this decade. It will be adults who lose out. Yet two in every three jobs to be filled in the UK over the next decade must be done by adults. There will be women returners, older people staying on or returning to work, and migrants. There are too few young people to fill all the vacancies when the baby-boomer generation retires.

It is a problem further education itself will need to address in its own workforce. The entitlement to a full level 2 qualification may meet the needs of some of these groups, but not everyone will be ready for that scale of commitment at the start.

Then again, as the government's imminent strategy for older people should make clear, silver surfers have much to gain: in financial education, in developing skills to volunteer, to keep fit, to care for others and to develop new skills. All this will need the imaginative help of educators able to work with adults. So, too, will the work flowing from the childcare strategy.

The mental health strategy highlights new roles for post-school education.

Neighbourhood renewal thrives where there is dedication to learning communities. Overall, the adult learning agenda is growing in importance, and we can ill afford to see a reduction in investment.

If there is no new public money to be found for post-school education and training, who else can contribute? Increased fees from employers and individuals would help, and both pay less than their counterparts in most other industrial countries. But if we are not to destabilise the system, their contributions will be modest in the short run. There is little hope of redistribution within education: schools and universities are powerful advocates for their own interests. Health investment will carry on increasing. It is hard to see a fall in defence spending until military adventures wind down.

So, to the dilemma. We need to argue for a larger share for adults. But if there is little prospect of shifting resources enough to make a difference, how do we manage best? Institutional leaders must be more assertive when defending local needs in talks with planners, and we need a recognition that sophisticated planning is inhibited by an obsession with targets. It is learning, not targets, that really matter.

18 February 2005

Don't let them disappear

Bad experience of education keeps too many adults away from training, says **Alan Tuckett**

Section: Wider World; Post-16 Under Scrutiny. Issue 4622, p8

'WHO IS not there?' It's the question research into adult education must always ask in any fair society. Policymakers and practitioners alike should be striving to give everyone the opportunity of enriching their lives through education. That is what the National Institute of Adult Continuing Education (NIACE) has been about for 20 years. Getting everyone involved is not easy, because we all come to adult education with baggage: our experience of compulsory education.

There is a persistent learning divide in the United Kingdom between the educationally excluded and the educationally involved. Those who had a good experience at school get opportunities for development at work, and continue to study in their own time.

As for the rest, as Helena Kennedy has said: "If at first you don't succeeed, you don't succeed."

Annual NIACE surveys show that the gap between the two halves has been deepened by a digital divide. Those who don't succeed in formal education are rarely skilled in information technology, and so fall further behind.

The future follows the past. Of those studying now, eight in ten expect to study again, but scarcely one in ten of those who have done no learning since leaving school expects to join them.

But there is nothing inevitable about the learning divide. NIACE research shows how institutions can embrace the excluded. Access to good childcare has long been a barrier for many women with children. But studies by NIACE and the Basic Skills Agency show that adults who use pre-schools as a springboard for their own development, as well as that of their children, benefit from peer encouragement and acquire confidence in their ability to learn.

Likewise with the digital divide. Our research shows that the buying of hardware and provision of initial training must be followed by courses that revise and update.

As society gets older, it's well worth overcoming the barrier between age and education. Older learners can benefit directly from training and also spread the benefit to other generations, as the NIACE research programme Older and Bolder proves. Parallel programmes examine how to widen participation through family learning, offering guidelines to practitioners.

NIACE research also supports adults with learning difficulties, looking at gender, race, self-esteem and the use of GPs' surgeries as a site for educational guidance.

Seriously useless learning

Consumers and providers alike have their blind spots. NIACE's work in the field of language, literacy and numeracy focuses on how best to give learners autonomy and how institutions can be made to see how they unconsciously exclude certain groups.

And then there are the policymakers, but even here there is hope. Nowhere is that clearer than in NIACE's work with adults with qualifications gained overseas, finally being followed up now, 15 years after its initial work was found too inconvenient to be published or supported by the government of the day. Then there is work on neighbourhood renewal, learning communities, effective outreach strategies, credit, the recognition of achievement, and work on retention, progression, and curriculum development. Taken together they present a simple message: if we want strategies that work to widen participation we have to match the rhetoric of a learner-centred system with the practice. Only then will we get a satisfactory answer to that small question: who is not there?

11 March 2005
Don't let young push old aside
by Alan Tuckett
Section: Viewpoint; Opinion; Further Education. Issue 4625, p4

JUST WHAT is happening to the government's lifelong learning strategy? We have a major demographic shift under way in the UK. We know that young people can fill only one in three jobs in the next decade. This is official, not some fuzzy estimate. From 2010, the impact of falling birth rates will have a sudden and inevitable impact on the labour market. At the same time, people born in the post-war baby boom will be hanging up their tools. In some industries, like engineering or further education, there is a concentration of skilled and experienced workers over 50. Replacing them will not be easy and requires effective strategies to get more women signed up, particularly from ethnic-minority communities. It involves persuading older people to stay in or re-enter the workforce. Yet, despite this, government policy concentrates more and more energy, and money, on the education of the young.

It is true that there will be a temporary bulge in the numbers of young people over 16 over the next four years. True, too, that the success of government policies sees more of them staying on at 16 – though far too many still opt out at 17. In addition, more young people are staying in school sixth forms. The result of these short-term pressures is that provision for many adults will get markedly worse over the next few years.

This is because the Learning & Skills Act in 2000 gave the Learning & Skills Council a statutory duty to ensure 'sufficient' education for 16-to-19s, and a responsibility to secure 'reasonable' provision for adults. But what is reasonable? The answer is, whatever the LSC thinks is 'reasonable' in the light of resources available.

A rise in young people's participation, therefore, comes at the cost of opportunities for adults. Those who choose to stay in school compound the problem because of the premium funds schools attract. All this is just about manageable with rising budgets. However, the tight budgets for FE from 2006 will lead to a decline in opportunities for adults. Tony Blair's recent proposal to create 100,000 new sixth-form places will make things worse. Who is going to fill them in five years time? How much unused capacity in schools will there be, then, when the country is crying out for resources to improve the skills of adults?

The National Employment Training Programme will also affect FE budgets. It will attract new money, but it will also lead to a shift of existing budgets from FE to employers. None of that money will come from budgets for young people. It can be argued that employers will spend this money on adults. Yet the discussions surrounding the first four industry sector skills agreements suggest that all of them expect to concentrate their recruitment strategies on young people.

Look, too, at the research evidence over decades, which shows that employers concentrate cash for training on the most qualified of their workforce. In fact, a huge number of employers offer their staff no chance for training and development. The only sensible conclusion from all this is that there will need to be a cultural revolution in attitudes among employers, and in the regulatory framework in which they operate, before the bulk of older workers can rely on the workplace as a secure source of opportunities to re-engage with learning.

An ageing society needs its older people not just for work, but to keep the fabric of civil society vibrant. Older people vote more. They maintain the voluntary sector through their contributions. They undertake a large proportion of the caring for older and much younger relatives and friends.

And they have spent a lifetime paying taxes for education without having much opportunity to benefit themselves.

Over the life of the LSC, there has been a welcome rising trend in older people's participation. That will inevitably reverse as 'other education' for adults bears the brunt of the funding pressures on the LSC. More money is needed to overcome the short-term pressures from 2006. And we must get better at planning – the challenges of an ageing workforce have not suddenly arrived over the horizon. Most importantly, you cannot have a life-long learning policy that focuses exclusively on the interests of the young.

Seriously useless learning

15 April 2005

A life in the best of all parallel worlds

by Alan Tuckett

Section: Viewpoint; Opinion; Further Education. Issue 4630, p4

I WONDER why we in England get work-life balance so badly wrong? I thought about this over Easter at a friend's house on Sandymount Beach, Dublin, pootling around the coast south of the city, visiting key sites from Ulysses, admiring my son's resilience in braving the sea.

Dalkey, the Beverley Hills of Dublin, is a sleepy village, full of good pubs and pretty vistas, but a symbol too of the success of the Celtic tiger economy. There is a marked difference between the time of day people give you here and back home. As so often when we are on holiday, the family agrees that we would like to spend more of our time doing things like this, and less time at work or waiting for delayed trains to whisk us hundreds of miles to meetings.

My second spur to thought was reading the new skills white paper alongside Richard Layard's new book, *Happiness: lessons from a new science*. The overwhelming rationale of the white paper is that we must strengthen the skills base in the British labour force to improve our productivity in order to compete more effectively with other industrial economies.

The paper argues that we must align post-school education and training much more closely with employers' needs. The result of all this has to be inferred, but must surely include a more prosperous society with less poverty and a population fulfilled by meaningful work. The paper does include a section that renews the current commitment to learning for personal and community development, particularly for pensioners. But at its heart is a utilitarian focus on workforce skills.

In *Happiness*, Layard wonders whether we have got the balance of public policy wrong. He suggests that public policy is broadly focused on securing the greatest happiness of the greatest number, but that until now the great difficulty has been in measuring happiness. He explains that economists have taken the overall rise in income as the most effective available proxy, and then points out the flawed nature of that approach.

He reports two experiments to show the difference between our attitudes to income and leisure. In the first, participants are offered a choice between two imaginary worlds, with constant prices applying in both. In one, you get $50,000 a year, while everyone else gets on average $25,000. The other world offers you $100,000, but others get $250,000. Most opt for the first, settling for fewer things but higher relative wealth.

The parallel experiment offers you two weeks' holiday a year while others get one, or four weeks' holiday while others get eight. This time, participants (and everyone with whom I have repeated the experiment) opts for the longer holidays. Income is relative, leisure an absolute good.

So why, he asks, do we organise so much of our policy around the challenge to increase overall prosperity? Layard's analysis suggests that the work-life balance in our learning policies is out of kilter. True, we still have classes where you can learn a language, improve your drawing or your parenting skills. But they are under intense pressure, as the push for vocational targets squeezes discretionary funding.

Take the case of adult education institutions, whose special character is protected in statute. These bodies – which include adult education centres in London, the Workers' Educational Association, and long-term residential colleges – all offer liberal education, as the cultural critic Raymond Williams put it, to understand the way the world is changing, to adapt and shape it.

At present, local LSCs are negotiating future programmes with these bodies, seeking greater commitment – from some at least – to achieving government targets. Why would any planner committed to social, cultural and civic education want to re-shape a distinctive beacon institution like the City Lit when competent colleges round the corner have their main focus on vocational qualifications?

But there are pressures – mainly because learning for fulfilment is no longer seen as a valid claim on the public purse. There is already evidence of a stark drop in pensioners' participation (7% year on year). And the trend will worsen as budgets tighten next year. For all of us, loss of opportunity impoverishes. It is too high a price to pay for any welcome improvement in skills for work.

13 May 2005

Scraps for the teenagers' table
by Alan Tuckett
Section: Viewpoint; Opinion; Further Education. Issue 4634, p4

THE NEW government must look urgently at the crisis facing adult learners. Across the country, news is flooding in of cuts in college budgets for adults, exacerbated by the Learning & Skills Council's demand that there be a further shift to 16 to 19-year-olds. In January, adult learning was promised a 5% funding increase, yet colleges in East Anglia report drops in adult funding, of between 5 and 16%. Wiltshire College, facing a £500,000 cut in its overall allocation, has been asked to shift a further £500,000 away from work with adults.

Initial Learning & Skills Council statistics for this year already show a 3% drop in adult numbers, with a 7% fall in college students over 60.

What happened to the assurance we were given that 2005-6 would be a transitional year, with budgets preserved? What do these changes mean for the guarantee to maintain the same volume of learning for its own sake? Or for the range of options available for people with learning difficulties? What kind of mess do we face in 2006-7, when the LSC's budget hole really widens?

The crisis has arisen because the bulk of adult education is below level 2 (GCSE-equivalent) and does not lead to a certificate. But the LSC is focusing adult spending on Skills for Life, the National Employment Training Programme and "full level 2" programmes that are equivalent to five good GCSE passes.

No one argues with the commitment to Skills for Life. Indeed, in relation to English for speakers of other languages, that commitment needs to be increased. Evidence also shows healthy demand for employment training pilots – though there is inevitable concern that public money may be replacing cash that some employers would have spent anyway. There are questions too about achievement rates in the pilots and their cost compared with similar courses.

But there is less evidence that adults feel able to commit themselves to a full level 2 course in colleges. Also why is this funding limited to people committed from the start to doing a full programme in a limited time, when we know adults study in bite-sized chunks, fitting learning in to busy lives?

The price of the current policy is a substantial loss of opportunities for thousands of adults who have found their way back to education and training. Yet, in colleges at least, these adults come disproportionately from less-affluent and less-skilled groups – exactly the people the Skills Strategy is designed to help.

Now, I am a keen supporter of the aims of the Skills Strategy. I agree that it is important for public funding to focus on those who benefited least from earlier education. I agree that level 2 qualifications are important, as a springboard to technician-level skills for which real demand exists.

But I do not believe the government has willed the means for the strategy to succeed. We are still well down the global league of average investment in post-school education and training.

Not all the money should come from the state. Individuals who can afford it must be encouraged to pay more. That, however, involves a change of culture in many places and staff need guidance on strategies that work.

Here, adult education services with years of experience could help – but the onus is on government and the LSC to secure that help. Employers should pay more but current policies offer mixed messages. The government must tell industry to bear its share of the costs.

The government also needs to invest more itself if we are to fill job vacancies of the next decade with skilled and confident adults. That has to be the clear conclusion of the Treasury's Leitch review of UK skills. Everyone who cares about adult learning should write to the review this month to make sure this is clearly understood.

Meanwhile, Adult Learners' Week this year comes at an opportune time to remind the new government we cannot build a lifelong learning culture if adults only get a chance to learn when there are scraps left over from younger learners' feast.

20 May 2005

Out of the shadows

Let learning give everyone the confidence to shape their own lives, says **Alan Tuckett**

Section: Adult Learners' Week (May 21-27); Skills For Life. Issue 4635, p2

A STUDENT of the great Brazilian educator Paolo Freire argued. "I want to read and write to stop being the shadow of other people." His interest was in reading the world as well as reading words. There is no doubt that confidence and skill in speaking the language, managing numbers and writing and reading really make a difference to the day-to-day experience and quality of life.

The Skills for Life strategy is now entering its second phase. The first national targets have been met. Thousands of tutors have been trained.

National standards that command confidence are in place, and a good deal of high quality learning material has been generated.

But we have still some way to go to give learners a larger role in shaping their studies – not least when they want to strengthen literacy, numeracy and language while studying for another goal. Embedding basic skills – so that the vocational curriculum and the literacy, language and numeracy skills are developed with equal confidence – is more of a challenge than meets the eye. But many learners do expect us to do better in designing programmes that work for them (perhaps this is what personalisation means?) and we would do well to engage them more in shaping the offer.

The second phase of the Skills for Life strategy is likely to be even more challenging. Some of the easiest-to-recruit learners have been reached.

There is a need to make sure that numeracy moves centre stage – not least as an anti-poverty measure. English for speakers of other languages (Esol) was excluded from the Moser Report in 1999, and when information and communications technology was added to the suite of basic skills, the official press release called it "the third basic skill" – so invisible was language. Esol needs sustained investment to build a tutor cohort large enough to meet the thousands ready now to learn, and to reach out to all the UK's linguistic minorities.

There is no doubt that skill and confidence in using the new technologies makes a difference to life chances, too. NIACE's annual participation survey highlights how the digital divide reinforces the learning divide that bedevils British education and society. But we are waiting for the development of a sustained programme of work to give life to the aim to make ICT a basic skill everyone has a right to.

Reading the world better is what all the dimensions of a wider definition of basic skills share in common. Making sense of the way stories are constructed in the media; understanding better our relations with other family members; dealing with bereavement and the torrent of financial choices that flood through our letterboxes – all point to the need for a confident population skilled in making sense of what is going on, and in how to deal with it. That surely is our common task.

27 May 2005

No fairness in adult funding
by Alan Tuckett
Section: Viewpoint; Opinion; Further Education. Issue 4636, p4

MORE BAD news for adult learning. In stark contrast to the inspiring tales of Adult Learners' Week, the messages from the funding front make hard reading. Doncaster College faces reductions in adult budgets this autumn, though it has no 'other' further education. Newcastle College has £5m less than the budget it anticipated. But, at least there is almost £40m left in the college's coffers. The worst news has come from local authority adult education services. In Essex there are cuts of up to 17% in certificated FE courses. Cumbria's cut is 'just' 12%. The most extreme case is North-amptonshire which faces a two-thirds cut in its budget. No one pretends that 2006/7 will be easier. Quite the opposite. It will be markedly worse for adults if present policies remain unchanged.

At first sight, it is surprising, given the guarantee enshrined now in two successive skills white papers to preserve adult and community learning budgets to keep a wide range of studies for community-based learning, and learning for personal fulfilment. To understand how the government and the Learning & Skills Council can meet the guarantee and yet introduce swinge-ing cuts in local authority adult services, it is necessary to revisit battles that dominated the early 1990s. At the time, colleges were incorporated and uncertificated adult education was left with truncated funding within the LEAs. Most adult education services adapted to offer certificated studies that qualified for Further Education Funding Council support under 'schedule 2' of the FHE 1992 Act. Over time, the greater security and new possibili-ties – offered by FEFC funding – saw many authorities expanding schedule 2-funded work while keeping the LEA-budgeted work relatively stable. Local courses accredited by the Open College Network qualified for FEFC cash. Many LEA services, therefore, adapted uncertificated courses, in languages, art, fashion and so on to qualify for funds.

When Labour came to power in 1997, it promised to sweep away the 'nonsense' of arbitrary qualification for funds under schedule. That promise was honoured in the Learning & Skills Act in 2000, when LEA adult education budgets were taken over by that Act. Schedule 2 was binned. LEA services continued to get two discrete budgets. Where they had received FEFC funds, they got an allocation from the FE pot. In addition, there was 'ring-fenced' adult and community learning money for the first three years of the LSC, and money assured through the skills white papers ever since.

By and large the adult community learning budgets are being broadly protected, but, ironically, the old schedule 2 work is now acutely vulnerable in many places as the LSC's plans are put in jeopardy by the current funding crisis. The curriculum divide, in adult learning is, clearly, alive and well in too many places.

As a result, language courses that lead to OCN accreditation are at risk, while holiday Spanish is safe. This is, surely, ridiculous. After all, the government's skills strategy is designed to improve the country's international competitiveness. Adult education services serve the business market in a far wider range of languages than are offered in schools. In addition, National Open College Network credit-bearing courses are used as early steps on the progression ladder by many students seeking better skills.

Surely, the time has come to re-integrate adult education services, and to trust learners and providers to strike the right balance of studies in community-based learning. In fairness, not every area faces misery and gloom. In Birmingham, the adult education service has a 1.8% cut in its adult and community learning allocation, and around 5% growth in its FE allocation.

There, the LSC supports local area planning partnerships. It has targeted developments to increase participation in the least well served communities. As a result, providers and planners have confidence in each other. Similar reports are emerging from central London. If these places can match policy with practice, why can't others? After all, that is why adult education was nationalised. Isn't it?

1 July 2005

A new dark age for adult learners?
by Alan Tuckett
Section: Viewpoint; Opinion; Further Education. Issue 4641, p4

FOR TEN years now, I have approved of the broad direction of public policy affecting adults. How then can it have come to this – that the Learn-

Seriously useless learning

ing & Skills Council writes round to principals to say one in ten adult learners can expect to see their learning opportunities disappear this autumn?

The nadir for adult learners came with the 1991 white paper when, but for the intervention of the Women's Institutes, the government would have made learning for personal development illegal, except between consenting adults in areas of extreme disadvantage, and only then if social services met the bill. Since then, things have got better. Slowly, the rampant utilitarianism of the time gave way to a recognition that adults' learning journeys are richer and more complex than the planners predict.

That is a message reinforced each year during adult learners' week. As the Conservative minister, Tim Boswell, remarked: "It stands to reason that people don't step back into learning ready straight away to take an NVQ3. They take their time, building confidence through modest steps, but, once the bug takes, there is no stopping them."

The pace quickened after 1997. David Blunkett told us it took time to turn round an oil tanker, but set about the system with brio. Since then, it sometimes seems, there has been almost an initiative a week to get people involved in learning. The government adopted a participation target to keep a focus on non-participants. The Learning & Skills Council was set up taking in uncertificated adult education as well as the training and enterprise councils and further education. The result was, for adults, an increase in participation of half a million adults, many from the least privileged groups. The Skills for Life strategy in particular has assisted almost two-and-a-half million people in its first four years. The two skills strategy white papers, too, have set an agenda for the country to invest successfully in people at work with few skills.

What then is wrong? Much more public investment is in place. Yet much of this is at risk this year and next because success in one arena of public policy is bought at the expense of reductions in work with adults. So we face the prospect of a quarter of a million learners lost this autumn, and all the gains since 1997 disappearing next year if the 2006/7 budget remains unchanged. Then, in 2007, changes to the European Social Fund put opportunities for a further 300,000 adults at risk. This is not just a short-term wobble, while colleges and learners adjust to a higher fee economy for those who can pay.

There is a real risk that the overall goal of policy in securing a learning society will be missed. One reason is that we have a funding and legislative regime where success in increasing volumes in one area is bought at the expense of another. It is not right for every full-time 17-year-old persuaded to stay on to be bought with the opportunities of ten adults. After so much creative work, so much effort, it can't be right that you can do holiday French or GCSE French, but the steps in between are disappearing, or priced out of reach. Even in the protected areas, like basic skills, cuts threaten opportunities – since so much provision is at the lowest levels, and providers act on what they think the Learning & Skills Council wants, and on what some local LSCs interpret national guidance to mean.

An example lies in the advice that 80% of the work should focus on courses related to the national standards framework. Too many providers and some local LSCs interpret that as meaning only courses leading just to the national tests. Yet, as John Bynner's important research for the National Research & Development Centre for Literacy & Numeracy shows, the link between poor literacy and numeracy, poverty, and the impact on their children's chances is strongest for people with skills below entry level 2 (GCSEequivalent). Funding and targets surely need to be focused on their learning first. Of course, the skills strategy is important – and employers need to bear their substantial share of its costs. Higher education matters, too, and needs investment. But not at the expense of the chance for adults to change their lives on their own terms. The time has come, now, to secure a new settlement for adult learning across the piece, and to give it time to flourish.

5 August 2005

Too important to be left to the DfES

by Alan Tuckett
Section: Further Education. Issue 4646, p32

POLITICS IS about establishing priorities, and targets have been this government's mechanism for making sure we don't forget them. In some areas, this has worked well. There is far more literacy, language and numeracy teaching, and of higher quality, than I, for one, thought possible a decade ago. The level 2 (GCSE-equivalent) target, which focuses on the needs of people without qualifications and mobility in the labour market, was welcome, too.

Welcome, that is, until it became clear that there is not enough money to pay for it – whether that money comes from the state, from employers, or from individuals. As a result of cash shortages, free tuition is only open to people able to take the equivalent of five GCSEs in a year or two at most. Yet most adults study in the spaces left after work and family demands are met. When the skills strategy was going through, everyone assumed it would support level 2 and all the studies leading to it. Not much point having a ladder for skills where the rungs begin just out of reach over your head.

It is perfectly reasonable for governments to make clear where priorities

Seriously useless learning

lie – which is why we face a shift in public funding from that great soup of courses called 'other'. Such courses don't fit into the increasingly arthritic National Qualifications Framework, which include most of the stepping stones learners take towards substantial qualifications. But how much is it reasonable to transfer without having negative effects that are wholly unintended?

In the absence of increased employer investment (and current policies risk securing less, not more, from employers), a tight public spending round and buoyant demand among young people, something has to give. Over the next three years, it seems certain that it will be adults who will miss out on learning. The arithmetic is simple. Each full-time 16- or 17-year-old staying in the system displaces ten adults. Each full level 2 enrolment displaces another four. The Learning & Skills Council calculates up to one in ten places will disappear this year.

And next year will be worse. Perhaps another 400,000 adult places will be lost then. Now that the spending review has been put back for a year, a further 400,000 could go in 2007-8. And 2007 brings to an end the current round of European Social Fund programmes. Currently, 284,000 adults study on ESF-supported courses, but Britain's share of ESF will shrink dramatically in the next round as the needs of the poorest regions in an enlarged European Union are addressed.

So, taken all in all, something like a million-and-a-half adults are at risk of losing their places – and fee rises won't save more than a modest proportion of them.

This is a picture, as Chris Hughes, chair of the national inquiry into adult education, suggests, where adult learning outside level 2 and Skills for Life is not just a lower priority. It risks being no priority at all.

Some of the courses that will be casualties are survival English for speakers of other languages, sign language and absolute beginners' literacy and numeracy work – as well as art, language, history and many of the courses where people meet to reflect on the meaning and purpose of life.

Even if the entire budget used for 'other' FE were spent on the level 2 entitlement, there would still be a major shortfall.

Yet the evidence for the value of adult learning to society continues to pile up. The National Mental Health Strategy recognises the role adult learning plays in maintaining health. The Home Office's citizenship strategy is built on a citizenship test backed by learning for adults.

Neighbourhood renewal programmes recognise the importance of learning in regeneration. The Financial Services Authority acknowledges the importance of financial education for young and old alike. In the Department of Culture, Media & Sport, learning for pleasure and personal enrichment is seen as a public good. Yet in adult learning, you almost feel the need to apologise for enjoying what you learn.

In local authority adult education, we used to believe that adult learning suffered acutely from being on the margins of the education budget. As a result, the service got little attention from politicians, since major budgets need major oversight.

We argued then that adult learners would be better served by being run from the chief executive's department, since learning benefits communities in areas beyond education.

So, since it is hard to establish a secure platform in the Department for Education & Skills for the adult learning that a civilised society and successful economy needs, the same logic should be in central government.

But where would adult learning go? Would we be better off being run directly from Number 10 or Number 11? We are not the only people wondering that, though, are we?

`16 September 2005`

Targeted learning for life's survivors
by Alan Tuckett
Section: Viewpoint; Opinion; Further Education. Issue 4652, p4

WHY IS it so hard to get a sustained focus on the variety and complexity of older people's learning needs? Daisy Bohm was a widely-read, well-educated survivor of the traumas of the mid-20th century, and an active student in her seventies at the Friends Centre in Brighton, when I went there to work in 1973.

The centre, which celebrates its 60th anniversary this year, is part of a diminishing band of independent centres, run by its students. Such centres are precious reminders that in the absence of state action, people can and do organise provision for themselves – and then properly look to the state for some support.

Like many others, Daisy used adult classes to keep abreast of the way the world was changing and for feeding new curiosities. After I had worked at the centre for a year or two, Daisy took me aside to ask me to label courses in the prospectus, to make clear whether they were lecture courses, where the tutor might be expected to do most of the talking, or the kind of interactive seminars where students were expected to play an active part.

When I asked her why, she made clear that she, and several of her friends, already knew what they thought themselves, and wanted authoritative expositions on the Arab-Israeli conflict or the flowers of the Sussex downland. It was a well-argued, assertive case for learning that suited one group of older learners.

By contrast, the largest group in the centre was a self-programming senior

Seriously useless learning

citizens group on Tuesday afternoons where different members among the 150 regular participants took turns to lead sessions. There was a period of formal presentation, followed by questions, then tea. Over tea groups of four to six pensioners took the subject of the week's talk as a springboard for reflection, reminiscence and challenge.

There was never a shortage of speakers and, despite the scale, new people were successfully included in the group's work. Neither Daisy's approach, nor that of the senior citizens group easily generated evidence of individual learning outcomes – but both demonstrated how effective learner-sensitive curriculum design can be.

When I moved to London in the 1980s, I was struck by three other examples of provision for older learners. Each focused, not on the third age of active and mobile younger retired people, but on people in residential settings in the later periods of their lives. The first, depressingly, was most common. Like many other London institutes, ours ran a programme in old people's homes, where the smell on crossing the threshold seemed all too often to be a noxious mix of ammonia and urine.Characteristically, we would offer just one or two keep-fit classes a week.

It was the kind of work defended brilliantly by Boris Johnson two or three years ago in the House of Commons. Important enough, but very limited in the range of the offer.

Nightingale Lane centre for retired Jewish people provided a stark contrast. There, learners from 70 to 100 and more took part in the widest range of activities from woodcarving to yoga, politics and poetry. It was and is an inspiring example of the kind of fourth age learning offer we might wish for ourselves and our parents. But the trend is for less work like that to attract public funding. Our crafts class in a hospice was inspiring, too. Learner retention was an issue – many students lived just a few weeks, but the impact was palpable. I tried to persuade our local authority to upgrade the tutor, but was refused, because "the work was insufficiently challenging".

There is, in my view, no more important job in education than supporting learners in managing the later years of their lives. There was a welcome renaissance of such work after 1997 – with a million more learners on Learning & Skills Council courses (particularly on short bite-size programmes). but the trend has reversed – with a 7% drop this year and the current cuts will bear heavily on older learners. Yet their needs get little policy focus. They deserve better – and so, sooner or later, will we ourselves.

14 October 2005

Why society needs awkward citizens
by Alan Tuckett
Section: Viewpoint; Further Education. Issue 4656, p4

THERE WAS a passage in Gordon Brown's eulogy at Robin Cook's funeral where the chancellor remembered the support offered him by Cook, then an experienced tutor-organiser in the Workers' Educational Association, when Brown's WEA class had attracted just one person to the first meeting.

Malcolm Wicks, too, was fond of remembering the disappointment when no one arrived for his first class in north Yorkshire, until, a quarter of an hour after the advertised start time, the branch secretary came in. As he took off his bicycle clips he said, apparently: "I never thought sociology would take in Thirsk."

In my own experience, when I offered a class with few takers, I was reminded of the old children's nursery rhyme: "Miss Smarty had a party. No one came. Her brother had another, just the same." It was frustrating, and hard to avoid feeling that the fault was my own in failing to connect with the zeitgeist. The disappointment experienced by tutors who spend hours preparing for a class that does not run is real, and the casual employment of most tutors means it is a disappointment reinforced too often by loss of earnings.

However, what is interesting here is not that some classes fail to recruit enough participants to be viable. It is, rather, that, like Neil Kinnock or Rhodes Boyson before them, major politicians recognised early on that a democracy is enriched by people working together to understand the forces shaping our future, and that learning and reflection are key dimensions in the political process.

The party conference season offered a reminder of the size of the challenges we face – to secure a sustainable future; to address the challenges arising from changing global economic conditions; and to find ways of living together in increasingly diverse communities. These issues have implications for what we do in our family and neighbourhood life, in the ways we organise our communities, and for national and international policy. Yet, as John Field notes in his excellent study *Social Capital and Lifelong Learning*, activists in the environmental movement, or in the campaign to 'Make Poverty History', learn as they go.

While the tutorial group and the study circle played important roles in the women's movement and in the earlier rise of trade unionism, they are little in evidence with the newer social movements. Rather, like people at work, many activists now prefer to learn on the job. I do not think, though, that this absolves adult educators from an engagement with political education.

Seriously useless learning

It may be that participation in social movements works for those who have already decided what they think. But what of the bulk of the population? What opportunities now exist to find out what you think, through dialogue with others? There are, of course, areas where such discourse is flourishing. The resilience of the residential colleges, the energies of voluntary sector organisations and the welcome resurgence of confidence shown by the WEA, are all testament to the continuing need for public education. Broadcasters, too, play an important role in securing an informed debate – but hardly one where dialogue with learners is developed.

I was heartened by the announcement of the Edinburgh conference, 'Dissenting Adults: Learning for Awkward Citizens', which takes place on 26 November at Moray House. Overall, though, there can be no doubt that opportunities to foster active, critical citizenship have a declining place in lifelong learning policies.

Yet we need awkward citizens every bit as much as we need a skilled workforce to test existing policies and come up with better ways of doing things. This is not a task to be delegated to think tanks. And all the blame for the marginalisation of such work cannot sit with government or its funding agencies. Some must lie with local providers, who move at the speed of light to adapt to changing priorities.

Nowhere is this clearer than in the spectacular decline over the past couple of years in the volume of 'other' further education offered in colleges. Of course, public money needs to be focused in the main on priority programmes. But where are all the learners displaced by the rush to certification to get the chance to learn? Where, too, will tomorrow's Gordon Brown or Robin Cook look to support the creation of an enlightened democracy? Education for citizenship – awkward citizenship – is every bit as important for adults, as for children, and we need urgently to rethink how best we support it.

11 November 2005
How Gordon can sort out funding
by Alan Tuckett
Section: Analysis; Further Education; Opinion. Issue 4660, p4

THE CURRENT funding crisis is well aired in these pages. It results from the success of providers in meeting public policy priorities. When Labour came to power in 1997, with 'education, education, education' as its three top priorities, the prime minister's concern clearly lay with school funding and performance. But, for David Blunkett, the mantra included a need to make lifelong learning accessible to those previously excluded.

Providers responded impressively to widening participation and, after the hair shirt of Labour's first two years, money increased and participation grew.

The Achilles heel, throughout the government's eight years in office, has been the overall volume of investment by the private sector and, in particular, by medium- and small-sized businesses; and in the British disease of investing more in those who have already had the benefits of extended education.

It is now 15 years since the Confederation of British Industry first complained of "the long tail of underachievement" in the UK economy – yet it is the comparative paucity of business-funded training that keeps the UK well short of the norm in the Organisation for Economic Co-operation & Development league tables of overall investment in post-compulsory education. The skills strategy sets out to address that concern but, like every government initiative for the past quarter of a century, its approach depends on the voluntary participation of employers and, in my view, overall, it isn't working. Much of the take-up of the employment training pilots so far has been by firms already training – in some areas 80 to 90% of the public funding just displaces money employers were spending previously, or would have had to to meet new statutory requirements.

Meanwhile, 46% of the 1.3m workers in the National Health Service still get fewer than two days training a year. With that background, and the impending impact of demographic change on many sectors of the economy, it seems short-sighted to cut public provision for adults.

Yet the Learning & Skills Council has little choice, since it has a cash limited budget, and the numbers of expensive younger students are rising, for the next two or three years, and one school based 16-to-19 student displaces ten part-time adults. So, providers' past success in meeting government goals to increase participation will lead over the next couple of years to a million or more adults losing their places. The policy may lead to the books being balanced, but it will surely lead to outcomes which are not in the public interest.

What is striking is how the government responds to this problem compared with its approach in other areas. Take school dinners – and the £280m found overnight, in response to the policy failure exposed by Jamie Oliver's television series. Look at foot and mouth, which was a crisis that had its roots in the de-regulation of the meat trade, and the lowering of health standards in the Eighties and Nineties. Faced with a problem that blew a hole in the budget of the Department of the Environment, the government properly stepped in and found the money. Or take the deeply unpopular, and questionably legal, adventure in Iraq. There, billions of pounds are found, at short notice, and in excess of the Ministry of Defence's budgets, to fund the war and its chaotic aftermath. That expenditure flowed from the misplaced belief that Iraq was developing weapons of mass destruction. Extraordinary, then, to read reports which suggest that a further £20bn will be needed to pay for a replacement for the UK's own weapons of mass destruction – even though we shall have no independent use of them. What foot and mouth and Iraq have in common is that events made clear that public funding was inadequate to meet the need – just as budgets in post-school education are clearly inadequate to meet the range of learner demands on them now. Surely the sensible thing to do is to find short-term money from Treasury reserves?

As finances are tight, here are two suggestions on where to find money from in the longer run. Recognise that employers respond to regulation – and make investment in staff development a pre-condition for trading in Britain. Contribute to arms reduction, and give a boost to the UK economy and to civic harmony by shifting that £20bn earmarked for nuclear weapons to create the infrastructure for a really world-class education and training system for all ages. Both measures are practicable – so, Gordon, why not announce them in your pre-budget statement?

9 December 2005
Foster forgot about the adults
by Alan Tuckett
Section: Viewpoint; Opinion; Further Education. Issue 4664, p4

THAT'S THAT then. Ruth Kelly has welcomed the Foster report. The education secretary made clear in answer to a Parliamentary question that Sir Andrew had addressed the main issues confronting further education colleges in his national inquiry. She took on the chin the report's criticisms of the Department for Education & Skills and the Learning & Skills Council – and promised a government response in the spring.

There is much to welcome in Foster, not least that he resisted the temptation to call for the post-16 sector – colleges and all – to be restructured. His focus on workforce development is all the more welcome because the training needs of teachers, lecturers and managers have been neglected for far too long.

The National Institute of Adult Continuing Education (NIACE) also welcomed Sir Andrew's call to listen more closely to learners. However, many in the sector face a daunting challenge in trying to give due weight to the views of all students – full-time and part-time, younger and adult. There is also a need to find ways of consulting potential learners.

Foster reflects a wide consensus when he says the main job of colleges and other providers is vocational education: preparing people for work and supporting education and training in the workplace. *Eight in Ten*, the recent report of the inquiry into adult learning in colleges and sponsored by NIACE, agreed that these were key tasks.

But our inquiry added a third task, representing a long and proud tradition in colleges: "Sustaining and enhancing cultural value". This has grown up in response to the demands of communities around the colleges. As Foster's own evidence from focus groups of learners young and old made clear, learners have more complex aims and recognise a broader range of achievements than those captured in government targets.

While Foster genuflects towards the need to widen participation, he gives it little attention. Yet so many of the people needed for the jobs of the next decade are under-represented in education and training. That may not be true of economic migrants in Esol (English for speakers of other languages) classes. But it certainly is the case with settled women from linguistic minority groups, and with people on incapacity benefits and older people inside and outside the workforce.

Then, despite telling us this was a report on what the post-16 sector must do over the next ten to 15 years, Foster is all but silent on the demographic timebomb. The Learning & Skills Council anticipates 500,000 adults being lost to FE over the next two years. We expect significantly more, since colleges, for understandable reasons, avoid the risks associated with charging fees by cutting more adult work than the LSC planners predict. That has certainly been the case over the past two years.

Meanwhile, the shortfall in labour market entrants that is already emerging in several sectors will accelerate, while we build capacity for 16 to 19-year-olds that will be surplus to need just three years from now.

The failure to think hard about the balance of funding for young and adult learners is the key weakness in Foster's thinking, and paralleled by much of the thinking in the Department for Education & Skills and LSC.

It is, of course, vital to give young people a good start in life, but a college system sensitive to the labour market must be better able to meet the needs of adults over the next decade. To do that, the system needs to support study that allows adults to fit learning in among the huge demands on their time. The new framework for achievement may help people build the qualifications they need over time.

But, until that is available, the level 2 (GCSE-equivalent) entitlement must be open to those only able to study for partial qualifications. Therefore, something must be done to secure the cash to pay for it – including more funds from employers and individuals. By contrast with Foster, there seems hardly to be a report from elsewhere in government that fails to recognise the adult skills and learning issue.

The Turner report on pensions makes firm recommendations that the LSC should give priority to training older workers. The Leitch committee's analysis recognises clearly that the skills adults need are central to the future health of the economy. The national mental health strategy recognises the impor-

Seriously useless learning

tance of adult education in preventing mental illness health, and in helping with recuperation.

Why then do we find it so hard to get adult learners a fair hearing in the post-school education and training policy debate?

13 January 2006
Freakish secret world of statistics
by Alan Tuckett
Section: Viewpoint; Opinion; Further Education. Issue 4668, p4

WHEN I told my daughter that I had had fun over the new year reading a book on economics, she said it was confirmation that I have become a sad case. "Bad enough to read the dismal science in the dog days of February," she said. "But in the festive season? Get a life."

Freakonomics, though, is an economics book with a difference. Like the work of the New Economics Forum in the UK, it recognises that, while conventional economics are good for some things, they are not so good at others.

Grand theory is eschewed. Economics, Levitt and Dubner suggest, is about the world as it actually is, morality and politics about how we might want it to be. And to my mind there is no doubt that adult learners' interests can be well served by the kind of divergent thinking Levitt and Dubner develop in a book full of memorable stories.

Their technique is to ask unusual questions, and to look for data that will help in answering them. So, while mayor Giuliani and his chief of police have been celebrated for their policy of zero tolerance of crime in New York, *Freakonomics* notes that crime rates were dropping in the USA before those innovative policies were introduced. Once the increase in police numbers was factored out, it concludes, New York's crime reduction was in line with national averages.

What, then, might account for the drop? The authors' analysis suggests that the major factor was the legalisation of abortion some 20 years earlier, reducing dramatically the number of unwanted poorer children born, and cutting the number of people most likely to be recruited to crime.

Other chapters ask why crack dealers live at home with their mothers (apart from a few, they do not earn enough to move out), and note how much higher the risks are of a child facing a fatal accident when visiting a friend with a swimming pool in the garden than a friend with a gun in the house.

They note that many of us have a fear of flying. More people die on the roads than in aeroplane crashes. But if you look at the hours spent travelling, road and air travel offer broadly comparable levels of risk, and both are safer than travelling on water.

Why, then, the fear of flying? *Freakonomics* suggests that we worry about risks where we have no control over what happens far more than those equal or greater risks where we have agency ourselves.

It is instructive to apply that principle to government thinking about lifelong learning policy. Everyone agrees that it makes economic and social sense to increase the skills base of the British workforce. As the interim report of the Leitch review of skills needs makes clear, increased investment in people with high, intermediate and low-level skills will be needed right through to 2020.

There is increasing acceptance, too, that while qualifications are the best proxy we currently have for the skills of the labour force, they are not an adequate one.

Employers highlight the need for teamworking skills, communication and problem-solving. Workers tell us that they like to learn incrementally and informally from their peers or managers, and that formal instruction has a place, but one much less central than our policy planners presume. We also know that many of the jobs we will be doing in 15 years' time have yet to be invented, making it hard to train for them. Why, then, is the welcome investment in strengthening the skills of workers and potential workers below technician level focused exclusively on the achievement of 'full fat' level 2 (GCSE equivalent) qualifications, often narrowly focused on technical skills fit for today's, rather than tomorrow's, economy?

Reading Levitt and Dubner, the suggestion occurs that we focus on the level 2 target because it can be measured, whether or not it is entirely fit for purpose.

For many in the workforce, this will result in no more than a confirmation of the skill levels workers already possess. Others will be excluded as a result of the inflexibility of the timing and structure of our qualifications, and the credit system to counter this still seems years off.

What is to be done? Sir Mike Tomlinson's report offered a major clue. Re-thinking the vocational curriculum for adults and young people alike would make for a good start, offering vocational students the breadth of studies we take for granted in schools and in higher education.

Trusting learners would help, too. As Foster recognised, they are central to the system, and should be listened to. They often understand better than the educators what studies will make a difference to their lives.

But, of course, that strategy brings risks. Since learners make choices that the planners do not expect, it is undoubtedly safer to stick with the targets. But is it wiser?

Seriously useless learning

17 February 2006

Migrant workers face language crisis

by Alan Tuckett

Section: Further Education; Viewpoint; Opinion. Issue 4643, p2

DRAZUTE ZARONAITE plays a key role helping migrant workers find decently paid jobs in rural Lincolnshire – where eight in ten people earn their living from farming, fishing and food processing. As a qualified senior social welfare officer in Lithuania, she was well respected and well paid, but she wanted to broaden her horizons. So, when Lithuania joined the European Union, Drazute took advantage of the new labour market mobility and moved to Britain.

Her job, which she loves, involves not only finding work for migrants but also helping them relate to people in the local communities. Everything seemed to be going fine. When Drazute arrived in the UK, she got a job and wrote to the Home Office to register as a permanent resident.

That was when her troubles began. So far, the Home Office has retained her passport for three months whilst it reviews her application. As a result, Drazute is unable to provide the proof of identity her bank requires for large withdrawals. With no passport, she cannot get a driving licence to replace one that expired. She could not change jobs – even if she wanted to – and she can't visit Lithuania (or anywhere beyond Dover), take on a mortgage or register with a doctor. Despite her key role at work, Drazute is left wondering if her identity has been taken, too.

She told her story at the recent national conference on migration, organised by the National Institute of Adult Continuing Education to mark the start of the European Year of Workers' Mobility. It illustrates a wide range of problems facing migrants and refugees.

The arrival of 280,000 migrant workers from the accession states, added to families of refugees and settled migrants, increases demand for overstretched English for speakers of other languages courses. In London, only a quarter of those who might require Esol classes get them. More courses and qualified tutors are needed. This puts more pressure on the Learning & Skills Councils' adult learning budgets, which are already being cut at an alarming rate.

Until now, Esol has been funded in the Skills for Life programme. It seems reasonable to expect highly skilled economic migrants, their recruitment agencies or employers to pay the full cost of language studies.

However, what if they can't afford to pay fees up front? Will we need to recover costs once they are in jobs? What if they go home, after a period of work and study? Will we chase them for outstanding loans? To refuse highly-skilled refugees access to the courses they need, or to charge the same rates for higher education courses as we charge overseas students stops many getting the very jobs that make full use of their skills – which this country needs.

Tony McNulty, minister of state for immigration and citizenship, has highlighted the gap between current priorities for Esol support and the practical help workers need, with the loss of skills essential to the UK economy. The current inquiry by NIACE into Esol will give helpful advice on the balance of needs for different groups and bring maximum benefit to individuals and the economy.

Refugees also have problems proving they are qualified – a difficulty everyone at the conference on migration recognised. People fleeing to escape persecution seldom arrive in the UK with a full portfolio of evidence of previous qualifications and experience. Unfortunately, employers look for UK references, and an account of the skills people have.

When migrants seek such recognition from professional bodies controlling qualifications, they are often set far more stringent tests than those set for 'domestic' professionals without evidence of qualifications.

In theory, labour markets are open; in practice, this is rarely so. Yet there are many inspiring illustrations of work involving a range of agencies – education, health, welfare – in partnership, to overcome such problems. Alas, as the conference heard, they are usually backed by short-term finance. Population changes and increasingly global markets will lead to steadily rising levels of migration. This is not new – as Australians in Earl's Court and the Bangladeshi community in Tower Hamlets illustrate – but the pattern and scale are different. The UK needs good educational strategies quickly, if we to bring maximum benefits to society and migrants themselves, whether high skilled or low skilled. The message of the conference on migration was that there are green shoots, but we urgently need an overall strategy.

Things are starting to happen. Effective education and training strategies to help migrants and refugees into work are emerging from the NIACE-led development programme, Progress GB, launched last June. Good practice has been identified which can now be shared. It shows common needs and challenges among the different groups – not least the need for good guidance for learners, employers and intermediary agencies. But, overall, a national strategy is needed, with cash to back it.

Everything must change

THE NEED for a public debate over the balance of public (tax) and private spending on adult education and training had become more urgent than ever by the spring of 2006. As everyone awaited the government's response to Foster, which education secretary Ruth Kelly had accepted in principle, there were growing concerns. Tuckett reiterated that Foster mentioned little about adult learning, unlike Leitch – in his report *Skills in the UK: the long-term challenge* – who said it was a must in order to prepare people for the new jobs. Then Chris Humphries, director general at City & Guilds, piled on the pressure, saying it would take 10% of GDP to develop an effective lifelong learning strategy.

A report of the NIACE inquiry, *Eight in Ten*, identified a third strand along-side employability and workforce development – sustaining and enhancing cultural values. But this was most vulnerable in the face of the cuts (typically, 16% in LEAs and £2.5m in a college such as Newham). Meanwhile, Esol was cut and teachers were quitting the Skills for Life programme.

Tuckett pointed out that there was still no career structure for teachers whose job was to help the harder to reach – essential in order to satisfy Leitch demands. On this front, he said, Foster did identify the need for seri-ous investment by FE in developing its own workforce. The Retro project, managed by NIACE for a year, gave a model; funded by the education department, it attracted new and inactive teachers, with peer-group mentor-ing, getting them into jobs. It showed that regional planning for teacher supply worked. He hoped that the coming white paper would include Retro-type staff development: "The policy paper *Every Child Matters* captured the aspirations of government. Let the FE paper be called Every Adult Matters – please."

In May, he pointed to what he saw as a contradiction that, while age discrimination at work had been outlawed, education and training opportu-nities to get the over-30s into work were being axed. There was an overall sharp decline while numbers of young people in learning grew. "Free tuition for all 19-to-25s is a good thing," he wrote, "but it is all part of moves to concentrate on under-30s and it will be paid for by cutting their childcare and transport support. The divide which reduced HE support for adults is spreading to FE." The white paper *Raising Skills, Improving Life Chances*, in response to Foster, put colleges on the pathway to greater specialisation and more emphasis on skills for work. The employer training pilots had spawned Train to Gain – targeted financial support for basic skills training in the workplace – and this was to grow, diverting cash from FE to employers. Tuckett issued a warning which became a prediction that would add to damaging criticisms for the Labour administration in the long run. "Expansion of Train to Gain is a good thing, provided it's not money employers would have spent anyway," he said.

So, would the white paper offer the necessary solutions and meet the range of urgent demands?

> *"Two 'timebombs' – the ageing population and rapid technological change – demand action for social and economic development. We all need to think how to support mass education for adults, with wider participation and greater achievement, sorting out who pays for what, when and where. Despite its strengths, the white paper does not take us far in addressing that task."*

As Tuckett knew Gordon Brown would be seeking big efficiency savings, he exhorted him to look as critically at schools and universities as he was at FE. Also, there was, he said, clearer than ever a need to support informal learning. But, by June, it was clear from pronouncements by Alan Johnson, education secretary, that the first target, yet again, was 'other' adult learning. Johnson, who had been a very effective FHE minister, was welcomed with open arms on his return as secretary of state – except for one big difference in emphasis.

Like so many ministers before and after him, he resorted to cheap shots to distract the media from the deepening crisis his department was facing. A senior official in his department admitted in confidence to the *TES* at the time that this was "precisely Johnson's purpose". Thus the education secretary made his assault – in good humour, as ever, to get a laugh and sweeten the pill – when he made his jibe about 'more plumbing, less pilates". But Tuckett would not let him off the hook. Johnson was continuing a tradition, he said:

> *"There is a deep-seated prejudice in Britain where administrators and politicians are sceptical of the learning people pick for themselves."*

Each generation singled out courses for opprobrium: tap dancing on the rates, willow weaving, under-water basket-weaving, flower arranging.

> *"In substance, Mr Johnson's speech was about re-balancing. In tone, it*

endorsed the loss of one in three adult places in further education over three years."

September would see the national roll-out of Train to Gain with government funds for individuals, primarily those in the 25-plus age band who did not already have a full level 2 qualification. In 2008, it would grow further to form part of the government's Employee Responsiveness training programme, by which time the volume of criticisms over deadweight would be deafening. It would also come at a price for the most disadvantaged and time-poor since it would spell the end of many short courses.

But at this stage, the Labour government was not going to be dissuaded from its utilitarian objectives. Leitch and the Treasury had defined the road to a skilled UK for the year 2020 and, in order to continue down that road, every department's objectives must change in order to maximise chances of success. Tuckett remained unconvinced and he was not alone in harbouring serious doubts.

There was evidence from a NIACE/Age Concern inquiry, Learning in Later Life, that employers were responding to skills shortages by outsourcing to the Indian sub-continent and hiring workers from the EU. There were very timely warnings about the changes in migration patterns, with Bulgarians and Romanians able to take advantage of EU labour mobility from January 2007. Polish communities had already settled. Was it really better than investing in post-school learning? What about Chinese cockle pickers who drowned in Morecambe Bay – able to phone China but unable to communicate for help here?

"As evidence to our inquiry makes clear, we are still dealing with the failure to support earlier migration from India, Pakistan and Bangladesh. A Department for Work & Pensions paper shows that just 4% of Bangladeshi and 28% of Pakistani women outside the labour force have the English fluency needed for successful engagement in it. It will be too late to start planning when the migrants move in."

After accepting two-thirds of the recommendations in a NIACE inquiry into Esol, Bill Rammell made a significant impact but only after a compromise, cutting all courses for asylum seekers among other changes. "While making a welcome commitment to prioritising those in need, the government decision risks further punishing the poor."

Lord Leitch published his final report, *Prosperity for all in the Global Economy: World Class Skills*, in December 2006. It called for the wholesale shake-up of the skills agenda with the departments for education and work and pensions, and the careers service, working in partnership. He set ambitious aims for literacy and numeracy, intermediate skills and HE expansion and called for a tripling of spending on basic skills and HE expansion to include the ageing workforce. Leitch also prescribed demand-led, employer-driven funding. "Was he right," asked Tuckett, "given the employers' track record?" It was a question that would still not be fully resolved four years into the next government, even though in 2006, he said, worrying evidence already suggested otherwise, as the fall in adult learners approached 1m, support for Train to Gain proved patchy and evidence from the Esol debate showed employers would only pay for job-specific skills. When asked in February 2007 whether he thought Train to Gain would work, Tuckett replied: "We must hope it will work since it has been purchased at a great price – diminished choice for older people."

In May, however, things were worse than expected. A NIACE/Association of Colleges prediction of 1m decline came in not three but two years. Moreover, Train to Gain netted just 89,000 new learners, 3,000 places for people with learning difficulties were lost, over-60s numbers halved and pre-entry level Skills for Life courses were axed. "Why has this happened when there is actually safeguarded funding for these adult groups?" asked Tuckett.

"Because of the summary ending of short courses. While every self-respecting professional is booking in for intensive one-day briefings as part of their competence updating, the tap has been turned off for Saturday schools and other short courses. Gone are the day schools on 'Reasons for the war in Iraq' or 'How to claim working tax credits'. Out, too, are courses such as an 'Introduction to Shakespeare's sonnets', or a 'Quick introduction to PowerPoint'."

They included a whole tranche of courses essential to mounting the skills ladder. Even so, with no state-funded short courses and 500,000 fewer adults taking any learning at all, a very stoical Tuckett found room for optimism in the work of the union leaning movement.

With government departmental changes and the arrival of John Denham, "a man of principle", as secretary of state for innovation, universities and skills, Tuckett was again more optimistic. Denham had made adult learning one of the government's four 'top priorities' many years earlier and, therefore, brought hope. Denham would carry out a thorough inquiry into the potential for informal adult learning, commission the U3A to create a training guide for informal adult learning tutoring and accepted that worthwhile learning need not be pinned to a qualification. It was part of a vision shared by David Blunkett that should have been pursued a decade earlier following *The Learning Age*. Unfortunately, it arrived amid a groundswell of cynicism and criticisms that it was an act of desperation rather than renewal.

Seriously useless learning

After all, wrote Tuckett, the Leitch/Forster agenda with contestability and sector skills councils deciding which qualifications count for public money, "is an analysis that leaves little room for creativity, democratic citizenship, the celebration of diversity, or widening participation". Train to Gain had achieved only 60% of expected take-up, while the NIACE annual survey showed overall participation down from 55% to 48% among part-time workers. Employers were proving hard to reach:

> "On the whole, the re-balancing of FE sector investment flowing from the skills strategy has shown little evidence that employers have been stimulated to increase investment, while individual learners have lost out. Meanwhile, the financial pressures on the LSC suggest adults face further misery with popular courses replaced by workplace provision that employers are not yet taking up, and routes back to the labour market disappearing for people a long way from work. That is just the kind of innovation and risk-taking the new department would do well to resist."

In January 2008, Tuckett reported on the NIACE/*TES* conference, FE in the 21st Century, which praised what achievements there had been around level 2 skills for life and apprenticeships; with Esol, though that was now capped; and the helpful consultation paper on how to support local decision making. But the verdict, voiced by Geoff Hall, principal of New College Nottingham, was "the rush for numbers leads to problems with quality and accountability", and financial irregularities that had been seen with individual learning accounts (ILAs) and Train to Gain.

If measures to explore a fuller role for informal learning came late in the day for Labour, so too did its proposal in March to row back from central government control and replace the LSC with the Skills Funding Agency and remove planning powers and micromanagement. It was a bit late in the day to restore Labour's reputation in government and – without a more strategic role for local authorities, said Tuckett – to restore the vast amounts of adult learning that had been cut.

As ever, it was raw politics that moved minsters faster on this agenda. After the drubbing in the local elections, Labour decided to listen and Denham launched the consultation paper on informal learning. Whitehall departments would co-operate with an expansion of reading groups and classes in libraries, museums and galleries. The U3A was on the rise and WEA had seen a renaissance. Voluntary groups saw prospects of state funds. "But there was much ground to make up with 1.5m lost adult learners and cuts to disabled classes, now dependent on a diminished safeguarded budget." Adult Learners' Week had the usual testimonies of restored dignity and departure from a life of crime – all "a reminder that quality of life has a claim on the public purse".

By contrast, there was more bad news for the government since there were now strong indicators that Train to Gain was substantially 'dead weight' and was replacing training costs employers previously paid for themselves. Furthermore, overall participation rates continued to fall and the proportion of employers who said they trained staff dropped from 42% to 38%. Post-25s, part-timers and the least skilled were seeing the sharpest fall in learning. Increased employer apathy and cuts in popular college courses compounded the felony. Tuckett concluded: "Government policies are not resulting in the expansion of learning opportunities that the country needs." Corroboration for this came in May 2009 when the UK Commission for Employment & Skills report, *Ambition 2020*, showed we were a long way from the Leitch aspiration to be in the top quartile of the 30 richest nations for adult learning, and the NIACE annual survey showed trends, far from creating fairness, gave most opportunities to those who succeeded first time round.

Labour were routed in the May 2010 general election and, for a brief period, the Coalition government made all the right noises for supporters of informal and 'other' adult learning. John Hayes, FE and skills minister, his boss Vince Cable and prime minister David Cameron, all piped up about 'strengthening bonds of community' and proposed an additional £100m for learning to be chosen by people themselves. The consultation document, *A Simplified Further Education and Skills Funding System and Methodology*, acknowledged "the need to balance the sensitivity to the diversity of learners and employer needs". Some £200m was cut from Train to Gain, part of the new government's planned £6.2bn austerity cuts for 2010-11.

Most of all, the safeguarded adult and community budget survived. But the conditions pushed Tuckett's stoicism to the limit. "Now it covers personal and community development, neighbourhood learning in deprived communities, family literacy, numeracy and language and wider family learning. Now online provision has been added and uncertificated provision. Where will it stop and will cash be adjusted upwards? We need safeguarding to be properly funded," he said appealing to all to say so loudly in the consultations. There were smaller than expected cuts to post-19 FE. Also, following the Browne review, HE loans were extended to part-time students on at least 25% timetable. Tuckett saw this as something of a red letter day following a 20-year battle backing equality for part-timers. The price was, however, a Treasury demand for more rigorous evidence showing initiatives reaching the marginalised and promoting Big Society.

It was soon clear that, despite the early rhetoric, the neoliberal economic ideology of the Coalition would plough the same furrow as Labour's utilitari-

Seriously useless learning

anism. Tuckett pointed to many of the negative aspects of the new strategy as "cuts to arts, social sciences and humanities threaten their survival for part-timers," he said. "The Skills Investment Strategy argues for basic skills to be fully funded, but the literacy rate is cut by a third and Esol by half, so the new funding and policy will have little impact on the 500,000 with greatest literacy needs."

There was a feeling that nothing had changed other than "for the worse". Colleges, particularly in areas of urban deprivation, tell of insurmountable difficulties in claiming their full adult-learning allocations from the Skills Funding Agency. This is the result of a toxic combination of changes to the eligibility criteria for fee reductions for learners, with cuts in the funding rates for those in literacy and Esol classes. It came on top of reductions planned by the previous government, the re-balancing of budgets attendant on the end of Train to Gain and increased investment in apprentices.

"Previously, they were poorly served by a regime that rewarded provision for those needing less help. Now the rate cut makes it difficult for institutions to commit the resources needed to make a difference."

Commentaries
10 March 2006 to 22 March 2014

10 March 2006

Every adult must matter to us, too
by Alan Tuckett
Section: Viewpoint; Opinion; Further education. Issue 4676, p4

EDUCATION WHITE papers were once rare beasts, but now they seem to come along almost as often as the Clapham omnibus. Since 2002, we have had *Success for All* and the two skills strategies. We are now awaiting another, the government's response to the Foster report. When the report was published, education secretary Ruth Kelly told us the government accepted Sir Andrew Foster's overall analysis – so it will be interesting to see what that means in practice. He focused on colleges' vocational education mission, but ignored demographic change.

The interim report of the Leitch review on the future skills needs of the country, by contrast, makes clear that the key to strengthening Britain's skills base lies in the education and training of adults. It argues, too, that even if the government achieves all its targets for skills, we will be only a mediocre performer internationally.

Chris Humphries, director general of City & Guilds, says that to develop an effective lifelong learning strategy would cost 10% of the country's gross domestic product. Clearly, the state won't meet all of those costs, the appetite for public taxation being what it is. But what should the balance be? There is an urgent need for a public debate on this which, with luck, the white paper might stimulate. I'd be keen to see a proposal for licences to practice, given their success in the construction and care sectors.

When colleges narrow their mission to vocational education, what will happen to the other things they now do? Who will hold the mission for what the NIACE-sponsored inquiry, Eight in Ten, identified as a third mission alongside access to employability and workforce development – to sustain and enhance cultural values?

Judging by this year's early allocations to local authority adult education services, education for citizenship, community development, and cultural enrichment look vulnerable, as LEAs nurse an average 16% cut in their FE budgets.

Prospects for adults in colleges, too, are bleak if Newham in London is in any way typical. There, cuts of £2.5m in post-19 budgets will inevitably mean cuts in English for speakers of other languages, and other basic skills.

Meanwhile, there is an acute shortage of English for speakers of other

Seriously useless learning

languages provision in the capital, and evidence of too many teachers leaving the Skills for Life programme across the country. There is, still, for all the success of the first phases of the Skills for Life campaign, an inadequate career route for such teachers. Too few full-time jobs, too little serious and sustained training, too little mentoring. Yet the challenges pile up for the next phase of the campaign – as we reach harder to serve learners, and develop skills for life in more workplaces, and with learners whose primary educational goal is not literacy, numeracy or language. And there are large numbers of people, already trained as teachers, who are not working in the profession.

Thankfully, Sir Andrew Foster made clear that FE needs serious investment in its own workforce. I hope the white paper will identify ring-fenced money for training. Otherwise, the risk is that the investment won't be made. But the white paper needs to explore innovative developments for increasing the numbers and the diversity of the teaching workforce.

The Retro project, which the NIACE managed for a year, provides a model worth building on, particularly to address the shortage in Esol teaching.

The project, funded by the Department for Education & Skills, focused on recruiting and training new and inactive teachers and getting them into jobs. It sought to increase the number of generic and specialist training programmes at level 4 (higher education) in each region, to build the numbers of teacher trainers, and to bring together the infrastructure for teacher supply in the three regions in which it was run.

Its lessons were stark. Regional strategic planning for teacher supply increases value for money. Retro showed the need for much more sustained investment and, alas, the continuing reluctance of sector institutions to invest in full-time staff. Not for the first time, the effectiveness of peer-group mentoring – and the value of reflective practice in strengthening teaching skills – was demonstrated. The Higher Education Funding Council needs to consider how to expand Skills for Life teacher training across the country. Government agencies must give sustained attention to staff development. I hope the white paper will include Retro 2, or something like it, not just for Skills for Life, but for all those other curriculum areas that need mature entrants. When something works, back it.

The policy paper *Every Child Matters* captured the aspirations of government. Let the FE paper be called Every Adult Matters – please.

5 May 2006

Too old to study once you hit 30

by Alan Tuckett

Section: Viewpoint; Opinion; Further Education. Issue 4684, p4

RECENT LEGISLATION outlawed age discrimination, yet here we are with rules on spending that block educational opportunities for adults over 30. There is plenty of help for people under that age. But, after that, support is distinctly harder to find.

This may not be the intention of government policy, but it is the effect – reinforced by the FE white paper. Latest official figures show that FE numbers on courses funded by the Learning & Skills Council fell 5.3% in the year to October 1, 2005. While the number of students under 19 went up 4.4%, overall post-19 participation fell 9% to 1.5m. Numbers decreased in every age group over 30. Those aged 45 to 49 fell 16%, participation among 55 to 59-year-olds fell 18.4% and numbers of adults over 60 in FE dropped 23.8%. This compounds a significant decline in the number over 60 in the previous year.

How does this decline help create the kind of learning society envisaged in earlier government policy statements such as *The Learning Age*? How, also, will this help give older people the educational opportunities they need to keep productively in work – when colleges are losing them in droves? Remember that adults must fill two-thirds of all jobs over the next decade. Politicians tell us it is all a matter of priorities. But numbers on full level 2 (GCSE-equivalent) courses beloved of government are up by just 3.4%, and those on full level 3 (A-level) by 6.8%, whilst Skills for Life courses – where the need is greatest – have seen a drop of almost 6%. Measures in the recent white paper will make things worse for the over-30s.

An entitlement to free tuition up to A-level for 19 to 25s is, of course, a good thing. It helps late learners catch up, as the skills task force reported five years ago. But it is all part of bigger moves to concentrate available cash on the under-30s.

That will be paid for by cutting childcare and transport support for older learners. The divide, which reduced higher education opportunities for adults, is spreading to FE.

The biggest cut to adult opportunities will be in 'other' FE. Much of it is at the most basic levels of need where the white paper promises some help.

But without the long-delayed credit framework, promised in successive white papers to sort out these courses, routes for adults will have closed down before the cavalry arrives to put things right.

Other good things for adults in the white paper include the return of individual learning accounts. It is not easy for governments to revisit past

Seriously useless learning

embarrassments, such as the security failures first time round. But they did raise motivation and encouraged otherwise reluctant adults back into education. What a pity the pilots are limited to people seeking level 3 qualifications. Why not a learning MoT for anyone over 50?

Welcome too are plans for the increased role of FE in HE, more students on governing bodies and increased cash for workforce development. The expansion of Train to Gain schemes for employers is also good news – provided the cash is extra to what is already spent by private companies and not a substitute for it. There is no doubt that many adults who missed out in initial education get their best chance to learn at work. But, overall, measures in the white paper fall far short of what is needed.

Two 'timebombs' – the ageing population and rapid technological change – demand action for social and economic development. We all need to think how to support mass education for adults, with wider participation and greater achievement, sorting out who pays for what, when and where. Despite its strengths, the white paper does not take us far in addressing that task.

19 May 2006
Rules of engagement

*Adult learning courses, in all their shapes and forms, have a core curriculum – building confidence and curiosity. But 15 years on, **Alan Tuckett** finds that financial restraints are still on the agenda.*

Section: Overview; Issue 4686, p2

THE FIRST Adult Learners' Week was held in 1992. It began at a time of struggle, when adults had to assert that they could be the best judges of what was worth studying, and that they had a right to claim modest investment from government to back them in their choices. This year, too, the week arrives when adult learning opportunities are at risk for too many people. As a result, once again it will generate intense debate.

Adult Learners' Week in 1992 was the culmination of a long winter of active and successful lobbying by adult students to make sure that adults had a right to expect courses for personal and community development as well as those leading to qualifications. It was born of an alliance between broadcasters committed to the broad education of the population, funders, practitioners and, above all, learners.

The week was featured on all the television channels, on radio, in the press and public, telling the extraordinary stories of how adults used learning to transform their lives, and describing how the winners of awards had used their learning to have an impact on their families, workplaces and communities. It touched a nerve.

Learners' experiences, stories told in very different ways, revealed common themes. Adult learning has a core curriculum – the building of confidence and curiosity – but it covers all sorts of subjects and takes all sorts of forms. And it became clear, too, that you can't tell the purpose of the student from the title of the course. People find modest art classes therapeutic when recovering from mental health problems. Older people use classes to keep alert, to develop new skills and to contribute to maintaining the fabric of our shared civic life. Workers solve problems at the workbench or in the office through learning together. Young adults, failed by schooling, recover an appetite for learning and catch the confidence to take a second chance. Women returning to work use courses as a way to put a toe back in the water and explore their options; people with learning difficulties use classes to support and enhance independent living.

The variety of learners' experiences and the stories they tell have had their impact on policy. You can see it in the budget, however modest, for personal and community development funding, and in the recognition that skills in literacy, language and numeracy are the right of every adult. You see it in the robust questioning of ministers' priorities when MPs on the Commons education select committee ask about the impact of the current white paper on adults' opportunities.

Perhaps the greatest impact of the week, overall, has been on learner engagement. The major support the week enjoys from the European Social Fund is for promoting learning to encourage people to get skills to improve their employment chances. The Adult Learners' Week award winners Scott Cator, Peter Fewell and Julie Cayman, all supported by ESF, illustrate the effectiveness of that strategy. The Department for Education & Skills, its ministers and officials support the week each year, too, to promote participation.

There has been substantial growth in participation over the 15 years, fuelled in part by current learners acting as ambassadors encouraging others to take part. Recognition that people like you take part successfully is often a first step to giving yourself permission to take up learning again.

But there have to be classes to join so adults can take the second step and can turn intention into participation. And for too many adults, that second step is no longer available. The changes in funding of further education in the last couple of years have already had a major impact, with a drop of almost one in four people over 60 participating this year alone, and further narrowing of the range on offer in the pipeline for next year.

The plan to pay attention to 'foundation level' learning is welcome, and should offer relief – at least for learners wanting a pre-planned progression route towards qualifications for employability – 'level 2', in the jargon. But the plan seems to be to ask sector skills councils which courses below level 2

Seriously useless learning

they recognise as stepping stones towards a qualification. That is part of the answer.

However, it ignores the key lesson of 15 years of Adult Learners' Week, that learners' journeys take myriad forms. Surely we need, too, real learner-centred planning, and funding for courses that help key groups to take the first steps back into learning.

Some groups, which are not well represented at present – like older workers, people on incapacity benefit, women from ethnic minorities, ex-offenders, and recent migrants – are vital to the economy, because they are bound to be a major source of the labour to fill the jobs of the next decade.

Others will look to learning for reasons not connected directly with the labour market at all, including the army of volunteers who keep our civil society going. Voluntary action takes many forms – from the role grandparents play in family learning; to the people who keep faith communities vibrant; from local councillors to visitors in hospices; from local historians to match day stewards, and coaches for sports teams. It includes, too, of course the army of volunteers making the University of the Third Age such a success. All these groups have learning needs – so it is welcome that the current white paper promises a fresh look at how best to combine the range of initiatives and local resources available to support adult learning to flourish. But fresh thinking is not to be matched by a fresh financial strategy.

So 15 years in, facing cutbacks in further education funding for adults over 30, and the chance to shape the agenda for learning for personal and community development, there is ample opportunity to make this year's Adult Learners' Week an occasion for lobbying again. How much provision can you expect within reach of where you live? How much can you be expected to pay? And how much should we expect employers to pay?

Everyone recognises the state can't pay for everything – but how much should we spend on adult learning? And, within that, how much on learning at work, for work, or in the community? These are questions for all of us. Adult Learners' Week provides an ideal framework to address them, and, as ever examples aplenty of the return on investment and impact on people's lives.

26 May 2006
A central piece in the jigsaw
by Alan Tuckett
Section: Viewpoint; Opinion; Further education. Issue 4687, p4

ADULT LEARNERS' Week comes at a time when funding for further education is under intense pressure, with a tough government spending review.

It is imperative that we all help by making clear the economic and social importance of adult learning to the chancellor Gordon Brown, who is leading the review. As always, the Treasury will want substantial 'efficiency' savings. In education, this debate is likely to focus on the ambition to reduce by 40% the number of adults at work without level 2 qualifications – equivalent to five good GCSEs.

When discussing possible savings, the Department for Education & Skills must scrutinise school and university spending with the same scepticism as it does further education. Savings should be spread across the board. The Treasury must acknowledge there has never been sufficient public money invested at level 2 and below. Remember why this target was adopted. While level 2 is a springboard to higher levels of learning, individuals and employers saw little or no return on investing below level 3 (technician or A-level-equivalent). Therefore, government agreed to fund an entitlement to full level 2. Yet, even if all uncertificated 'other' adult courses were scrapped, there would still be inadequate public money to meet the target.

The Treasury should recognise that, without a better framework for assessing achievement, much of the success of the government's skills strategy goes unrecorded in the target. Overwhelmingly, adults study part-time, and pick up their achievements in bite-sized chunks. Remember, too, that the biggest group of people in work without such qualifications are already doing jobs requiring skills at level 2 or above.

Most importantly, the Treasury must recognise that qualifications are a proxy for the skills, knowledge, understanding and creativity that the country needs. As the Small Business Council never tires of saying, a huge amount of learning at work is informal, and many workers choose to learn from colleagues rather than formal courses. Part of the spending review debate must focus on how best to adapt the targets to include less formal learning. That, after all, is the whole point of education: adaptation in the light of what we have learned.

The Skills for Life target needs overhauling, too, despite being a success story. It ignores those in greatest need. We need more money and new 'sub-targets' for learners below entry level 2 and for the burgeoning numbers of students lacking the most basic English language and information and communications technology skills. They urgently need the right support.

How much we should pay remains a vexed question that needs resolution. Sorting out fees for individuals, and remissions policies that don't unintentionally reduce provision for people with disabilities must be priority of the spending review. Measures must also be introduced to ensure that employers share the burden of improving the skills of employees, since they will, without doubt, share the benefits.

It must be remembered that two in three of the jobs of the next ten years will be filled by people who are adults today – among them women outside work, migrants, older workers, ex-offenders and people on incapacity benefits. Each needs a learning strategy that starts from their personal experience.

Finally, the challenge is for the Treasury to take off its blinkers.

Adult learning supports a wide range of other government targets – in health promotion, community cohesion, engagement of older people, among a number of others. That support is vulnerable if the focus on formal qualifications is not accompanied by a rich offering of less formal education, provided by well-trained and properly paid staff.

The Treasury is more likely to respond to these arguments if they are made consistently, by a number of different voices. As long as they do take the advice, though, adult learners have little to fear from the spending review.

30 June 2006

Creative workers come at a price

by Alan Tuckett
Section: Viewpoint; Opinion; Further Education. Issue 4692, p4

ALAN JOHNSON'S speech to the recent Quality Improvement Agency conference shocked me. I was delighted when he came back to education and skills as secretary of state. As minister for further and higher education, he had been straightforward, open-minded, tough and good with people.

The day after he got the new job, he was heading the Skills Alliance of ministers, quangos and leaders of national associations. He demonstrated a grip on the economic and social challenges facing the country by making lifelong learning a reality for many. At the heart of his contributions was a desire to discover what works best.

No one argues with the substance of the case he made to the conference. He insisted: "There must be a fairer apportionment between those who gain from education and those who pay for it – state, employer or individual." Few would disagree. Indeed, we have waited for decades for employers to take their share. And government's share in funding adult learning surely cannot continue to vary wildly from year to year, depending on the level of demand from younger learners.

There is, however, less agreement about what the balance of funding should be – which is why the National Institute of Adult Continuing Education launched a big conversation in Adult Learners' Week, asking how much adult learning should be on offer, and who should pay.

Governments are elected to make their priorities clear, and Mr Johnson's were straightforward: "We must rebalance taxpayer's money towards the subjects where there is greatest need." My problem lay with his illustrations.

"More plumbing, less pilates" makes for a good headline – it is alliterative, and rolls off the tongue. "Subsidised precision engineering, not over-subsidised flower arranging" – government apparently wants hard vocationalism, not soft leisure courses. Then, remembering that there is more to the British economy than manufacturing, he backpedals: "Except, of course, where flower arranging is necessary for a vocational purpose."

Just in case we have missed the point, he concludes: "Tai chi may be hugely valuable to people studying it, but it's of little value to the economy."

And here is the rub. Anyone looking at the statistics on days lost to the British economy through bad backs will conclude that more pilates might lead to more productivity. And if tai chi has little to offer the economy, why is the government campaigning so hard to limit obesity?

But the real point is that you don't need to denigrate learning for personal and community development to make the case for a skilled economy.

Employers endlessly tell government that 'soft skills' are what the system fails to develop. The skills of team working, communicating effectively, problem solving, working flexibly and applying creativity are at the heart of good working practice in the modern economy. Such skills can be developed in liberal-education classes, at least as well as in vocational ones. And learning is not a neat business; learning leaks. Skills and confidence acquired in one place apply elsewhere. Managers know this, which is why so much money is spent on executive awaydays building castles in the air. And, for young people and adults alike, you cannot tell the purpose of the student from the title of the course.

There is, alas, a deep-seated prejudice in British education. Just like the academic-vocational snobbery that has bedevilled initial education here, there is a long-standing administrative and political scepticism about the value of adult learning that learners choose for themselves. It has a common theme. In 1980, in Sussex, the mantra was that people didn't want tap dancing on the rates. In 1991, it was flower arranging again, until we found a merchant banker who had retrained to become a florist at Lambeth evening classes. Under-water basket weaving and Australian cake decorating have had their moment of opprobrium. When the Foster review was launched, willow weaving took centre stage – though 80% of the tiny number of willow-weaving courses on offer are vocational.

These illustrations fail to do justice to provisions that prolong active life for pensioners; offer a space for rebuilding relationships to people recovering from mental health problems; offer a route to learning languages; a chance to overcome obesity for people who can't afford the gym; opportunities for rehabilitation for offenders; and stimulus for people stuck in dull jobs.

In substance, Mr Johnson's speech was about re-balancing. In tone, it endorsed the loss of one in three adult places in further education over three years. It needs an act of faith now to believe the government still wants learning that is life-wide as well as life-long.

28 July 2006

Brilliant advocate for cause of adults

Naomi Sargant, one of the great post-war figures in FE, died this week.
Alan Tuckett *pays tribute*

Section: Further Education. Issue 4696, p29

NAOMI SARGANT numbers among the most distinguished adult educators of the post-war era. She pursued her passion for learning to the very last moments of her life. Naomi learned last week that her cancer was inoperable – that she was dying. Characteristically, she set about making the best possible use of her time. She drew up a list of visitors to see and issues to sort out.

Hours before she passed away last weekend, she told one visitor, fresh in from New York: "The challenge is to bring the worlds of adult learning and vocational education much closer together, and to make them sexy." Not a bad agenda for *FE Focus* and not a bad description of an important theme in her life's work.

Naomi was an exceptional authority in so many arenas. First, as an academic, her groundbreaking work shaped much of the debate about adult participation for three decades. Second, as a broadcaster, she had an outstanding track record of innovative educational programming. Third – as someone who recognised very early how technology would break the boundaries between computing, broadcasting and telephony – she saw the potential for an electronic revolution in adult learning. And, fourth, as a public citizen, Naomi shaped the evolution of policy to challenge inequality of opportunity wherever she found it.

Born of a Czech mother and English father in 1933, she fled the Nazis as a child in 1938, travelling in a locked railway carriage across Europe. It had a profound influence, making her a passionate advocate for the rights of refugees, which she pursued to the end as vice-chair of the campaign group MediaWise Trust.

Educated at Friends School, Saffron Walden, Essex, and Bedford College, London University, where she took a BA (Hons) Sociology, Naomi soon moved to adult education.

Her early career was influenced by working closely with the great social entrepreneur, Michael Young. His eye for unmet need and her skills in market research led to her leading role in the National Consumer Council. She then took that experience to the Open University, and championed the educational aspirations of the working class, women and other under-represented groups.

I met her first when she was pro vice-chancellor at the OU, at a Ruskin history workshop conference on women's history, just as the women's movement was flowering. She was passionate, brilliant, argumentative, engaging and infuriating in turns – but always memorable.

In 1976, she was appointed to the Advisory Council for Adult & Continuing Education, established by the then education secretary Shirley Williams to address exactly the question Naomi highlighted in her final hours. How do you bring together strategies to strengthen learning throughout working life with liberal adult education's concerns with active citizenship, second-chance education, and cultural enrichment?

Naomi led the council's work on future trends, with the first major national detailed studies on adults' experiences of learning. With Richard Hoggart, she played a central role in shaping the council's final report, *Continuing Education – from policies to practice*.

Naomi went on lead the new Channel 4's educational work as one of its first senior commissioning editors. Her groundbreaking work led to education being included in the full range of the channel's programming – complementing broadcast programmes of great flair with off-air back-up materials, helplines and networks.

Her success can be seen from the way these techniques have shaped the whole industry. We have memorable series on history, adult numeracy and consumer rights, programmes for people with more time than money, and programming for people with disabilities.

Her work in broadcasting led naturally to her concern with the potential of the new technologies. She advised successive national policy initiatives on e-learning, notably Dame Helena Kennedy's seminal work on widening participation in FE and Professor Bob Fryer's advisory group on continuing education and lifelong learning. Naomi's interventions changed the detail of successive broadcasting bills in adult learners' favour, most notably by securing a media literacy remit for Ofcom just two years ago.

While enjoying a close family life – married to the current broadcasting minister Lord McIntosh – she was active in local government, held office with the National Gas Consumer Council and played a leading role in the National Extension College.

She was also deputy chair of the University of East London and of the National Council for Voluntary Organisations, and chaired Great Ormond Street's hospital trust, and the Open College of the Arts.

Naomi has also been a towering influence on the development of the National Institute of Adult Continuing Education for the past two decades, leading its quantitative research, helping to create Adult Learners' Week and prodding, challenging, encouraging, in her writing, speaking and forensic committee skills. She led a life rich in ideas and relationships, dedicated to the public interest.

No one did more for adult learners in her time. She was exceptional, a polymath, and a dear friend.

6 October 2006

Let's not learn the hard way about migration

by Alan Tuckett
Section: Further Education; Opinion. Issue 4706, p4

WE ARE faced with an imminent and dramatic decline in the number of school leavers over the next decade, just as the post-war bulge begin to leave the labour market. Yet the Foster report on the future of colleges and the subsequent white paper substantially ignored its implications for adult learning, concentrating attention and intensifying expenditure on the young. People from all adult education interests met recently for a 'Big Conversation' organised by NIACE. They were asked what should be done about this.

As part of the debate, NIACE published with Age Concern *Learning in Later Life*, and this week we published the findings of our inquiry 'English for speakers of other languages: More than a language'. Together, they have important messages for the world of work. Some planners are relaxed about the skills and labour shortages, confident that the market will find solutions.

In the short run, the evidence is that firms are responding by recruiting from new members of the EU, and by outsourcing jobs to the Indian subcontinent or China.

Migration within the European Union will be boosted, too, if Bulgarian and Romanian workers are able to take advantage of EU labour mobility next January. Of itself, migration will not solve all the pressures on the labour market, but it does, it's argued, offer an alternative to overhauling postschool learning. Or does it?

The case of the Chinese cockle pickers drowned on Morecambe Sands, able to communicate by phone with China but unable to get help on the beach, highlights the importance of language skills, and the protection of employment rights for migrants.

As evidence to our inquiry makes clear, we are still dealing with the failure to support earlier migration from India, Pakistan and Bangladesh. A Department of Work & Pensions paper shows that just 4% of Bangladeshi and 28% of Pakistani women outside the labour force have the English fluency needed for successful engagement in it.

The Learning & Skills Council now spends £279m a year on Esol, yet there are few places available for the marginalised, and waiting lists are growing.

In five years time, the numbers of young people entering work will have dropped dramatically, and the transitional measures that allow France, Germany and Italy to limit migration from the accession states will have ended. Will migrants moving to Britain now move to take advantage of opportunities in those countries?

Where will British business fill its jobs from? Despite the early success of Train to Gain in engaging older workers, we will need to do more to retrain and retain older workers, and find routes to work for people a long way from it.

It will be too late to start planning when the migrants move on, and desperate if we condemn our new neighbours to the poverty, isolation and alienation so many earlier migrants experienced.

3 November 2006

Power battle risks punishing those most in need

by Alan Tuckett
Section: Further Education. Issue 4710, p4

MIKE NEWMAN'S writing first inspired me 30 years ago. His latest book, *Teaching Defiance*, begins from the understanding that in all kinds of contexts decisions made or imposed result from the exercise of power. That power is not equally shared and you can teach people the tools to better defend their interests and to assert their needs.

What follows is a brilliant combination of practical workshop exercises and a relaxed account of the pedagogical and philosophical underpinnings of the methodology. I think it should be essential reading for adult educators.

Different forms of power – deriving from formal authority, fiscal clout, media influence, co-operative action, or innovative social forms – are brought to bear on conflicts of interest.

Analysing them helps to see who are the winners, and who are the losers, in order to better plan what to do about it. This is adult education for democracy – work just as vital to the health and well-being of the country as the skills strategy, but work that has shrivelled in university extra mural departments, colleges and local authorities alike.

One area where this kind of strategic thinking is essential is in policy for adults learning English as their second or subsequent language. That was the reason NIACE commissioned its committee of inquiry into English for speakers of other languages (Esol).

I was encouraged that minister Bill Rammell wrote accepting well over two-thirds of the 39 recommendations made by the inquiry, and for his personal engagement with the issue. Many will improve things for those learners who make it through the door and get a class.

One very welcome development is the recognition that employers need to do more in one area at least. The Learning & Skills Council's annual statement of priorities promises to make sure that employers pay for their workers to learn English.

However, there were two areas of disagreement. The government will cut all courses for asylum seekers, while we argued that where the Home Office failed to process a decision within eight weeks, it should pay for Esol until a decision is made.

It is not that anyone questions Home Office aspirations to process claims quickly, just that for some people judgment can be delayed for months and years.

The second disagreement was over fees. NIACE argued that adults who can afford to should pay, but that everyone needed an entitlement to free provision up to level one. The government has decided to charge fees for all Esol learners not on benefits or income support. It is a difference that will have an impact on low-waged workers, with the weakest language skills, whose lack of the language will inhibit them from accessing the evidence which they would need to claim exemption.

In our view, while making a welcome commitment to prioritising those most in need, the government's decision risks further punishing the poor.

12 January 2007
Will monies go to Leitch or be leached?
by Alan Tuckett
Section: Comment; Opinion; Further education. Issue 4719, p6

SOMETIMES, THE best way to find out what you think about a pressing issue of the day is to immerse yourself in other things. Lord Leitch's report on the skills Britain needs over the next 20 years generated intense debate when published last month. Then silence, as the demands of the festive season took over.

Now back to work, the report's ambitions for literacy and numeracy, intermediate skills and expansion of higher education still look impressive. Gordon Brown accepted the targets in his pre-budget statement.

Excellent news, provided the chancellor backs his commitment with enough cash. This is no small proviso, given the promise of extra money for schools, the need to renovate the country's transport system and the apparent commitment to yet another generation of nuclear weapons.

Lord Leitch is right to say the departments for Work & Pensions and Education & Skills need to share coherent policies. Benefit claimants need help getting jobs and the skills to keep them in work. He is right to say the adult guidance service needs a shake-up. Right, too, that we should triple our spending on adult basic skills and extend higher education access to a rapidly ageing workforce. All good stuff – if there is the money.

But is he right to suggest that all cash for adult vocational education be shifted to demand led funding? He puts huge faith in the capacity of employers to recognise the skills the UK and its workforce need. This is not the first initiative to put employers centre stage. Will it prove more successful than earlier ones? Their past record leaves little room for optimism.

Lord Leitch gives qualifications a lot of weight. However, there is overwhelming evidence that workers and employers value most the skills gained informally at work. Generic skills such as teamwork and problem solving are learnt best by doing the job, not by taking structured courses.

The UK earns more from its creative industries and financial services than from manufacturing, and for both it is the skills a general education brings that are industrially valuable. Will a qualifications-driven adult skills strategy secure the breadth, ingenuity and flexibility a vibrant economy needs? Not on its own.

The cost of Leitch's proposals will squeeze other further education yet again. There will be learner accounts, where those who benefit most will be those who do what government wants. But what about divergent thinkers, or adults returning to study but uncertain of their learning intentions? What about migrants? And older people? The Leitch report is light on the needs of such groups.

Not surprisingly, he has little to say on the role of education in promoting well being, confident active citizens, or the pursuit of happiness. Yet happy people work productively; they miss fewer days at work. And anyway, we work to sustain lives worth living. Lord Leitch is properly ambitious and the cost of acting on it will be large. But will the budget stretch to enable providers to respond to the real needs of students, trainees and enterprises? The jury is out.

16 February 2007

Older learners pay a high price of Train to Gain

by Alan Tuckett
Section: Comment; Opinion; Further education. Issue 4724, p4

WHERE HAVE all the learners gone? Adult student numbers fell by 735,000 last year, and we can expect worse this year. It mirrors the squeeze on adult

Seriously useless learning

education budgets to pay for a rise in the number of young people. But it scarcely reflects the recent sharp shift of priorities, away from courses which gave individuals freedom of choice and towards learning that meets the needs of employers.

We can expect losses of a million adult learners or more in less than three years.

Many of the losers are older people. Yet we know that learning stimulates good health and active citizenship, quite apart from any role it plays in helping people rethink their later working lives.

There is evidence that the cuts are not only in art, languages, crafts and liberal studies, but in short courses that lead to the progression the government is keen to see. Taken together, the cuts in courses in colleges and community centres represent a massive shift of policy.

This is highlighted in the Learning & Skills Council's latest consultation paper on demand-led funding. It shows how government funding for vocational programmes will be channelled through an expanding Train to Gain programme and learner accounts. Learners will get support only if they study what the government wants them to learn.

There will be minimal protection for spending on personal and community development learning and new foundation learning courses. For anything else, adults can expect to pay full fees.

It is astonishing how little fuss this shift of policy has provoked. Colleges are busy enough addressing other priorities, and politicians' postbags are hardly groaning with complaints.

There is, as yet, only patchy evidence of employers using Train to Gain to offer workers substantial additional skills (rather than assessing existing ones). And we have yet to see figures on the programme's value for money. Despite this, there has been little sustained appraisal of just how employer demand – and willingness to pay for training – will be driven up.

In fact, the evidence of the debate on funding English for speakers of other languages suggests that many employers remain deeply resistant to paying for anything other than job-specific training.

The last time I saw a million or so people was during the great demonstration against going to war in Iraq. It was a formidable sight and they made a formidable noise. The lost learners are not visible in the same way. They have gone quietly, releasing resources for the grand experiment on which the system is embarking.

Will it work? No one can be sure, since there is little evidence to draw on, despite government enthusiasm for evidence-based policy. But we must hope it will, since we do know that the new policies have been bought at a high price, in lost opportunities for willing learners and in diminished choice for older people in particular.

23 March 2007
Adversity with a smile
As the WEA's Sheffield branch celebrates its centenary, adult education campaigners prepare for fresh battles. **Alan Tuckett** reports

Section: Further Education. Issue 4729, p5

EVERYWHERE I go, people describe the prospects for adults in further education with gloom and despondency coupled with pessimism about the near future. Curiously, the analysis is mixed with an abundance of energy, determination and gallows humour. What do they think of the demand-led funding consultation paper? "Appalling stuff," they say. And what of the lack of coherence between the Leitch review of UK skills and the Lyons review of local government? "It is bound to end in tears," comes their reply.

This blend was, perhaps, understandable when the Workers' Educational Association celebrated its Sheffield branch centenary by asking what the future holds for adult education.

Local MP and former education secretary David Blunkett was there, still flying the flag for the organisation's ambitions. It was he, remember, who created Labour's 'visionary' lifelong learning policies a decade ago. He insisted the abiding role of adult education was to create and sustain communities that were compassionate, civilised and curious.

The WEA boasts 19,000 members in 640 branches who share his view. But there was anger at the impact of cuts in funding. As one student put it: "If you take away my class, you take away my reason for getting up in the morning."

There was little expectation that things would be mended quickly, despite evidence of the benefits of adult learning. The success of union learning representatives evinces widespread respect. But it is hard to understand why the parallel work of community learning champions created by this government is so hard to fund.

Bill Rammell, the minister, argues it is all about priorities – that the expansion of Train to Gain and the Skills for Life Strategy inevitably put pressure on other areas. And while John Hayes, the Conservative shadow minister for learning and skills, argues passionately for adult education, it is unclear whether his party is committed to maintaining the provision currently on offer.

One reason for cheer is the evidence that public debate makes a difference. Mr Rammell's agreement to modify the government's proposals to introduce fees for classes in English for speakers of other languages came as a result of hot public debate. There has been a race impact assessment exercise, a thousand people at a Universities and Colleges Union parliamentary lobby, backed by large numbers of MPs and peers, and powerful advocacy from learners.

Seriously useless learning

The changes to Esol funding are welcome, of course, but as Paul Mackney, former Natfhe general secretary, says, it is not a matter of shuffling the limited budget for adult learning, to give privileges to some learners at the expense of others. The time has come to squeeze serious money from the spending review. Maybe this prospect explains the gallows humour abroad in the land.

4 May 2007

Tap turned off for short courses

Older learners lose out as skills training absorbs increasing chunks of funding

by Alan Tuckett

Section: Commentary; Opinion; Further Education. Issue 4738, p6

EVERY YEAR, the Learning & Skills Council's data on student numbers shows the winners and losers resulting from changes to funding and policy. This year, the figures showed that we at the adult education body NIACE and the Association of Colleges were wrong to suggest a million adult learners would disappear in three years. This sharp decline was achieved in just two. The figures also give early evidence about the Train to Gain programme, which had reached 89,000 people by January this year.

Everyone recognises that it costs more to fund a substantial qualification than a taster course. However, the contrast between a million adults lost to FE and 89,000 gains in workplace training is striking. It raises many questions. What will it cost, at current levels of investment, to secure the skilled workforce the country seeks? Do we have the right balance of public investment between work-based learning and community-based activity?

Digging into the figures, we find that 3,000 places for adults with learning difficulties have been lost across the country. Participation in FE by the over-60s has halved in just two years. In addition, institutions that focused on the needs of pre-entry-level Skills for Life students in London face budget cuts.

It is too early to make judgments about the overall impact of Train to Gain. But development is patchy. Skills brokers are too ready to offer a one-size-fits-all solution to employers' needs. Meanwhile, continuing cuts in 'other further education' add to the pressure on organisations to spend money for adult learning wisely.

Those cuts in FE for adults make the safeguarded budgets for adult and community learning, family and neighbourhood learning in deprived communities look reassuringly secure. All right, there has been no inflation for the past two years. But, otherwise, budgets have been stable.

Why then do the LSC figures show big falls in participation over two years for every age cohort over 25? These figures show a peak, with a drop of 30% for people in their 50s taking safeguarded courses.

One major reason for the decline is the summary ending of funding for short courses. While every self-respecting professional is booking in for intensive one-day briefings as part of their competence updating, the tap has been turned off for Saturday schools and other short courses.

Gone are the day schools on 'Reasons for the war in Iraq' or 'How to claim working tax credits'. Out, too, are courses such as an 'Introduction to Shakespeare's sonnets', or a 'Quick introduction to PowerPoint'.

There is, apparently, little statistical evidence of a link between such courses and the progress we all want learners to make. But they are brilliant at engaging older people – and at a time when much community provision is being reduced, the argument for making a little go a long way is a powerful one.

It would help reverse the decline in adult participation – and put a little adventure back into some tired programmes.

25 May 2007
Drive towards wider horizons
by Alan Tuckett
Section: Further Education; Adult learning. Issue 4738, p2

ADULT LEARNERS' Week comes this year at a challenging time. It is hard to encourage new participants when a million places for adults have been lost from Learning & Skills Council courses in just two years. Short courses are no longer part of the portfolio of publicly supported study. Waiting lists for lessons in English for speakers of other languages stretch beyond next year's Adult Learners' Week.

This year, we found in our annual adult participation survey that 500,000 fewer people are taking courses of any kind.

However, it is not all bad. There is evidence that many committed adult learners react to cut classes by finding self-organised solutions to carry on learning. The union learning movement goes from strength to strength, and Train to Gain – which supports employers who train staff up to level 2 (GCSE-equivalent) – may be experiencing a slow start but does seem to be helping older workers gain access to training.

One other key group can look forward to a new entitlement this year. These are the workers who support adult learning. The introduction of an entitlement to 30 hours a year of continuing professional development for full-time teachers sets a minimum benchmark. More impressive, perhaps, is the extension of that entitlement to tens of thousands of part-time teachers, who get at least six hours a year, however modest their employment.

For those struggling to complete formal teaching qualifications by 2010, this will not be enough. I spent three days in Germany, helping manage

Seriously useless learning

a major European Union-sponsored conference on qualifying the actors in lifelong learning. It convinced me that our debates are painfully insular. The focus of the event was on the skills needed to support effective adult learning and teaching – by policymakers and planners, organisers, tutors and support staff alike. And on how we might best learn from each other in constructing a European framework of support for teachers and their allies.

One group report focused on the needs of support workers. It took the form of a job advert. "Wanted: support worker. Tasks to be undertaken: hard to define. Skills needed: someone flexible, skilled in multi-tasking, likes working with people; good at process control; able to create effective learning environments; good at marketing; at ease with the media; able to undertake counselling; an experienced information broker; good at networking and good with languages. Conditions: insecure. Pay: variable. Training: good idea."

Adult educators know that secretaries and caretakers play a critical role in supporting learning, and any institution worth its salt should develop training strategies that enrich their contributions.

We looked at advice from the Organisation for Economic Development on what's needed for a globalising economy. It goes beyond the conventional basic skills. You need, they say, to learn to act independently, to use tools interactively and to interact in heterogeneous groups. But to interact you need to meet – yet I was the only Briton at an event, in English, with participants from 26 countries.

Are we uniquely uninterested in other countries? Or are we so embarrassed by our weakness in languages that we stick to the familiar? I am convinced our sights are still set low and our attention span is too narrow. Changing that is exactly why we have an Adult Learners' Week – for learners, teachers and administrators alike.

13 July 2007

Changes bring hope of return to creativity

by Alan Tuckett
Section: Further Education; Viewpoint; Opinion. Issue 4745, p7

WHAT PRICE adult learning in the next few years? As the new Cabinet announcements were made, I thought adult learning and skills had disappeared into business and enterprise, and had visions of the last remaining bits of liberal education being drummed out of court.

It was not such a fanciful idea if the vision in Sir Andrew Foster, and the recommendations from Lord Leitch were followed through. A commission on employment and skills, sector skills councils deciding which qualifications count for public money, contestability for everything, it is an analysis that leaves little room for creativity, democratic citizenship, the celebration of diversity, or widening participation.

What a pleasure, then, to find that adult learning will now nestle in a department of innovation, higher education and skills.

Good, too, that the department is to be led by John Denham, a politician of principle. The changes in the machinery of government give us an opportunity to review the balance of current public policy as it affects adults. After all, a million adult learners have been lost from Learning & Skills Council funded provision in the last two years. The annual NIACE participation survey showed a drop from 55% to 48% among part-time workers.

Recruitment to Train to Gain is reported as barely 60% of planned numbers (125,000) and completions are low, too. Indeed, many are no more than the assessment and accreditation of existing skills. The LSC's success in getting through to over 60% of 'hard-to-reach' employers is set in context when you realise that 'hard to reach' means "not engaged in vocational training leading to a qualification or holding Investors in People recognition" over the last 12 months. And skills brokers, the key to the success of the Train to Gain policy, have variable performance so far.

On the whole, the re-balancing of FE sector investment flowing from the skills strategy has shown little evidence that employers have been stimulated to increase investment, while individual learners have lost out. Meanwhile, the financial pressures on the LSC suggest adults face further misery with popular courses replaced by workplace provision that employers are not yet taking up, and routes back to the labour market disappearing for people a long way from work.

That is just the kind of innovation and risk-taking the new department would do well to resist.

18 January 2008

Throw open the windows of opportunity

Alan Tuckett reflects on the three NIACE conferences, supported by FE Focus, on the future of post-19 education

Section: Future of FE. Issue 4771, p6

TWO YEARS ago, the National Institute of Adult Continuing Education's independent inquiry on the state of adult learning in colleges published *Eight in Ten*. The title was taken from the proportion of adults in further education. Like the Foster report on the future role of FE colleges published shortly afterwards, *Eight in Ten* argued that colleges had key roles to play in

Seriously useless learning

vocational education and workplace learning. Unlike Foster, it argued that colleges had a third core function: to create and sustain cultural value.

Foster's view chimed with the Skills Strategy, was reinforced by the Leitch review of skills, and was backed by the government. The result is that if the NIACE inquiry was to publish a similar report today it would be called *Six in Ten, and Falling!*

The NIACE and *TES* conference series on Further Education for the 21st Century, the last of which was held yesterday, has reviewed developments affecting adults and looked at future prospects. They have shown just how creative and responsive colleges can be in meeting the needs and aspirations of adults when they are given the chance to get on with the job. They have shown, too, how often and quickly the goals set by the system have changed and that there are risks when government seeks to force the pace too quickly.

Geoff Hall, principal and chief executive of New College Nottingham, argued tellingly that a rush for numbers leads to problems with quality and accountability, and that the financial irregularities experienced with individual learning accounts and franchising were likely to be reproduced with Train to Gain. It is clearly government's responsibility to set the direction of travel, but the lesson of recent years is that it is best to go slowly.

Cuts in funding for 'other further education' – which is not directly associated with government targets and priorities – have been dramatic. Add in sharp fee increases in many areas and the result has been a big decline in adult learning opportunities: there was a 40% reduction in Learning & Skills Council-funded numbers in further education for post-19s between 2003-04 to 2006-07; for over 25s, it was 43%, and for the over-60s, it reached 58%.

Low-waged earners working for employers who decline to invest in training have missed out significantly. The loss of 1.4m adult students – when the LSC estimated a loss of 200,000 – devastated colleges' capacity to respond to locally expressed need, and the innovation, universities and skills secretary's grant letter suggests there is more pain to come over the next three years for anyone whose needs are not met within the targets. That will affect the poor and marginalised more than the affluent.

There have, of course, been successes. In Skills for Life, level 2 (GCSE equivalent) and apprenticeship participation has been buoyant and achievements on target.

Until this past year, colleges had had great success in meeting demand for courses in English for speakers of other languages, but that demand is now capped. The government has, however, produced a helpful consultation paper on how to support local decision-making in giving priority to settled migrants with language learning needs. Particularly welcome is the inclusion of asylum seekers on the list of priority groups.

Colleges should be trusted to set their own priorities, not just for Esol, but also in other areas. Current policies are dangerously narrow in scope for a country which needs its citizens to be well informed and its communities to get on with each other.

The key lesson of the conferences was, as the veteran socialist Tony Benn suggested, that the time has come to campaign. We need a broad alliance of colleges, communities, faith organisations and the wider voluntary sector, unions and businesses to reassert that we need public support for learning for the good of our society – for life as well as work – and we need it now.

21 March 2008
Adults must not lose out again
by Alan Tuckett
Section: Comment. Issue 4780, p4

THE PROPOSALS announced this week to replace the Learning & Skills Council with new bodies for young people and adults after 2010 risk the further erosion of the government's commitment to lifelong learning in England and threaten to marginalise the interests of adults as learners outside higher education.

Since the incorporation of colleges, every change to the institutional infra-structure has initially resulted in damage to provision for adult part-time students. The experience of NIACE is that any measures that set the needs of one group of learners against another generally results in adults losing out.

Further education colleges are used overwhelmingly by adults but are driven by the needs of younger full-time students preparing for entry to the labour market.

In spite of this, they have been outstandingly effective in widening participation and achievement for all. NIACE is concerned that the new arrangements may inhibit colleges from continuing to meet the needs of learners from all sections of society. For the government's proposals to succeed, Whitehall departments, local government and new funding bodies and agencies will need to display greater levels of flexibility than has occurred in the past.

The absence of a planning role for the proposed Skills Funding Agency will lead to more confusion.

A demand-led funding system needs to respect the full range of adult demand, not simply that prioritised by government's public service agree-ments. While local authorities are not the most appropriate bodies to lead on the entire skills agenda, they do however understand the needs of the communities they serve.

Seriously useless learning

To better safeguard adult learners' interests, NIACE proposes that government should give local authorities a statutory duty to advise and comment on the plans of the Skills Funding Agency with regard to the sufficiency of local arrangements for the education and training of adults – within their areas – in the welfare of communities.

16 May 2008

Still a poor show for enrichment

Next week's focus on adult learners shows there is a long way to go to create a culture of lifelong education

by Alan Tuckett
Section: Viewpoint. Issue 4788, p7

IN THE wake of the recent local election results, ministers have promised to pay more attention to what people think. It is to John Denham's credit that he has already created the perfect opportunity for this through the consultation on informal learning. As secretary of state for innovation, uiversities and skills, he understands that there is a good deal to be listened to and acted on.

On the plus side, there is the prospect of closer co-operation and planning between the Department for Culture, Media & Sport and Mr Denham's own, as libraries report an expansion of reading groups, and museums and galleries explore how to enrich the learning experience of their adult users.

A number of voluntary organisations are encouraged by the paper, hoping that being noticed may be a precursor to being funded. Self-organised groups such as the University of the Third Age report steady expansion, and there is evidence that developments in online social networking offer new forms for co-operatively managed learning on the web. It is a major strength of the paper to re-assert the connection between publicly funded provision and the riches of less formal learning on offer outside structured education.

There is, of course, another side to take into account. First, however welcome it is, the consultation comes at a time when almost 1.5m adult enrolments on Learning & Skills Council courses have been lost in just two years, and the plans are for more losses over the next three.

Meanwhile, disabled students who have been displaced from the classes that have been cut can only be catered for under the safeguarded budgets for adult education for personal development. And, since that work is more expensive, overall numbers in that area are falling.

Adult Learners' Week provides reminders aplenty of what those learning opportunities mean to people's lives. They include Paul Lee, who left school with one O-Level, worked in the building trade until he did his back in, took an Access to Higher Education course in history, and is now off to

Cambridge. Then there is Momotaz Begum, who took a culture and textiles class that led to paid work in the rag trade. There's Anthony Benfield, who used his time in a maximum security prison to study through the Open University, and to develop a database for translating hieroglyphics now used by museums and universities all over the world.

Quite apart from the exceptional stories captured in Adult Learners' Week, people all over the country tell us how their lives have been enriched and stimulated by classes in art, tai chi or industrial archaeology. They care about being taught by skilled teachers – and can't understand why the modest support their courses have attracted has been withdrawn at the very time education budgets overall have expanded. They remind us that quality of life has a claim on the public purse, and that "when people feel valued, the common good is fed" – to quote John Hayes, the Tory further education spokesman. In response, the government argues that every spare penny must be committed to improving the employability of the adult workforce.

It has been successful so far with the Skills for Life strategy. Apprentice-ships, too, are a success. But government money is increasingly focused on Train to Gain, which provides work-based skills.

While increasing numbers of people are undertaking state-subsidised workplace training, there are lingering worries about whether public money is replacing costs that employers were previously meeting themselves.

Overall, we have a mixed picture in which fees are going up for individual adult students, employers are increasing their investment in training, and the state continues to provide more funding. Despite this, the overall participa-tion rates, which cover public and private learning, are significantly down this year. The proportion of employers who say they are providing training, or have recently done so, has fallen from 42% to 38%.

Most worrying is that the numbers are down most sharply over two years for full-time and part-time employees, for social class C2 and for adults between the ages of 25 and 34. These are, of course, exactly the groups targeted by the Train to Gain programme.

As government expands provision for a minority in these groups and employers report an increase in spending on training for others, a larger number are losing opportunities, whether because of a changing balance of employer-funded training or because these groups are big users of the open-class programme lost in colleges and adult education.

It seems that improved opportunities for some are being bought at the expense of widening opportunities for others and government policies are not resulting in the expansion of learning opportunities that the country needs.

Learning for work does matter, but so too does quality of life. The informal learning consultation offers Mr Denham and his colleagues, having listened, the chance to re-examine the balance of public investment across adult provision as a whole, to reverse the decline in participation, and encourage the culture of adult learning to which we all aspire.

15 May 2009

Good policy is born of shrewd measurement

by Alan Tuckett
Section: Comment. Issue 4839, p6

NUMBERS MATTER. In a world where there are always more things to do than money to pay for it, good metrics help policy-makers to decide who gets what on a rational basis. That is what evidence-based policy means. However, choosing the right measures is the key to good policy-making. After all, as Einstein observed, not everything that counts can be counted, and not everything that can be counted is worth counting.

Each year, Adult Learners' Week (which we have been marking this week) provides an opportunity to reflect on adult participation and achievement in learning, on the balance of government policy, and on what can be learnt from people who have overcome obstacles and transformed their lives through adult learning.

There have been numbers aplenty to inform any debate. The industrial challenge was highlighted in *Ambition 2020*, a report from the UK Commission for Employment & Skills published last week. It showed that Lord Leitch's ambitions – for the UK to be in the top quarter of the skills league table for the 30 richest countries by 2020 – remain challenging.

Despite real gains, the UK has slipped to sixth in the gross domestic product league table; we have the 12th highest proportion of highly skilled workers; we rank 18th for intermediate skills; and 16 other countries that belong to the Organisation for Economic Co-operation & Development have smaller proportions of low-skilled adults. The government can point with pride to the numbers gaining level 2 (GCSE equivalent) qualifications and basic skills as a result of their rebalancing of funding since 2005. Yet, to achieve the Leitch aim to be among the top eight in each league, we have a very long way to go.

All well and good, but are these the right numbers to measure? Qualifications are important, certainly, but they are not enough; and skills are not the only measure of the learning needed for a healthy society. In the past 12 years of prosperity, we have slipped from 10th to 21st in the United Nations' human development index, which measures longevity, literacy rates and GDP. *Ambition 2020* also shows the UK is in the bottom quartile when you measure inequality by comparing rewards for the best and lowest paid. In the main, countries with high levels of productivity and employment are ones where the benefits of affluence (and opportunity) are shared most evenly.

The annual NIACE survey on adult learning highlights not only who is benefiting from participation but also who isn't. This year's survey confirms the trend that, far from creating fairer access to learning, the sum of public, private and informal learning benefits those who did best first time around. Gains in basic skills and at level 2, which target the least skilled, have been bought at the expense of opportunities for a larger number of adults from the same communities.

Balancing intensive investment for some adults with diverse and accessible but more modest opportunities for the many cannot be done by central planning alone. *Ambition 2020* is right that we need more responsive skills and, I would argue, education provision. That means more discretion for providers to maximise participation and progression, backed by a national participation measure.

Sixth formers and university students are trusted to decide what is worth studying. If we want a learning society for all, with the flexibility to meet challenges of changing economies, and the pressures they generate for community and family life, we need to extend that trust to adult learners everywhere.

8 October 2010

Will safeguard for adults be all-inclusive?

by Alan Tuckett
Section: Comment. Issue 4911, p6

COALITION MINISTERS are clear about the value they place on adult learning. John Hayes says: "To build a bigger society ... we must recognise the value of community learning ... Learning is a powerful glue that can bind us together as families, as friends, as communities." Vince Cable recalls the impact adult education had on his mother's recovery from mental ill-health.

David Cameron agrees: "Learning isn't just about consuming chunks of knowledge to be able to do a job. It's about broadening the mind, giving people self-belief, strengthening the bonds of community ... Over the past 13 years, so many learning places have been lost because they haven't been deemed useful." Hence the Tory proposal for £100m for additional adult learning chosen by people themselves.

The vision is clear. The shift from target-driven utilitarianism is marked, and comes with promises to trust providers to respond to demand from individuals, communities and employers alike. Yet the consultation document *A Simplified Further Education and Skills Funding System and Methodology* shows how hard it is to shift officials' mindsets. Providers are encouraged to "focus their offer to learners and employers rather than trying to navigate the funding system", and the paper acknowledges the "need to balance the sensitivity to the diversity of learner and employer needs". Excellent. But the devil is in the detail.

It says there are two options for funding adult learning. The first gives providers a single adult-responsive budget, the second keeps a safe-guarded budget for provision for adults outside the Qualifications & Curriculum Framework (QCF), and shifts substantial volumes of work currently made under the adult learner-responsive (ALR) budget into the safeguard – but says nothing about why, or what this means for budget totals. The first option is a bad idea; the second begs questions and will only work if there is enough money attached.

Adults often lose out when budgets are tight, unless they have ringfenced protection. This is why then-minister Ivan Lewis adopted a safeguard in 2003 for adult provision at risk. But 1.5m adults did lose out from unprotected FE provision between 2004 and 2007 as young people and employers were prioritised and, increasingly, only courses leading to approved qualifications were funded. In the proposed FE budget, ALR funding will still be for QCF-approved qualifications, leaving community- based provision vulnerable if the safeguard goes.

Central bureaucracy may be lightened, but diversity of offer will be chal-lenged if four in ten providers are demoted to the status of sub-contractor, when many are small local providers effective at meeting the needs of marginalised groups.

The safeguard was initially set at 3% of the Learning & Skills Council budget, then about £300m, and shrunk each year to its current cash-limited £210m. Without it, and a fund for innovation like the Transformation Fund, it is hard to see how ministers' vision can be realised, or local aspirations met.

The safeguard covers personal and community development learning for adults, neighbourhood learning in deprived communities, family literacy, language and numeracy, and wider family learning. Last autumn, online basics was added. Now it seems the uncertificated provision for adults is to be added, too. That might not matter if budgets are adjusted to take account of the new strands of work. But the document is silent about what is to be included, and how much cash is to shift. Yet if formal first steps means entry-level literacy, language and numeracy, that will be critical, since this work accounts for a major slice of the adult-responsive budget.

For adults, this consultation reads like business as usual with a few frills. We need a safeguard, certainly, but clearly defined and properly funded. Everyone determined to see a broad and inclusive provision for adults should respond and say so.

7 January 2011

The new face of adult learning is emerging

by Alan Tuckett

Section: Comment. Issue 4923, p4

AT FIRST sight, last year was kind to adult learners. For a start the new team of ministers in the skills area arrived with a genuine passion for adult further education. John Hayes quoted Yeats, asserting that "education is not the filling of a pail, but the lighting of a fire", and called for a new aesthetic in revaluing practical learning. And if words sometimes come cheap, actions followed.

Community-based adult learning survived the July budget and the comprehensive spending review with no reductions in overall investment. So did the Unionlearn budget. The wider field of further education saw smaller-than-expected reductions in funding for 19-plus education, too – once the closure of the employer-based Train to Gain programme was taken into account.

Then, in higher education (HE), following the Browne review, the government extended access to loans to students taking just 25% of a full-time course. Since we, along with many others, have spent 20 years arguing for equal treatment for part-time students – overwhelmingly adults – this could be seen as a red-letter day. So too could the extension of loans to FE students – though part-timers will wait to be included in that sector. Taken together, these measures look like the first building block in years towards the creation of the tertiary system of comprehensive post-school education this country needs.

All good stuff. And yet there can be no doubt that there will be a great deal for adult educators to scrutinise in 2011 to make sure that headline wins don't roll out as localised losses for their students. The Department for Business, Innovation & Skills' battles with the Treasury on behalf of adult learning were bought at a price. Apparently the Treasury wants more rigorous and formal audits of adult learning, and a review of how budgets are committed, to ensure it meets the needs of marginalised groups, contributes to the Big Society and secures curriculum breadth.

While the improvement in access to loans is welcome, there are real risks of reductions in part-time HE as public funding for arts, social science and humanities teaching in the sector disappears. Progression will be difficult since Access courses will be wholly funded through loans – and the scale of debt incurred in progressing to HE could be a real disincentive to older participants. Teacher training in HE loses all public subsidy, just as retiring baby boomers in the FE workforce leave gaps. Can they be filled with new teachers funding their own training with loans? I doubt it.

Seriously useless learning

The Skills Investment Strategy argued that basic skills would be fully funded, but the funding rate for literacy has fallen by 33% and public support for English for speakers of other languages has fallen by 50% over two years. While new technologies can surely be exploited to enrich teaching, and to secure more for less for many learners, current policy and funding have had little impact on the 500,000 adults with the greatest literacy needs. For them, we surely need more, not fewer, resources. The NIACE independent literacy inquiry, chaired by Lord Boswell, will look at this along with other developments in the ten years since the Moser report.

For people on benefits, the strategy focuses support on people seeking work, which will exclude most lone parents with pre-school children. Given the importance of parents as educators, this must be a policy to reverse.

Despite the dramatic drop in the size of the age-cohorts available for labour market entry each year during this decade, and the resulting need to keep older learners at work for longer, budgets have shifted away from the post-25s to 19-to-25s. And the closure of Train to Gain weakens mechanisms for reaching workers in their 40s and 50s.

Adult educators have their work cut out to secure enough opportunities for learners who missed out earlier, to protect equality and diversity in the sector. But how much easier it would be with a fully-fledged, stable and coherent lifelong learning strategy that values the role learning can play across the life cycle.

6 May 2011

Don't erase opportunities for those in need

by Alan Tuckett
Section: Comment. Issue 4940, p6

NO ONE can doubt FE minister John Hayes's passionate belief in the role adult learning has in transforming lives, illustrated recently at the final Community Learning Champions conference. Funded for two years under the previous government's Learning Revolution, this project demonstrated that the work of union learning representatives, providing peer group guidance on returning to learning, could be effective in communities. It showed the impact that the champions had on the lives of neighbours and friends, inspiring them to return to study, and the marked effect on the self-esteem and prospects of the champions themselves.

The minister attended the conference and stayed to watch a powerful film. At the end, Mr Hayes asked to speak again. Visibly moved, he promised to ensure the work would continue. That, of course, is the hope of every short-term project with a successful outcome, but you need a minister with sufficient empathy and clarity of purpose to make such a commitment there and then.

The same commitment, shared with business secretary Vince Cable, was evident when they saw off the Treasury's campaign to reduce the 'safe-guarded' £210m for uncertificated adult education. It was evident in the protection of the Union Learning Fund, and in universities minister David Willetts's move to offer equitable loans to part-time, overwhelmingly adult students in higher education – and to plan a comparable move in FE. It was there, too, in the plans for an all-age careers service.

So where have the problems come from? Colleges, particularly in areas of urban deprivation, tell of insurmountable difficulties in claiming their full adult-learning allocations from the Skills Funding Agency. This is the result of a toxic combination of changes to the eligibility criteria for fee reductions for learners, with cuts in the funding rates for those in literacy and Esol (English for speakers of other languages) classes. It comes on top of reductions planned by the previous government, the re-balancing of budgets attendant on the end of Train to Gain and increased investment in apprentices. More is to come in 2012/13, when lone parents, among others not 'actively seeking work', will be hit by the new regulations.

We are still waiting for an equality impact assessment, but if half of Esol students cannot afford to study next year, it will sit uncomfortably with prime minister David Cameron's exhortations to everyone living in Britain to learn English. And while it is reasonable to concentrate public support on those actively seeking work, conventional Department for Work & Pensions meas-ures capture men's routes to the labour market. It is women, as 'inactive' claimants or the wives of low-wage workers, who will bear the brunt of the changes.

Changing the funding rate for adult literacy students may make sense for those topping up on skills missed at school, but it will be inadequate to help those who need it most. Previously, they were poorly served by a regime that rewarded provision for those needing less help. Now the rate cut makes it difficult for institutions to commit the resources needed to make a difference.

Adults with learning difficulties face another set of barriers. The admin-istrative muddle responsible for securing the rights to learning of 16 to 25-year-olds are paralleled by a policy void for those aged 25 and over, not to mention the financial challenges of the Access route to HE and the absence of effective strategies for workplace learning for people in their 40s and 50s.

Mr Hayes and his colleagues urgently need to revisit the changes to regu-lations and rates, to prevent equality and diversity from becoming optional extras.

Seriously useless learning

22 March 2014

TES Opinion

Alan Tuckett, president of the International Council for Adult Education, writes:

THE RECENT Office for National Statistics report showing the productivity gap between Britain and the USA, France and Germany is now more than 30% is only the latest evidence that our national skills strategy is a disaster.

The first and fundamental mistake, at the heart of skills policy since 2003, was to teach industry that training staff is something the state pays for. This was, initially, the product of the Treasury-inspired Train to Gain programme, which rewarded employers financially for certifying workers for skills they already possessed.

It was a truly bizarre initiative. Both Tesco and the Army were persuaded to take public money from the training ministry (the names of the relevant department of state ministry changed every year or two) for training that they were already doing, just so the ministry could demonstrate to the Treasury that it was hitting its targets. And this flagrant abuse of the public purse was funded by cutting further education courses for adults who were keen to learn new skills in their own time at colleges.

In vain we argued for co-financing by employers, with a reducing state share. In vain we complained about dead weight; indeed, I was told by the senior civil servant responsible that the Treasury was relaxed about the 90% dead weight (displacement of private investment by public finance).

Once the scheme was eventually wound up, in the wake of the 2008 bankers' crisis, it was perhaps unsurprising to find that many small and medium sized businesses had got out of the habit of investing in the development of their own staff.

And government went on to repeat the mistake, at least in the initial phases of the apprentices programme, where employers were once again able to take public money for certificating adult staff without necessarily adding to their skills.

The second major mistake made in our skills policy has been to focus public investment increasingly narrowly on securing more formal certification.

Ever since the CBI-inspired National Education & Training Targets of 1988, we have been hell bent on improving the qualifications of the workforce, as the key route to productivity improvement.

At first sight this seems to make sense. There is after all only a limited amount of money available for investment in skills. Far better, then, to concentrate it on supporting studies that relate directly to workplace skills, or so you would think.

Over the 26 years since we first adopted national targets focused on formal qualifications, there have been impressive gains in the numbers of adults in the workforce with qualifications.

At the same time, a national curriculum has been introduced in schools, and children are subject to a regime of intensive testing, backed by external inspection, public league tables of qualifications gained, and endless new initiatives to strengthen literacy and numeracy.

But as the latest OECD study of adult skills (Programme for the International Assessment of Adult Competencies, 2013) showed, England is unique in OECD countries in having 15 to 24-year-olds with no more skills in literacy, numeracy and problem solving than its 55 to 64-year-olds. And whatever comfort we offer ourselves for the qualifications gained, when adults' actual skills in these areas are measured, we languish in the OECD league tables mid-twenties of the 30 countries studied.

This latest evidence is confirmation of a key finding of the national Skills for Life survey of adult literacy and numeracy skills (DfES, 2003). It found that among the post-school population the age cohorts with the highest skills levels in both disciplines were those who had been schooled in the Plowden era – when teachers were trusted to set their own curricula, when HMI spent 80% of their time on supporting development, and when there was no national curriculum, no league tables, no targets. Curiously, that connection was not highlighted in the conclusions of the government report, but it is there for all to see.

The third weakness in the strategy is its obsession with targets. They are of course comforting. They generate data to justify investment. Yet as John Denham said, when he was briefly the responsible minister, "you can hit the target and miss the point". Or as Einstein put it: "Not everything worth counting can be counted, and not everything countable counts."

So what is to be done? First, copy our more productive partner countries. Leave investment in the skills of workers to the firms that employ them, but secure the public interest through licence to practice schemes as a guarantee to employers and consumers alike.

Even the USA has twice the proportion of its workforce covered by these schemes than the UK. Second, spend the money saved in recreating public education opportunities for adults and invest in certificated and uncertificated courses alike.

Third, trust teachers to get on with the job, and scrap the paraphernalia of over-testing, over-inspecting. Copy Finland, train teachers well, give them ongoing space and time for reflection and development, in schools and FE, and then trust them to do a good job.

Conclusions
by Ian Nash

ALAN TUCKETT'S writing is a homily to the powerful about how best to use that power for the public good. And they read him and listen. Every minister responsible for adult learning over the past two decades or more has sought an audience with him, regardless of politics, and most have come up with fine and, occasionally, visionary ideas in the process.

From the Labour education secretary David Blunkett to the Tory John Hayes, Coalition government minister for FE and lifelong learning, all have paid homage to the man and to the inspiration and flexibility of mind he brings to discussions and writing on policy. When politicians fall short and dismiss aspects of adult and community learning as a distraction from the nation's skills training priorities ("More plumbing, less Pilates"), the heavy hand of the Treasury is invariably close by.

Tuckett's writing and his patient persistence in telling the world story of lifelong learning – and the snail's-pace progress we make towards a broad entitlement for all – also exposes a folly of our age of utilitarianism and economic determinism. Of course we must live within our means and we need skills to generate wealth. While the Treasury may, however, offer guidance on overall spending levels, it does not have the competence to determine the means.

And yet, as we see so clearly in Tuckett's columns for the *TES*, this is exactly what each chancellor attempts though annual and triennial ministerial horse-trading, plea bargaining and budget setting. Worse, the UK model of economic management at this level reinforces a silo mentality that, top-down, breeds distrust and militates against joined-up government at departmental and local level.

When Tuckett writes about such issues, he never does so in the abstract and always gives living examples; as when he cites NIACE research showing how effective it is to use GPs' surgeries as centres for educational advice. Substantial evidence shows education can be a better and far cheaper remedy for ill health than costly medicines. However, since this requires co-operation and spending beyond traditional departmental boundaries, it rarely happens.

Similarly, when it comes to education and training, Tuckett insists learning cannot be neatly divided into silos such as 'skills', 'other', 'vocational' or 'academic'; nor can anyone predict the purpose or career intentions of learners from the course content or the level at which they are studying. He stresses time after time that people can and should be trusted to decide for themselves the best course of learning at any stage in life.

Some, particularly the most disadvantaged, will at times need a helping hand along the way; indeed, everyone could benefit from good advice and guidance. He stresses that good labour market information is essential if we are to encourage more people to acquire the right skills for individual and national economic and social gain.

What emerges, however, from Tuckett's columns are very telling images of a system of political oversight built on distrust, constant change, impossible targets, unrealistic deadlines and very poor long-distance vision. Information, advice and guidance systems rarely survive for long – certainly not beyond the life of a Parliamentary term – before the next round of political interference, and they are invariably too poorly funded.

A question emerges loud and clear from his writing, without actually being uttered: after decades of multi-million pound skills training initiatives based on forensic analysis and evidence such as the Leitch review of skills needs to the year 2020, why are we still said to be in a state of crisis? A second equally telling question emerges: is there really a shortage of skills or a shortage of employers willing to reward people adequately for such skills?

Tuckett's equanimity in all this is remarkable; but then he knows that there is no point railing against the inadequacies and short-termism of political systems without constantly pressing home the fact that there is a better system. Rather, he fights a war of attrition in the hope that the persistence will inch things along in the right direction, even if at times it feels like one step forward and two steps back.

What also keeps him going – and should be a source of embarrassment to ministers – is the overwhelming sense of injustice in the education and training system spawned by the narrow skills-based approach in recent years, with its focus on employer training.

As his most recent *TES* column entry in this book says about Train to Gain, it was "a truly bizarre initiative" where the likes of Tesco and the Army were persuaded to take public money from the training ministry for training that they were already doing. "This flagrant abuse of the public purse was funded by cutting further education courses for adults who were keen to learn new skills in their own time at colleges."

His power to keep explaining and campaigning stems not from any belief that politicians can or will change any time soon, but from the sheer joy that he sees in the faces of those people who return to learn and find that it changes their lives. The best of his writing emerges when he is describing the achievements of learners. As he wrote in May 2006 and is worth reiterating here:

> *"The first Adult Learners' Week was held in 1992. It began at a time of struggle, when adults had to assert that they could be the best judges of what was worth studying, and that they had a right to claim modest investment from government to back them in their choices."*

Now on the world stage and, at the time of writing, president of the International Council for Adult Education, Tuckett is courting a larger audience and exhorting them to avoid a narrow path and commit to a broad entitlement of lifelong learning for all.

Index

Seriously useless learning